FROM THE LAND OF THE LABYRINTH

MINOAN CRETE, 3000–1100 B.C.

FROM THE LAND OF THE LABYRINTH

MINOAN CRETE, 3000–1100 B.C.

ALEXANDER S. ONASSIS PUBLIC BENEFIT FOUNDATION (USA)

HELLENIC MINISTRY OF CULTURE

ARCHAEOLOGICAL MUSEUMS OF CRETE

Published by the ALEXANDER S. ONASSIS PUBLIC BENEFIT FOUNDATION (USA)

In collaboration with the HELLENIC MINISTRY OF CULTURE, the ARCHAEOLOGICAL MUSEUMS OF CRETE

This catalogue is issued in conjunction with the exhibition *From the Land of the Labyrinth: Minoan Crete, 3000–1100 B.C.* held at the Onassis Cultural Center, New York, March 13–September 13, 2008

EXHIBITION

Organizing Committee
Maria Andreadaki-Vlazaki
Vili Apostolakou
Nota Dimopoulou-Rethemiotaki

Scientific Committee
Maria Andreadaki-Vlazaki
Vili Apostolakou
Christos Boulotis
Nota Dimopoulou-Rethemiotaki
Lefteris Platon
Giorgos Rethemiotakis

Designer
Daniel B. Kershaw

Graphic Designer
Sophia Geronimus

Lighting
David Clinard

Installation
David Geiger

**Chief Conservators in
the United States**
Leslie Gat
Ursula Kugler

Chief Conservators in Greece
Stephania Chlouveraki
Charalambos Kalogerakis
Anna Mylona
Alexandros Nikakis
Georgios Noukakis
Georgia Pahaki
Panayiotis Sinadinakis

Conservators in Greece
Veta Kalyvianaki
Charalambos Karaiskos
Georgios Marakis
Nearchos Nikakis
Yannis Rogdakis
Eirini Savou
Eirini Sinadinaki
Konstantinos Tsallos
Ephie Tsitsa
Christina Volitaki

CATALOGUE

Editors
Maria Andreadaki-Vlazaki
Giorgos Rethemiotakis
Nota Dimopoulou-Rethemiotaki

Essay Authors
Maria Andreadaki-Vlazaki
Philip Betancourt
Christos Boulotis
Nota Dimopoulou-Rethemiotaki
Athanassia Kanta
Nanno Marinatos
Photini J. P. McGeorge
Clairy Palyvou
Irini Papageorgiou
Lefteris Platon
Jean-Claude Poursat
Giorgos Rethemiotakis
Metaxia Tsipopoulou
Andonis Vasilakis
Peter Warren

Catalogue Authors
Maria Andreadaki-Vlazaki
Emmanouela Apostolaki
Vili Apostolakou
Katerina Athanasaki
Eirini Galli
Irini Gavrilaki
Epameinondas Kapranos
Panagiota Karamaliki
Maria Kyriakaki
Deukalion Manidakis
Nektaria Mavroudi
Christina Papadaki
Yiannis Papadatos
Eleni Papadopoulou
Lefteris Platon
Sophia Preve
Eftychia Protopapadaki
Giorgos Rethemiotakis
Evi Saliaka
Chrysa Sophianou
Dimitris Sfakianakis
Vasiliki Zographaki

Bibliography
Ariadne Gazi

Translation
Colin F. Macdonald
J. Alexander McGillivray
Maria McGillivray
Alexandra Doumas
Emmanouela Apostolaki

Text Editor
Barbara Burn

Editorial Assistant
Eleni Mathioudaki

Designer
Sophia Geronimus

Photographers
Yannis Patrikianos
Yannis Papadakis (cat. nos. 137, 158, 194)
Chronis Papanikolopoulos
    (cat nos. 101b, 107b, 137, 157, 159)

Image Editing
Panagiotis Gregoriadis
Michalis Dinos

Color Separation by Colornet in Greece
Printed by Petros Ballidis in Greece
Bound by Stamou in Greece

PUBLICITY SPONSOR
www.ert.gr

ISBN 978-0-9776598-2-1

Front cover: cat. no. 205
Back cover: cat. no. 194

Frontispiece: detail of cat. no. 22

CONTENTS

LENDERS TO THE EXHIBITION

Haghios Nikolaos Archaeological Museum, Crete, Greece
Herakleion Archaeological Museum, Crete, Greece
Hierapetra Archaeological Collection, Crete, Greece
Khania Archaeological Museum, Crete, Greece
Kissamos Archaeological Museum, Crete, Greece
Rethymnon Archaeological Museum, Crete, Greece
Siteia Archaeological Museum, Crete, Greece

CONTRIBUTING AUTHORS — CATALOGUE

Maria Andreadaki-Vlazaki, Director, 25th Ephorate of Prehistoric and Classical Antiquities, Khania, Crete, Greece
Emmanouela Apostolaki, Archaeologist, Herakleion Archaeological Museum, Crete, Greece
Vili Apostolakou, Director, 24th Ephorate of Prehistoric and Classical Antiquities, Haghios Nikolaos, Crete, Greece
Katerina Athanasaki, Archaeologist, Herakleion Archaeological Museum, Crete, Greece
Eirini Galli, Archaeologist, Herakleion Archaeological Museum, Crete, Greece
Irini Gavrilaki, Archaeologist, 25th Ephorate of Prehistoric and Classical Antiquities, Rethymnon, Crete, Greece
Epameinondas Kapranos, Archaeologist, 25th Ephorate of Prehistoric and Classical Antiquities, Rethymnon, Crete, Greece
Panagiota Karamaliki, Archaeologist, 25th Ephorate of Prehistoric and Classical Antiquities, Rethymnon, Crete, Greece
Maria Kyriakaki, Archaeologist, 24th Ephorate of Prehistoric and Classical Antiquities, Haghios Nikolaos, Crete, Greece
Deukalion Manidakis, Archaeologist, Herakleion Archaeological Museum, Crete, Greece
Nektaria Mavroudi, Archaeologist, Herakleion Archaeological Museum, Crete, Greece
Christina Papadaki, Archaeologist, Herakleion Archaeological Museum, Crete, Greece
Yiannis Papadatos, Archaeologist, 24th Ephorate of Prehistoric and Classical Antiquities, Haghios Nikolaos, Crete, Greece
Eleni Papadopoulou, Archaeologist, 25th Ephorate of Prehistoric and Classical Antiquities, Khania, Crete, Greece
Lefteris Platon, Lecturer in Prehistoric Archaeology, Department of History and Archaeology, University of Athens
Sophia Preve, Archaeologist, 25th Ephorate of Prehistoric and Classical Antiquities, Khania, Crete, Greece
Eftychia Protopapadaki, Archaeologist, 25th Ephorate of Prehistoric and Classical Antiquities, Khania, Crete, Greece
Giorgos Rethemiotakis, Archaeologist, Herakleion Archaeological Museum, Crete, Greece
Evi Saliaka, Archaeologist, 24th Ephorate of Prehistoric and Classical Antiquities, Haghios Nikolaos, Crete, Greece
Chrysa Sophianou, Archaeologist, 24th Ephorate of Prehistoric and Classical Antiquities, Haghios Nikolaos, Crete, Greece
Dimitris Sfakianakis, Archaeologist, Herakleion Archaeological Museum, Crete, Greece
Vasiliki Zographaki, Archaeologist, 24th Ephorate of Prehistoric and Classical Antiquities, Haghios Nikolaos, Crete, Greece

The civilization of the third and second millennia B.C. in Crete became known through the excavations of Sir Arthur Evans at Knossos, at the beginning of the twentieth century. A mythic and greatly ravishing new world that came into view became known as the Minoan civilization. Excavations and research continued thereafter by Greek and foreign archaeologists attracting international interest. Certainly, it is not an easy task to describe the Minoan life. We trust, however, that the present exhibition offers a palatable feeling of this unique world.

Over the course of approximately two millennia, the bright and colorful Minoan civilization enchanted the Eastern Mediterranean world with its peaceful motifs, its naturalistic works of art, and its innovative approach to things. Minoan art returned many times over what was "borrowed" from Egypt and the Levant. Furthermore, it created the models for Greek art and provided inspiration for artists of the Western world.

The undeniable cultural freedom of Minoan artisans is evident through the variety of forms and the search for new means of expression, which resulted in the development of Minoan vase-painting and sculpture, as well as the operation of brilliant local workshops of all kinds throughout the island. The remains of this civilization reveal the artistic sensitivity of people, who felt intense love for ephemeral life but also dealt with death by creating art for eternity.

The Alexander S. Onassis Public Benefit Foundation (USA), which has always distinguished itself by its significant multifaceted activities and its ceaseless effort to project the Hellenic civilization, is the gracious host of this important exhibition.

The exhibition and its catalogue are the results of a fruitful collaboration of the Onassis Foundation (USA) with the Greek Ministry of Culture, together with a team of eminent archaeologists who worked with great enthusiasm and dedication. The 281 artifacts on exhibit, most of which are presented to an international public for the first time, are drawn from the most important collections of the Archaeological Museums of Crete. Representative examples of daily life, economic activity, religion, and art offer visitors a unique opportunity to take a fascinating trip into the distant past, a journey through the "Land of the Labyrinth."

Michalis Liapis
Hellenic Minister of Culture

It is common ground that classical Greece has given us democracy and most of the fundamental principles and tenets of our social and political life. But if the fifth century B.C. witnessed the human quest for truth and beauty, in the preceding millennia the Greek lands of the Aegean archipelago experienced the blossoming of the first buds of civilization on European lands.

The Island of Crete, lying on the edge of the Aegean Sea and in the middle of the Eastern Mediterranean Sea, is at the same time one of the south boundaries of the European continent. Its central geographic position in the middle of the sea across three continents (Europe, Asia and Africa) has allowed the Cretans to enjoy the strategic privilege of easy access to these lands while being protected from warlike expeditions by land. Indeed the Cretans gave us the first examples of unwalled cities, an example which was again followed only in the late 19th century A.D.! It is demonstrably the first palatial and urban civilization on European soil. Commerce and trade led to the exchange of ideas with other older civilizations and the nurturing of civilization.

The Minoan civilization (3000–1100 B.C.), born on the island of Crete, has enchanted countless generations with its complexity, elegance, and vigor.

Cretan civilization provides us with a thread (μίτος) which leads us out of the labyrinth of today's civilizational mix towards the foundation of our heritage and in so doing helps us to restore our sense of balance. Artistic modes, trading relations, some of the very words we still use today, come originally from Crete. In fact research has proven that the Cretan written words are at the basis of parts of our alphabet and bear a striking similarity to words still in use today, and not only by the Greeks.

Through the Minoan era and the wonderful myths of the union of Zeus with Europe, her son the great King Minos, the Minotaur, the Labyrinth, Daedalus and Icarus, Crete is linked with the very roots of our common Hellenic and humanistic past. The Cretan land is thus entitled not only to an important share of Europe's cultural heritage, but it can even lay claim to the very name of our venerable old continent.

In this context it is difficult to over emphasize the importance of the exhibition "From the Land of the Labyrinth: Minoan Crete, 3000–1100 B.C."

The Onassis Foundation is proud to be able to offer this magnificent cultural and archaeological event to the American public. Unique artifacts from all the Cretan archaeological museums are brought together for the first time in the U.S. The Onassis Foundation is most grateful to the Hellenic Ministry of Culture, and all the curators, and distinguished archaeologists who made this achievement possible.

Anthony S. Papadimitriou
President
Alexander S. Onassis Public Benefit Foundation

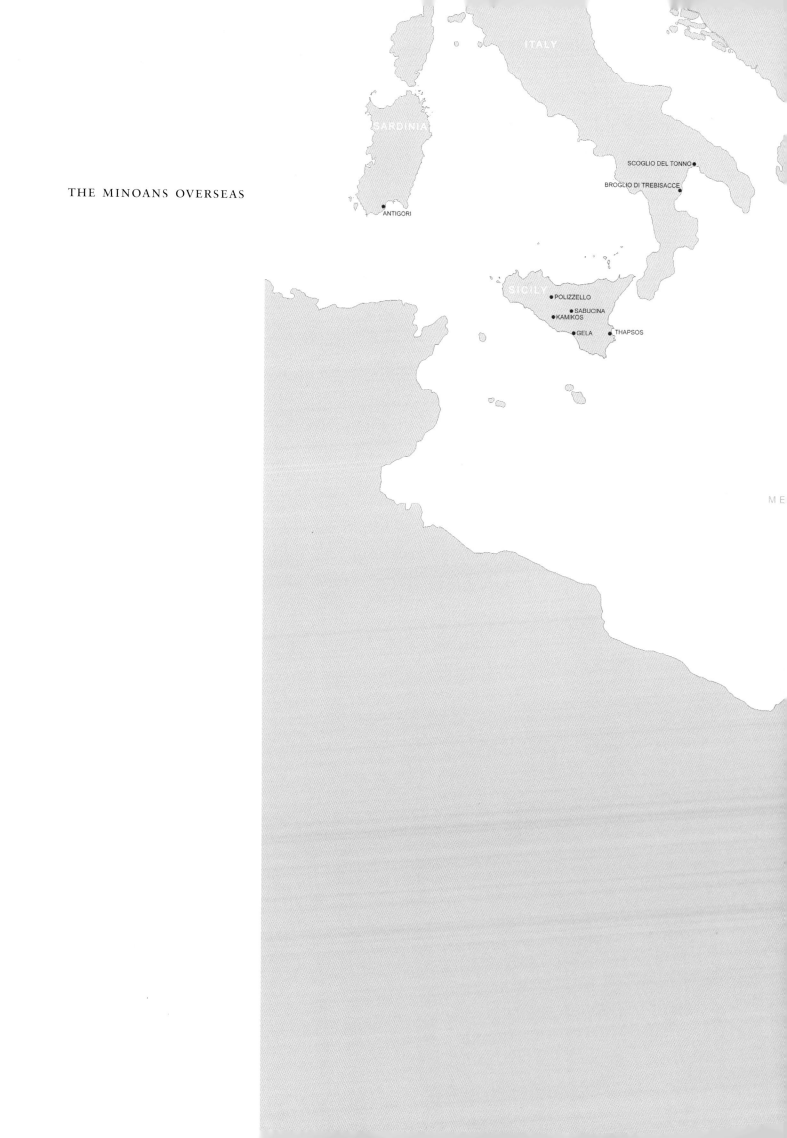

THE MINOANS OVERSEAS

ITALY

SARDINIA

SCOGLIO DEL TONNO●

BROGLIO DI TREBISACCE●

●ANTIGORI

SICILY

●POLIZZELLO

●SABUCINA
●KAMIKOS

●GELA ●THAPSOS

ME

SAMOTHRACE

HATTUSHA

TROIA

LEMNOS

PEUKAKIA

KALAPODI
ORCHOMENOS
MITROU

CARCHEMISH

MITANNI

IZMIR (SMYRNA)

THEBES
ELEUSIS

ICHOS DYMAION

AEGEAN SEA

ASIA MINOR

ALEPPO

MESOPO

MYCENAE
AIGINA
KEOS

SYRIA

ARGOS
TIRYNS
LAVRION

CAPE IRIA

ALALAKH

MILETOS

CYCLADES

PAROS
NAXOS

IASOS

ORONTES

UGARIT

MARI

VAPHEIO

ANO
KOUPHONISI

KOS

QATNA

MELOS

IOS

KNIDOS

KYTHERA

THERA

RHODES

CAPE GELIDONYA

ULU BURUN

ENKOMI

PYLA

CRETE

KARPATHOS

KITION

CYPRUS

HALA SULTAN TEKKE

KYDONIA

POROS

MAA-PALAIOKASTRO

BYBLOS

KNOSSOS
MALIA

KASOS

KALORIZIKI

BEIRUT

KOMMOS
PHAISTOS

ZAKROS

PALAIPAPHOS
SKALES KOUKLIA

NEAN SEA

TEL KABRI

JORDAN

MARSA MATRUH

AVARIS/TELL EL-DAB'A

GIZA

EGYPT

TELL EL-AMARNA

ASSIUT

NILE

ABYDOS

THEBES
LUXOR

TÔD

ASWAN

CHRONOLOGICAL CHART

Early Minoan I	3000–2600 B.C.	**Prepalatial Period**
Early Minoan II	2600–2300 B.C.	
Early Minoan III	2300–2100 B.C.	
Middle Minoan IA	2100–1900 B.C.	
Middle Minoan IB	1900–1800 B.C.	**Protopalatial Period**
Middle Minoan II	1800–1700 B.C.	
Middle Minoan III	1700–1600 B.C.	**Neopalatial Period**
Late Minoan IA	1600–1525/1500 B.C.	
Late Minoan IB	1525/1500–1450 B.C.	
Late Minoan II	1450–1400 B.C.	**Final Palatial Period**
Late Minoan IIIA1	1400–1375 B.C.	
Late Minoan IIIA2	1375–1300 B.C.	
Late Minoan IIIB	1300–1200 B.C.	**Post Palatial Period**
Late Minoan IIIC	1200–1100 B.C.	

INTRODUCTION

Crete, "the Land of the Labyrinth," is the large island in the center of the eastern Mediterranean Sea where the first great palatial civilization in Europe flourished during the third and second millennia B.C. The size, the fertile soil, and the topography of the island favored the development of agriculture, which led Crete to a self-sufficient and independent economy. At the same time, Crete's advantageous location between three continents at the junction of sea routes in the Mediterranean and the Aegean encouraged contact with the cultures of neighboring regions, from the Aegean archipelagos and the Asian coast to the vast territory of Egypt. These factors, which the Cretans exploited to the fullest, formed the basis for the development of a unique cultural expression in the Bronze Age societies of Crete from 3000 to 1100 B.C. This was the brilliant Minoan civilization, which was named for Minos, the legendary king of Crete, ruler of Knossos.

Crete's archaeological history begins in the Neolithic period, which lasted from about 7000 to 3000 B.C. Small communities of hunters, farmers, and breeders of livestock spread throughout Crete during that time, slowly developing the foundation of the island's culture. By the end of the fourth millennium B.C. and the beginning of the third, however, new settlers arrived in Crete, possibly from western Asia Minor, via the Cycladic islands. These tribes are believed to have introduced revolutionary techniques in the treatment of metals. Together with the original Neolithic population, they became the first Minoans, creators of the Minoan civilization of the Bronze Age. The first chronological period of this civilization—which extends through the third millennium B.C., is called Early Minoan or Prepalatial. The innovative metal technology made possible the development of appropriate tools for the improvement of farming and industrial activities. The Cretans became proficient in sailing and trade, which enabled them to import raw materials, export their products, and share technology. The new tools and techniques, along with imported bronze, gold, silver, semiprecious stones, and ivory, encouraged industrial production and made possible the arts of metallurgy, seal engraving, jewelry making, stonecutting, pottery, and the creation of miniature works of art. Developing alongside farming and stock breeding, industrial production led to the formation of new social groups, including specialized craftsmen, merchants, and sailors.

Gradually, the increase in wealth, urbanization, and religious and political structures brought about the rise of influential social classes and ruling groups. These early elites demonstrated their status by displaying luxury objects, such as silver and bronze daggers, sophisticated ivory seals, precious jewelry, and exquisite small stone vases and figurines that have been recovered in Early Minoan tholos tombs. From these groups arose regional rulers, and this led to the establishment of the first palaces in the beginning of the second millennium B.C.

The Middle Minoan, or Protopalatial, period was a time during which the Minoan socio-political system was configured and consolidated. The first palaces were erected soon after 2000 B.C. in the large settlements at Knossos, Phaistos, and Malia, where they served as the seat of rulers and as centers of civil and religious authority. The continuing economic growth and the widening of Crete's trade network resulted in the development of a bureaucratic system based on clay sealings and hieroglyphic script. Public worship was practiced at open-air peak sanctuaries, where votaries deposited figurines seeking divine protection. Settlements increased in number and population; harbors under the control of the palatial centers became gateways for circulating goods. Precious, exotic raw materials came to Crete, and Cretan artifacts were shipped to mainland Greece, the Aegean, the Levant, and Egypt. The palatial rulers demonstrated their power and wealth by displaying such prestigious objects as the elaborate swords from the palace at Malia and the splendid polychrome Kamares Style pottery used in the palatial feasts at Knossos and Phaistos.

The destruction of the first palaces by an earthquake about 1700 B.C. did not reverse the cultural dynamics of Minoan Crete. On the contrary, it marked the beginning of a great new era during which the Minoan civilization reached its zenith. In the Neopalatial period (ca. 1700–1450 B.C.), the three centers rebuilt palaces that were larger and more imposing and featured important architectural and structural innovations. Palaces were also built in other areas, including Zakros and Petras in eastern Crete and Galatas and Archanes in central Crete; a palace may also have existed in Kydonia (Khania) in western Crete. The palace at Knossos, however, was the most significant and monumental of all, and for more than three hundred years it represented the preeminent center of power in Minoan Crete.

The new Minoan palaces were impressive complexes, decorated with frescoes and housing multiple administrative and religious activities, from daily routines to formal rituals. Ceremonies and feasts were held in official palace halls, and spacious courts hosted public gatherings of a social or religious character. During this period, religion was consolidated in an organized system that accommodated outdoor cults with meaningful religious symbols, such as the double axe, the sacred bull, the horns of consecration, and the sacral knot. The ruler and the palatial court stood at the top of the social hierarchy and displayed an elaborate and refined way of life. Their palaces applied a bureaucratic system to the control of internal and external trade, the circulation of goods, and the production of sumptuous artifacts. Records were kept in the Linear A script, and the authentication of transported products was achieved by sealing lumps of clay. At the same time, large buildings with spacious rooms and storage areas, called villas, played an administrative role in rural areas by controlling the transport of agricultural products and livestock, occasionally involving the keeping of records. Specialized workshops in the palaces, the harbors, and the large settlements produced splendid pieces of small-scale artworks in stone and metal, as well as seal engraving and jewelry made of precious materials from Egypt and the Levant. Minoan artifacts, manufactured by inspired and skillful artisans and craftsmen, traveled to the markets of the Aegean and the eastern Mediterranean, where a network of Minoan trade posts was established. Crete's domination of the sea routes and its expansion throughout the Mediterranean basin are reflected in later histories of Greece that refer to the Minoan Thalassocracy.

At the peak of its political power, economic growth, artistic creation, and cultural influence, Minoan Crete was struck down about 1520 B.C.—according to traditional dating—by a natural disaster, the eruption of a volcano in Thera, the closest Cycladic island to the north. Minoan civilization did not collapse immediately but lasted for a few more decades, although it seems to have passed its prime. The general destruction of the Minoan centers, palaces, settlements, and villas occurred about 1450 B.C., perhaps resulting from a combination of natural factors and socio-political unrest. The palace at Knossos survived and continued to function for another century or more, but now Mycenaean cultural elements began to prevail, indicating the presence of a Mycenaean dynasty. During this Final Palatial period (ca. 1450–1350/1250 B.C.), changes can also be seen in burial practices that involved a new type of grave, which related to those on mainland Greece, and rich "warrior graves," which are thought to represent the Mycenaeans and their "military spirit." Definitive evidence for the Mycenaean presence on Crete and the practice of central control is proven by the Linear B tablets, which were inscribed in

Greek, the language of the Mycenaeans. Another important Mycenaean center with intense trade activity was founded in Kydonia in western Crete, the location of modern Khania. Documents on tablets and sealings found there suggest the existence of a palatial administration. The warrior graves of Kydonia, like those of Knossos, signify the authority of individuals of high social class and office.

The Mycenaean palatial centers decayed from the end of the fourteenth century through the thirteenth century B.C. Post Palatial Crete, especially after 1200 B.C., had assimilated the cultural idioms of the Mycenaean world, along with survivals of the Minoan past. The island's population was divided into small communities, which lacked any central control. Worship was practiced in small domestic shrines that housed idols of the goddess "with raised arms." Life was no longer lived at a high level: metals had become rare, imported raw materials disappeared, and grave offerings with few exceptions comprised ordinary jewelry made of glass and standardized pottery types.

The circle was completed about 1100 B.C., the twilight of the Bronze Age. The advent of the Dorians, an early Hellenic tribe, at the beginning of the first millennium B.C. placed Crete in a different cultural framework, one that would eventually become part of the ancient Greek world.

The vigorous Minoan past survived, however, through ancient Greek literature in the form of inventive and appealing myths and legends. King Minos, the son of Zeus and Europa and the ruler of Knossos and Crete, was reputed to be a fair judge of souls in the netherworld. The Labyrinth of Knossos, built for Minos by the gifted artisan Daedalus, was the fabled home of the Minotaur, a man-eating monster with a human body and the head of a bull, said to be the offspring of a bull of Poseidon and Minos's wife, Pasiphae. When Minos's daughter Ariadne fell in love with Theseus, an Athenian prince, she incurred her father's wrath in helping Theseus escape from the Labyrinth by unrolling a magic ball of thread, another of Daedalus's inventions.

This mythic Minoan Crete and its material culture, which has survived in many beautiful and intriguing objects, is presented for the first time to the American public in this exhibition, *From the Land of the Labyrinth: Minoan Crete, 3000–1100 B.C.*, organized by the Alexander S. Onassis Public Benefit Foundation (USA), the Hellenic Ministry of Culture, and the Archaeological Museums of Crete. For this purpose, 281 Minoan artifacts from the permanent collections of the Cretan museums have traveled to the United States, most of them for the first time. Through jewelry and signet rings;

seals and clay sealings; stone and bronze vases; pottery, fig-urines, and ritual vessels; weapons and tools; inscribed tablets; painted sarcophagi and even colorful frescoes, the wondrous Minoan world and its superb art are revealed in all their splendor.

The exhibition is organized chronologically and themat-ically in eleven parts, which cover aspects of administration and bureaucracy, script, religion and cult, arts and technol-ogy, daily life, and death and burial practices. The "Pots and Potters" section includes, among other objects, vases of the splendid Kamares, Floral, and Marine Styles. "Masterpieces in Stone" presents the marvelous works of Minoan stonecut-ters from the Prepalatial period onward, while tools, molds, and materials are exhibited in the section "In the Domain of the Craftsman." "Warriors and Weaponry" presents exam-ples of Minoan military equipment, such as a long sword with a gold-covered hilt, copper and silver daggers, and a rare boar's-tusk helmet. A vivid picture of daily life is given in "Alimentation and Aromatics," which features food-preparation vessels, articles for the production of aromatic substances, samples of pulses and fruits, and a fragmentary mural depicting an olive tree. The section entitled "Scripts and Weights" includes clay tablets with Linear A and B scripts, which were used to number and record products, clay sealings for the transported products, weights, and even a bronze scale. A representative series of seals made of ivory and semiprecious stones, as well as signet rings and seal impressions in clay, are presented in "Seal Engraving: Great Art in Miniature." The celebrated Minoan craft of jewelry making is represented in "Jewels for Life and Death" by fine pieces made of gold, semiprecious stones, and colored glass. "The Colorful World of Murals" offers an example of the great art of wall painting with the famous "Partridge Fresco," one of the most charming compositions in Minoan iconography. The important section "Religion and Ritual Practice" is illustrated with idols and representations of deities, human and zoomorphic figurines and other votaries, replicas of cult symbols, and golden rings with religious compositions, as well as magnificent ritual vessels, among them a rare rhyton in the shape of a bull's head from the palace at Zakros. The exhibition ends with "A Glance into the Afterworld," a section dominated by three painted clay sarcophagi.

We hope that this exhibition about Minoan civilization presented by the Onassis Cultural Center of New York will enable the American public to become acquainted with ancient Cretan history and culture, as well as with modern day Crete.

We would like to thank the Greek Minister of Culture, Mr. M. Liapis, for generously allowing the loan of artifacts from the Cretan museums and for his support of the project, as well as the former Minister of Culture, Mr. G. Voulgarakis, for his initial approval of this undertaking. We are also grate-ful to the Alexander S. Onassis Public Benefit Foundation (USA) and its President, Mr. A. Papadimitriou, for his initia-tive in presenting the first major exhibition about Minoan culture in the United States. The successful completion of this project owes much to the continuous active interest and ardent support provided by the Executive Director of the Onassis Foundation (USA), Ambassador L. Tsilas, and the Founda-tion's Cultural Director, Mrs. A. Cosmetatou, whom we cordially thank for the fruitful collaboration. We also thank Dr. Chr. Doumas, Professor Emeritus at the University of Athens. We would also like to stress the interest, assistance, and collaboration of the General Director of Antiquities, Dr. V. Vassilopoulou; the Greek Ministry of Culture-Directorate of Museums, the Director Mrs. M. Pandou and her assistants; the Greek Ministry of Culture-Directorate of Conservation, the Director, Mr. N. Minos and his assis-tants; the former Director of Antiquities, Honorary Ephor Mrs. K. Romiopoulou, and the Director of the Twenty-third Ephorate of Prehistoric and Classical Antiquities of Herakleion, Mrs. M. Bredaki. Thanks are also due to Mr. D. Kershaw for the exhibition design, to Mrs. S. Geronimus for designing the exhibition catalogue, and to Ms. B. Burn for editing the texts.

We are especially grateful to all contributors, including the authors of essays and catalogue entries and the archae-ologists in Crete, as well as conservators, photographers, and translators, for their substantial contributions to the successful completion of this venture.

THE ORGANIZING AND SCIENTIFIC COMMITTEE

Maria Andreadaki-Vlazaki   Nota Dimopoulou-Rethemiotaki
Vili Apostolakou   Lefteris Platon
Christos Boulotis   Giorgos Rethemiotakis

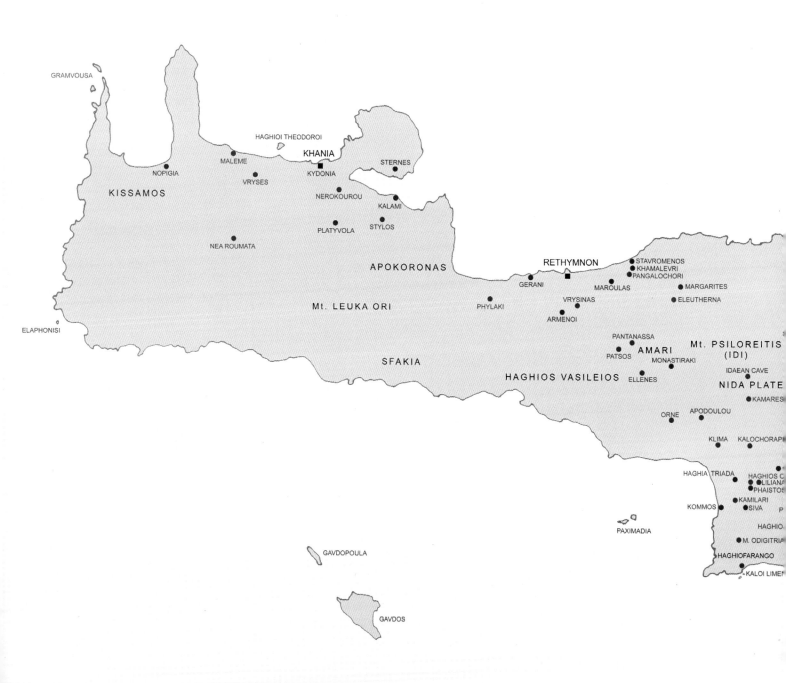

GRAMVOUSA

HAGHIOI THEODOROI

KHANIA

MALEME
NOPIGIA
VRYSES
KYDONIA

STERNES

KISSAMOS

NEROKOUROU
KALAMI
PLATYVOLA
STYLOS

NEA ROUMATA

APOKORONAS

RETHYMNON

STAVROMENOS
KHAMALEVRI
PANGALOCHORI
GERANI
MAROULAS
MARGARITES
Mt. LEUKA ORI
VRYSINAS
ELEUTHERNA
PHYLAKI
ARMENOI

PANTANASSA
Mt. PSILOREITIS
AMARI
(IDI)
SFAKIA
PATSOS
MONASTIRAKI
IDAEAN CAVE
HAGHIOS VASILEIOS
ELLENES
NIDA PLATE

KAMARES

ORNE
APODOULOU

KLIMA
KALOCHORAPI

HAGHIA TRIADA
HAGHIOS C
LILIANA
PHAISTOS
KAMILARI
KOMMOS
SIVA
P

ELAPHONISI

HAGHIO.

M. ODIGITRIA

HAGHIOFARANGO
PAXIMADIA
KALOI LIMEN

GAVDOPOULA

GAVDOS

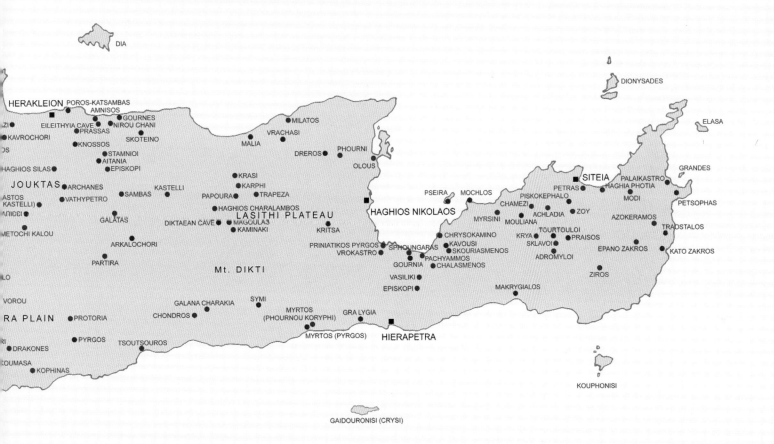

DIA

DIONYSADES

ELASA

HERAKLEION POROS-KATSAMBAS
AMNISOS
GOURNES
EILEITHYIA CAVE NIROU CHANI
KAVROCHORI PRASSAS
SKOTEINO
KNOSSOS
HAGHIOS SILAS STAMNIOI
AITANIA
EPISKOPI
JOUKTAS ARCHANES
VATHYPETRO SAMBAS
KASTELLI
GALATAS
METOCHI KALOU ARKALOCHORI
PARTIRA

MILATOS
VRACHASI
MALIA
DREROS PHOURNI
OLOUS
KRASI
KARPHI
PAPOURA TRAPEZA
HAGHIOS CHARALAMBOS
DIKTAEAN CAVE MAGOULA3
KAMINAKI
LASITHI PLATEAU
KRITSA

Mt. DIKTI

SITEIA
PETRAS PALAIKASTRO
HAGHIA PHOTIA
PISKOKEPHALO
MODI
PSEIRA MOCHLOS
CHAMEZI
ACHLADIA ZOY
MYRSINI MOULIANA
AZOKERAMOS
HAGHIOS NIKOLAOS CHRYSOKAMINO TOURTOULOI
KRYA PRAISOS TRAOSTALOS
PRINIATIKOS PYRGOS SPHOUNGARAS KAVOUSI SKLAVOI
EPANO ZAKROS
VROKASTRO PACHYAMMOS SKOURIASMENOS ADROMYLOI KATO ZAKROS
GOURNIA CHALASMENOS
VASILIKI ZIROS
EPISKOPI MAKRYGIALOS

GRANDES

PETSOPHAS

VOROU
RA PLAIN PROTORIA
GALANA CHARAKIA SYMI
CHONDROS
MYRTOS
(PHOURNOU KORYPHI) GRA LYGIA
PYRGOS TSOUTSOUROS
MYRTOS (PYRGOS) HIERAPETRA
DRAKONES
KOUMASA KOPHINAS

KOUPHONISI

GAIDOURONISI (CRYSI)

The production and decoration of ceramics was ideal for the expression and application of specialized artistic creativity and high-quality craftsmanship. This began with the coarse handmade ware of the Prepalatial period (third millennium B.C.), with its thick walls and plain geometric decoration that was burnished, incised, or painted, as well as the fine, mottled embellishment deliberately produced by uneven firing in ceramic kilns. By the Protopalatial period (ca. 1900–1700 B.C.), however, pottery production resulted in splendid polychrome vases, which became known as Kamares Ware, named for the Kamares cave of southern Crete, where they were first found. This development followed the mastery of wheel making, which made possible the production of sophisticated shapes and vessels with very thin eggshell-like walls and the imitation of metal objects.

Innumerable combinations of curvilinear and floral motifs, such as spirals and rosettes, were painted on the polished black surfaces of vessels with such originality and creativity that, despite the hundreds of pots found to date, no two pieces are identical. The polychrome ware was, in fact, part of the "royal" sets that were destined for the conspicuous feasts organized at the two major Cretan palaces, those at Knossos and Phaistos, where the majority of the most elaborate examples have been found.

In the Neopalatial period (ca. 1700–1450 B.C.), the predominant decorative styles were the Floral Style, which featured vegetal motifs, mainly reeds, and the Marine Style, whose themes were inspired by undersea life. Octopuses with tentacles spread over the surfaces of pots; tritons, argonauts, dolphins, and starfish swim among corals and seaweed, which move gently with the movement of the current. The variety and originality of these stylized compositions, combined with an apparent *horror vacui*, or fear of empty space, combine to produce an especially decorative result without much concern for accuracy. Dense, painted compositions of reeds and endlessly repeated geometric motifs express the same decorative spirit.

The two great phases of Minoan pottery, Kamares Ware and the era of Floral, Marine, and Geometric Styles, led Cretan ceramic production to a superior level of artistic accomplishment. In no other region of the eastern Mediterranean basin did potters or vase painters achieve such high standards of quality. It has been established that these vases and implements were not objects intended for daily use but were a material means of projecting prestige and power.

In the Final Palatial period, from about 1450 to 1350 B.C., a series of amphorae were produced in the so-called Palace Style, with stylized floral and marine patterns executed in a relatively grandiose manner. Around 1300 B.C., decoration tended to primarily linear and abstract forms, but the last brief flourish of vase painting about 1200 to 1100 B.C. brought on a renewed tendency to exaggerated decoration, for the third time in the history of Minoan pottery production. Large, impressive kraters and smaller vessels were decorated in the distinctive Close Style, in which dense, symmetrical arrangements of birds and curvilinear and geometric motifs were enriched with fine linear ornaments carefully painted in a calligraphic manner.

Detail of cat. no. 31

1 **Burnished Jug**
   Final Neolithic period (ca. 3600–3100 B.C.)
   Clay
   Max. h. with handle 0.184 m
   Lasithi, Kastelli Fourni, 1959
   Herakleion Archaeological Museum, HM 14076

Complete, closed vase, biconical shape with high cylindrical neck and flat base. Perforated projection opposite the base of a raised strap handle, at the junction of the neck and body. The black surface is highly burnished.

Careful burnishing of clay vases before firing was widely practiced in the Neolithic period. Burnishing increases a vase's impermeability, which could not be achieved otherwise because of the low firing temperatures of that time (firing in heaps or inside pits at 700 to 800° C).

   This jug was found inside a Final Neolithic well, together with about thirty vases of the same period whose shapes indicate that they were designed for drawing and transporting water.

   The digging of a well at a height of 300 meters above sea level in the Fourni plain during this period indicates that the region's prehistoric inhabitants knew how to exploit the subterranean water sources when surface water was not sufficient for household use and farming. This was a typical practice of the Final Neolithic in Crete, which saw an increase of the population and the occupation of new sites, particularly hills with adjacent fertile plains that were appropriate for cereal cultivation.

Selected Bibliography
Betancourt 1999; Hayden 2003; *Κρητ. Χρονικά* ΙΓ΄(1959): 388 (Platon); Mantelli 1992.

Eirini Galli

2 Haghios Onouphrios-Ware Jug

Early Minoan I period (ca. 3000 B.C.)
Clay
Max. h. 0.188 m
Kanli Kastelli, Kyparissi, burial tomb, 1951
Herakleion Archaeological Museum, HM 10853

Finely made jug, complete. Conical upper body angles abruptly into a rounded bottom, which is smaller than the maximum diameter. The short, narrow neck ends in a raised spout. The evenly fired yellowish surface is decorated with groups of vertical red lines that converge under the base to form a net pattern.

This jug, which comes from the burial cave at Korphi tou Vatheia, near the village of Kyparissi in central Crete, is a typical example of Haghios Onouphrios Ware. The excavated deposit included human bones, a large number of vases, and other types of grave gifts, such as metal weapons and jewelry, obsidian tools, and stone necklace beads.

The production of pottery with painted decoration is one of the earliest developments of Minoan material culture and a significant indicator of the Early Minoan period. It also indicates a relatively high degree of technical knowledge, a distribution system for manufactured goods, and the organization of pottery manufacture, which appears to have been fairly complex even before the establishment of the early palaces.

The jug is the most popular shape in Haghios Onouphrios Ware and occurs in both domestic and funerary contexts. This particular shape, very popular in the northeast Aegean and western Asia Minor, may have inspired the flask-shape gourd, which had been until recently used as a container.

Haghios Onouphrios Ware, named after an archaeological site in the Mesara Plain, is characterized by painted decoration of orange-red to brownish-red motifs on a light background. The red paint is achieved by creating an oxidizing atmosphere within controlled firing conditions and is among the earliest evidence for the use of a closed kiln. In the earliest examples, the linear motifs are organically related to the shape of the vase and consist of groups of lines that often cross each another to create grids that recall basket weaving. Similar painted decoration occurs in the Syro-Palestinian region.

Vases of this ware are found in burial caves in northern and central Crete.

Selected Bibliography

Alexiou 1951, p. 277, pl. 13, fig. 1.1; Alexiou–Warren 2004, pp. 72, 125–26; Betancourt 1985, pp. 29–31; Day–Wilson–Kiriatzi 1997; Wilson–Day 1994, pp. 84–85.

Eirini Galli

3 Barrel-Shape Vessel

Early Minoan I period (ca. 3000 B.C.)
Clay
H. 0.104 m, l. 0.087 m
Lendas, Mesara 1959, Tomb II
Herakleion Archaeological Museum, HM 15385

This clay barrel-shape vessel has a cylindrical neck and disc-shape sides, each with a pair of tiny horizontal perforations and four small feet protruding beneath the body. Almost complete.

The vessel is decorated in the so-called Lebena Ware style with white linear motifs on a red ground. The cylindrical body bears cross-hatching with X motifs in between; the disc sides have three successive bands and closely arranged chevrons, and the neck has a zigzag pattern and two bands at the lowest part.

Barrel-shape vessels make up a rare category in Cretan ceramic production of the Early Bronze Age and recall similar vessels from Troy and the islands of the northeastern Aegean, where this ceramic type is attested more frequently.

In the Early Minoan period, personal items for everyday use are found among grave gifts, as are miniature objects specially manufactured for funerary use that imitate larger utilitarian objects. This seems to apply as well to the barrel-shape vessels, which functioned either for practical, individual use or as miniature versions of larger utilitarian vessels of unknown size.

Selected Bibliography
AΔ 16 (1960): 257–58, fig. 14 (Alexiou); Alexiou–Warren 2004, p. 62; Podzuweit 1979, pp. 231–32, pl. 241; Schliemann 1880, pp. 404–5, nos. 439–40.

Katerina Athanasaki

4 Footed Cup ("Chalice")
End of Early Minoan I–beginning of Early Minoan IIA
period (ca. 2700–2600 B.C.)
Clay
H. 0.235 m, max. diam. 0.185 m
Early Minoan cemetery of Haghia Photia, Siteia, Tomb 134
Haghios Nikolaos Archaeological Museum, 4157

Biconical body, with a slim waist and a triangular, perforated
protuberance below the rim. Incised decoration of fifteen irregular parallel incisions on upper part of body. Mended and restored
in gypsum.

It is of local clay and belongs to a Minoan ceramic form found
in cemeteries. It is of the so-called Pyrgos Style and has a gray,
well-burnished surface. Similar vessels have been found at many
sites in central, southern, and eastern Crete.

The Haghia Photia tombs are subterranean chamber
tombs, elliptical in plan, cut into the soft limestone bedrock of
the region. Their entrances were usually sealed by large stone
slabs. Entry into the burial chamber was through a small
antechamber, which was filled with soil and stones after the
interment. This cup was found in pieces on top of the stone fill
in the upper part of the antechamber. This location shows that
the vessel was not one of the grave offerings that accompanied
the deceased but was used in a ceremony of some kind, perhaps
a final offering that took place above the tomb after the dead
was buried and the entrance sealed. It also seems very likely that
the smashing of the vase was not accidental but a deliberate part
of the ceremony.

Rites of a similar sort seem to have been quite common at
Cretan cemeteries of the Early Bronze Age and included the use
of cups, pouring vessels, kernoi, and zoomorphic and anthropomorphic rhyta.

Selected Bibliography
Alexiou 1951, pl. XIV; Branigan 1993, pp. 61–63, 76–80; Davaras
1971; Davaras–Betancourt 2004, p. 118, no. 134.5, fig. 286;
Galanaki 2006, pl. IV; Soles 1992, pp. 247–51; Xanthoudides
1918a, figs. 8–11.

Yiannis Papadatos

5 **Incense Burner**
   End of Early Minoan I–beginning of Early Minoan IIA
   period (ca. 2700–2600 B.C.)
   Clay
   H. 0.20 m, max. diam. 0.175 m
   Early Minoan cemetery of Haghia Photia, Siteia, Tomb 104
   Haghios Nikolaos Archaeological Museum, 3845

Brownish-red, smoothed surface, with thin red slip. Conical foot
and piriform body. Vertical strap handle below lip, with a protuberance above. The neck has triangular fenestrations.

The vessel is made of semicoarse clay with many limestone
inclusions. Although petrographic analysis has been unable to
ascertain beyond a doubt whether the vessel is local or
imported, this particular clay mix with limestone is a predomi-
nantly Cycladic characteristic. It should be noted that vessels of
the same shape from similarly early contexts have been found in
many Cycladic cemeteries, whereas on Crete the shape has been
found only at Gournes, Herakleion, in a cemetery that has many
points of similarity with Haghia Photia.

   The vessel was likely used as an incense burner, probably
for burning aromatic substances, judging from the traces of
burning on the interior, as well as from the fenestrations on the
neck allowing oxygen in and smoke out. Also, the protuberance
above the handle and neck would have given greater protection
to the fingers against the heat that was developing inside. The
existence of incense burners in cemeteries may indicate that they
served both practical and ceremonial purposes. Burning incense
may have helped offset the smell that lingered in the closed
chamber tombs, yet it may also have had something to do with
funeral customs and rites. Thus the use of such vases at Haghia
Photia suggests a particularly strong relationship between this
site and the Cyclades, not only in terms of material culture but
also in burial customs.

Selected Bibliography
Branigan 1987; Davaras 1971; Davaras–Betancourt 2004, p. 98,
no. 104.2, fig. 229; Day–Wilson–Kiriatzi 1998; Doumas 1977,
pp. 63–64; Galanaki 2006, p. 230; Marangou 1990, pp. 94, 102,
108, no. 106.

                                                    Yiannis Papadatos

6 Bird Vase

End of Early Minoan I–beginning of Early Minoan IIA
period (ca. 2700–2600 B.C.)
Clay
H. 0.15 m, l. 0.21 m
Early Minoan cemetery of Haghia Photia, Siteia, Tomb 216
Haghios Nikolaos Archaeological Museum, 4890

Gray surface, well burnished. Bird-shape body supported on
three short legs. Two vertical tubular excrescences on the belly.
Short conical neck on top. Incised body decoration depicts the
bird's plumage. Mended and restored in gypsum.

This vessel lacks precise parallels, although its shape is a rare
variation of a common Cycladic vase form with a piriform body
(also known as a bottle). This form is relatively rare on Crete
and is found in cemeteries with marked Cycladic features, such
as Gournes and Pyrgos, Herakleion. Moreover, the vessel is
made of semicoarse clay with numerous limestone inclusions, a
mix that is typical of Cycladic pottery. On the other hand, we
should note that no Cycladic site has yielded a similar vessel and
that bird vases are generally absent from the repertoire of the
Cyclades, unlike Crete. From this point of view, the vase in
question could be a creative marriage of a Cycladic form with a
Cretan potting tradition.

Selected Bibliography
Davaras 1971; Davaras–Betancourt 2004, p. 197, no. 216.10,
fig. 485; Day–Wilson–Kiriatzi 1998; Doumas 1977, pl. XXXVId;
Galanaki 2006, p. 230; Sakellarakis 1977, fig. 133; Zapheiropoulou
1984, p. 35, fig. 3a.

Yiannis Papadatos

7 Spool-Shape Pyxis with Lid

End of Early Minoan I–beginning of Early Minoan IIA
period (ca. 2700–2600 B.C.)
Clay
H. 0.04 m, l. 0.095 m
Early Minoan cemetery of Haghia Photia, Siteia, Tomb 2
Haghios Nikolaos Archaeological Museum, 2491 and 2510

Well-burnished, brownish-red surface. Cylindrical body, with
projecting base. Lid symmetrical to the body, with cylindrical
vertical walls and projecting upper surface. Incised decoration
on the lid, comprising vertical incisions and bands of zigzag
lines on the walls and a fifteen-ray star on the upper surface,
framed by two concentric circles, one of small dashes and
another of a continuous zigzag line. Small amount of restoration
in gypsum.

The vessel was made of semicoarse clay with limestone inclusions. Cycladic influences are confined not only to the clay but
also to the incised decoration, particularly the star, a favored
motif on the clay "frying-pans" of the Cyclades during the
Kampos phase. In Crete similar vases have been found only in
tombs displaying Cycladic influences—at Kyparissi, Pyrgos, and
Gournes, Herakleion.

Selected Bibliography

Alexiou 1951, pl. XIV:2:13; Davaras 1971; Davaras–Betancourt
2004, p. 10, nos. 2A.19 and 2A.38, fig. 9; Day–Wilson–Kiriatzi
1998; Galanaki 2006, pl. IV:2e; Marangou 1990, p. 173, no. 180;
Xanthoudides 1918a, fig. 9; Zapheiropoulou 1984, p. 35, fig. 3b.

Yiannis Papadatos

8 Potter's Wheel

Early Minoan IIA period (ca. 2600–2400 B.C.)
Clay
Diam. 0.23 m, th. 0.029 m
Early Minoan settlement of Phournou Koryphi, Myrtos,
Hierapetra (Room 49)
Haghios Nikolaos Archaeological Museum, 6957

Complete. Clay circular disc with flat upper surface; curved underneath. The center of the underside has traces of damage from turning. Its decoration consists of a broad strip around the edge and a cross in the center.

This piece of equipment was likely used as a potter's wheel to make clay vases, a proposition supported by the traces of damage on the base. The absence of a hole indicates that it was not used as a fast wheel but rather as a slow one, which was manually turned by the potter in order to lift up the walls of the vessel. The fast wheel made its appearance in Crete about five hundred years later in the Middle Minoan I period.

Seven other similar discs, presumably used in the same manner, were found in the same room (Room 49), which dates to the earlier phase of occupation of the settlement (Early Minoan IIA). Therefore, it could have either been a ceramic workshop or a place used for the storage of such equipment.

Selected Bibliography
Warren 1969a; Warren 1972, p. 214, dr. 98, fig. 75c, no. 14.

Yiannis Papadatos

9 **Footed Pyxis**

Early Minoan II period (ca. 2600–2300 B.C.)
Clay
H. 0.145 m, body diam. 0.18 m
Platyvola cave, Kerameia, 1966–67
Khania Archaeological Museum, Π 2002

Pyxis with spherical body pressed onto a high conical foot, and twin pierced vertical handles—excrescences attached at the middle of the belly. The decoration comprises eight zones of incised designs (herringbone, small angular lines, and lozenges) on the upper body. Mended from several fragments.

The vase is in fine gray ware, which was relatively widespread throughout Crete early in the Early Minoan II period. Incised decoration is very popular and characterizes many of this ware's products. The pyxis, a form shared with the Cyclades, where it originated, played a special role during this period. Also, the discovery of Early Helladic "sauceboat"-type vases in the Platyvola cave strengthens the view that west Cretans and Cycladic islanders had close relations during this period.

Selected Bibliography
ΑΔ 23 B2 (1968): 415–16, pl. 376a (Tzedakis); Betancourt 1985, p. 40, pl. 3H.

Eftychia Protopapadaki

10 "Teapot"

Early Minoan IIB period (ca. 2400–2300 B.C.)
Clay
H. 0.177 m, max. diam. 0.266 m
Early Minoan settlement of Phournou Koryphi, Myrtos
Hierapetra (Room 91)
Haghios Nikolaos Archaeological Museum, 7224

Brownish-black surface, well polished, with mottled decoration comprising orange circles with black blots at the center. Piriform body with ring base, large protruding spout, and vertical handle on the opposite side.

This vase, an example of so-called Vasiliki Ware, was found inside a small room that was filled with sixty-six small and medium-size utensils for consuming and serving food. The room next door, where a built altar and a figurine of a goddess, known as the "Myrtos Goddess," were revealed, has been interpreted by the excavator as a shrine area. It is, therefore, likely that our vase belongs to a wider range of equipment that was kept there for use in rites in the neighboring cult area of the settlement.

Vasiliki Ware is among the finest artistic products of the Prepalatial period. The manufacture of such vases goes beyond the boundaries of domestic production on a small scale, since it called for very specialized technological expertise, both in throwing the pot and in firing it, as well as in the creation of the mottled decoration, which was achieved by the correct application of a slip rich in iron oxide. The high degree of specialization is supported by analyses that have shown that the Vasiliki Ware was produced in only a few centers, whence it was exported to the whole of central and eastern Crete.

This particular vase, like all Vasiliki Ware found at Myrtos, was manufactured and imported from the north part of the isthmus of Hierapetra, at least twenty kilometers from Myrtos. The fact that almost half the pottery found at Myrtos is imported from this region shows how extensive the networks were and how frequent exchange was in Crete as early as the middle of the third millennium B.C.

Selected Bibliography

Betancourt et al. 1979; Warren 1972, p. 150, fig. 63c, no. P656; Whitelaw 1997.

Yiannis Papadatos

11 **Jug**

Early Minoan IIB period (ca. 2400–2300 B.C.)
Clay
H. 0.306 m, max. diam. 0.175 m, base diam. 0.08 m
Early Minoan settlement of Phournou Koryphi, Myrtos,
Hierapetra (Room 80)
Haghios Nikolaos Archaeological Museum, 7214

Red surface, well polished, with mottled decoration of orange
circles with black blots in the center. Ovoid body with ring base,
high spout and vertical handle at the back. Mended and restored.

This vase is an example of Vasiliki Ware. See catalogue
number 10 for the technology required for the manufacture, circulation, and significance of this type of pottery.

Selected Bibliography

Betancourt et al. 1979; Warren 1972, p. 131, fig. 49a, no. P399;
Whitelaw et al. 1997.

Yiannis Papadatos

12 Kamares Ware Tray

Middle Minoan IIB period (ca. 1750–1700 B.C.)
Clay
Diam. 0.385 m
Phaistos, Old Palace, Great Destruction, west of Court I, 1966
Herakleion Archaeological Museum, HM 18593

This circular tray has low vertical walls, a horizontal rim with three parallel grooves, two horizontal handles, and a tubular spout, now largely broken. Mended and restored.

A row of white roundels with a reserved double-axe motif occupies the walls' outer surface; simple white discs decorate the walls' inner surface. White dots on the rim and white lines on the handle complete the secondary decorative motifs. A dense radiating ornament consisting of vegetal and geometric motifs occupies the entire interior base. Four hatched, sinuous bands connect a central orange roundel, which contains a red lozenge

and a white circle with four identical roundels in the periphery. Each peripheral roundel develops into petals and spirals that end in a rosette. This symmetrical composition is based on the antithetical twisting and turning of the various decorative motifs. The composition's spiraling and radiating movement gives the impression that the multicolored motifs are floating on the black background.

Undoubtedly one of the finest examples of mature Kamares vase painting, this exquisite vase exemplifies the quality and dynamic of Phaistos's palatial workshop. It was probably intended as an ostentatious prestige item rather than as a utilitarian vessel. The spout implies a liquid content, which may have been a factor in demonstrating the "floating" decoration. Unusual in the palatial apparatus, it may have also had a ritual use.

Selected Bibliography
Levi 1976, pp. 567, 594, pl. LVII.

Dimitris Sfakianakis

13 Kamares Ware Amphora

Middle Minoan IIB period (ca. 1750–1700 B.C.)
Clay
H. 0.435 m
Phaistos, Old Palace, Room XVI, 1907
Herakleion Archaeological Museum, HM 5836

Complete, tall, and narrow ovoid vase with elliptical rim and two vertical handles, decorated with white and orange paint on a black background. Brown discoloration on the lower half indicates uneven firing. A large star with white rays, an orange interior outline enclosing a similar motif, and a white circle with an orange center dominate the decoration. The tips of the stars curve slightly in different directions, creating the impression of antithetical movement. The same motif occupies the wall on the opposite side between the handles. By contrast, a simpler ornament comprising two concentric white circles decorates the walls under the handles. Four circles connected by sinuous bands decorate the base of the neck.

This amphora was found inside a storeroom of the Old Palace of Phaistos, beneath and to the west of the later palace's storerooms, together with drinking cups, serving vessels, and storage jars. The rim is pressed inward on two opposite sides, so that it forms two lobes, or spouts, which allow for increased control when the contents are poured out and which makes the vase more functional. The tall, narrow body and the markedly pushed-in rim place this example in the late period of Kamares Ware production. It is one of the precursors of the elongated amphora with elliptical rim that dominates the subsequent ceramic phase.

Selected Bibliography
Pernier 1935, pp. 264–68, pl. XVIc; Walberg 1976, p. 54, fig. 5.

Dimitris Sfakianakis

14 Beak-Spouted Jug
  Middle Minoan IIB period (ca. 1750–1700 B.C.)
  Clay
  Max. preserved h. 0.281 m, diam. base 0.069 m,
  max. diam. 0.185 m
  Phaistos, Palace, Room IL
  Herakleion Archaeological Museum, HM 10198

Beak-spouted Kamares Ware jug with an ovoid body and low neck. The decoration—white motifs on a black ground—consists of two large antithetical crescents on either side of two connected, upright and pendent triangles that form a biconcave altar. Two pairs of short oblique lines joining a horizontal band and two applied bosses, painted white, decorate both sides of the spout. Restored spout and handle.

With its minimalist, symmetrical decoration, contrast between black and white, and precise, balanced form, this vase is a simple, but characteristic example of the Kamares Style.

Selected Bibliography
Levi 1976, pl. 87.

Christina Papadaki

15 Beak-Spouted Jug

Middle Minoan IIB period (ca. 1750–1700 B.C.)
Clay
H. 0.218 m, diam. base 0.077 m, max. diam. 0.236 m
Phaistos, Palace, below the staircase of Room LV
Herakleion Archaeological Museum, HM 10594

Kamares Ware beak-spouted jug with spherical body, low neck, and vertical handle, decorated with white and orange-red motifs on a black ground. Two horizontal bands decorate the lower part of the body, and another with pendant semicircles underlines the neck. On the belly, below the spout, a white lozenge, filled with a central dotted rosette and four half-rosettes in the corners, is surrounded by four floral ornaments alternating with four solid orange-red semicircles. Horizontal lines and two concentric circles decorate, respectively, the handle and its base. Part of rim and spout restored.

This is a typical example of the mature Kamares Style, in which plant motifs are arranged in a symmetrical tectonic composition.

Selected Bibliography

Levi 1976, pl. 86; Walberg 1976, p. 167 (no. 12); Walberg 1986, p. 15, fig. 11.

Christina Papadaki

16 Bridge-Spouted Jar

Middle Minoan II period (ca. 1800–1700 B.C.)
Clay
H. 0.319 m, max. diam. 0.366 m, base diam. 0.257 m
Phaistos, Palace, Room XXVII
Herakleion Archaeological Museum, HM 5834

Vessel with Kamares Style decoration, ovoid body, two horizontal handles, and one smaller, vertical handle opposite the bridge spout. The painted decoration consists of white and orange motifs on a black background. Pairs of concentric circles decorate the area under the horizontal handles, and pairs of antithetically placed spirals ending in a spiraling plant motif decorate the front and back, below the spout and vertical handle. Mended and restored.

This jar was found together with a large group of richly decorated vases in a room near the west entrance of the old palace at Phaistos. It has been suggested that the room was used either for storing ritual objects or for preparing rituals of worship.

The bridge-spouted jar is one of the most characteristic shapes of Kamares Style pottery (Kamares Ware). The vase shape was already established by Middle Minoan II, when it acquired this particular form, with a spherical or ovoid body and a vertical handle opposite the spout. Most examples of this form, including the most richly decorated examples, date to this time.

The broad surfaces of the bridge-spouted jar provide space for the frontal, large-scale rendering of decorative motifs. The variety of ornaments used and the combination of geometric and floral motifs in different arrangements produce a unique decorative effect on nearly all of these vessels.

Selected Bibliography

Betancourt 1985, pp. 96–101; Carinci 1997; Gesell 1985, pp. 124–25; Levi 1976, pp. 58–69; Pernier 1935, pp. 142–50, pl. XVI; Walberg 1976, pp. 51, 57, figs. 28, 37, 43.

Deukalion Manidakis

17 Bridge-Spouted Jar
   Middle Minoan IIB period (ca. 1750–1700 B.C.)
   Clay
   H. 0.43 m, max. diam. 0.46 m
   Phaistos, Palace, below Room XXVII
   Herakleion Archaeological Museum, HM 5833

This wide-rimmed bridge-spouted Kamares Ware jar has an ovoid body, flat rim, two slightly raised horizontal handles, and one vertical handle set opposite the spout. The Kamares Ware decoration consists of white and orange-red motifs on a black ground. Three horizontal bands occupy the lower part of the body, and spirals combined with flower buds adorn the belly and shoulder. Vertical bands and opposing spirals, which reach the belly, decorate the handles. Mended and restored.

This is a characteristic example of the mature, or classical, Kamares Style of the Middle Minoan IIB period, which was created in the palatial workshops of Phaistos and Knossos. The style's main feature is the use of complex rotating-radiating motifs in various original, often unique combinations, which constitute a truly unlimited artistic vocabulary.

Selected Bibliography
Banti 1939–40, p. 37, fig. 46a.

Christina Papadaki

18 **Askoid Vase**
   Middle Minoan II period (ca. 1800–1700 B.C.)
   Clay
   Max. h. 0.122 m, max. w. 0.173 m, base diam. 0.061 m
   Phaistos, Palace, Room IL
   Herakleion Archaeological Museum, HM 10162

Closed carinated vase with a conical lower half and convex upper half. Restored and mended. Two raised horizontal handles and a funnel-shape trefoil spout. The painted Kamares Style decoration is made up of white and orange motifs on a black background, which is divided into three zones. A row of vertical, arched plant motifs is arranged radiating upward from the base on the lower body. Crescent-shaped motifs alternate with small leaflike patterns on the upper part. At the top, fine orange and white lines form a cross.

The vase was found inside a room in the old palace at Phaistos, together with a large group of decorated vases and ritual vessels, such as offering tables and bull-shaped rhyta. The rooms in this area of the palace, near the West Court, are thought to have been used for storing ritual objects or for preparing religious rituals.

This vase combines the basic tendencies of the highly decorative mature Kamares Style, as it developed in the palatial ceramic workshops. The finely executed decoration is arranged, according to the so-called built syntax, in zones that correspond to the vase's different parts, emphasizing its structure. The decorative motifs radiate and twirl around the axis, creating antithetical movements that balance each other in an impressive, unified composition.

Selected Bibliography
Banti 1939–40, p. 15; Betancourt 1985, pp. 96–101; Carinci 1997; Gesell 1985, pp. 124–25; Levi 1952, p. 13, fig 18; Levi 1976, pp. 43–58, pl. 148b; Walberg 1976, pp. 17, 112, 143, figs. 27, 30, 42.

Deukalion Manidakis

19 Three-Handled Miniature Pithos

Middle Minoan III period (ca. 1700–1600 B.C.)
Clay
H. 0.095 m, diam. rim 0.069 m, diam. base 0.038 m
Phaistos, Palace
Herakleion Archaeological Museum, HM 17971

Three-handled miniature pithos with a piriform body, low foot, broad neck and vertical handles. The Kamares Style decoration consists of white and orange-red motifs on a black background. A broad band decorates the foot. On the body, two horizontal bands support three large crocus buds, which fill the space between the handles. Bands decorate the neck and the rim's interior. Complete, rim restored.

Endemic to southeast Europe and western Asia, the crocus is a bulbous perennial plant with a short stem; its leaves have fine white veins. The purple flowers are collected in the autumn for their three valuable orange-red stamens, which contain saffron, a strong coloring substance known since antiquity for its dyeing and healing properties. Six or seven species of wild crocus grow in Crete today.

Crocus flowers are a popular motif in Minoan art, particularly on clay vessels and faience objects. Women and, in one rather unrealistic representation, monkeys are depicted gathering crocuses in wall paintings (Knossos; Akrotiri, Thera). Scholars have identified these crocuses as the species *Crocus cartwrightianus*, which occurs in western Crete, and *Crocus oreocreticus*, which grows in the island's central and western mountainous regions. The crocus flower also appears as an ideogram in the Minoan scripts. It undoubtedly had a practical and possibly symbolic significance for the Minoans. On this miniature three-handled vase from the Phaistos palace, the large white crocuses—the only motif on the black ground—produce the highly decorative effect that characterizes Kamares Ware in its mature phase.

Selected Bibliography

Evely 1999, pp. 102–4; Levi 1976, pl. 205b; Psilakis–Psilaki 2000, pp. 97–98.

Christina Papadaki

20 Kamares Ware Cup

Middle Minoan IIB period (ca. 1750–1700 B.C.)
Clay
H. 0.073 m
Phaistos, Palace, Room LV, beneath staircase, 1955
Herakleion Archaeological Museum, HM 10606

Cylindrical cup with slight splaying, a very thin body, and a vertical strap handle. The painted decoration consists of white and orange motifs on a black ground with a metallic sheen. Two large white antithetical spirals, which emerge from the white band that encircles the handle, fill the cup's sides. The spirals are united above and below by an orange-red disc, from which sprout two palmetted half-rosettes. Mended and restored.

A large number of neatly stacked utilitarian vessels, which had fallen from the story above, were found in the area below the staircase in the old palace. Several cups were found one inside the other. A superb drinking vessel, this cup shows a remarkable variety of form. This particular type is probably a more refined version of the cylindrical cup, the result of the form's lengthy development in the pottery workshops of Phaistos and Knossos. The imitation of metal prototypes is evident from the squat, shallow cylinder with vertical wall to the deep cup with slightly curved walls. The strap handle, the thin walls, and even the decorative spiral motif further demonstrate the influence of metal prototypes.

Selected Bibliography
Levi 1956, p. 249, fig. 24; Levi 1976, pp. 91–96, pl. 126f.

Dimitris Sfakianakis

21 Kamares Ware Cup

Middle Minoan IIB period (ca. 1750–1700 B.C.)
Clay
H. 0.061 m
Phaistos, beneath New Palace Room 11, 1939
Herakleion Archaeological Museum, HM 10089

Carinated cup with vertical strap handle. The lower part of the body is conical, and the upper part has concave walls. A decorative motif occupies the wall opposite the handle. This motif consists of an orange circle, with solid white semicircles on the periphery, that surrounds four cross-shape ornaments radiating from a four-petaled rosette with a central red disc. Pendant solid white semicircles are below the rim, and a white band outlines the base. Mended and restored.

The floor of the old palace room in which this cup was found, beneath the New Palace Room 11, yielded large quantities of exquisite Kamares Ware pottery. These were products of the last years of the palatial workshop, before the palaces' complete destruction. Carinated cups are the most characteristic of the Protopalatial ceramic drinking vessels. This shape was abandoned when the new palaces were established. The thin walls, vertical strap handle, and sharp carination reflect metal prototypes. The carinated cups from the Phaistos palace, probably the most impressive examples of this type, demonstrate both the ostentation of the palatial apparatus and the endless imagination of that period's potters. Here the motif occupies the entire height without taking into account the cup's main structural feature, its carination. This is an example of the so-called unified decoration, as opposed to structural decoration, in which the decorative motifs are arranged in zones. The unified syntax is a peculiarity of Minoan vase painting of that period.

Selected Bibliography
Guarducci 1942, p. 231, fig. 4; Levi 1976, pp. 365, 368d, pl. 131f.

Dimitris Sfakianakis

22 **Spouted Pithos**
   Middle Minoan II–III period (ca. 1800–1600 B.C.)
   Clay
   H. 0.90 m, rim diam. 0.57 m, base diam. 0.29 m
   Aitania
   Herakleion Archaeological Museum, HM 29752

Conical pithos with slightly curved sides, a small bridged spout and three handles below the rim—two horizontal handles on the sides and one vertical handle opposite the spout. The white-painted decoration on a dark-brown ground consists of a leafy band at handle level, a retorted running spiral that covers most of the body, and three horizontal bands directly above the base. Solid-painted arcs cover the outer side of the rim. Mended and restored.

This pithos is one of the finest examples of burial pithoi that were used mainly during the Middle Minoan III and Late Minoan I periods, and were common in many different sites of the island, although rare in western Crete.

Selected Bibliography
AΔ 53 B3 (1998): 853 (Rethemiotakis); Christakis 2005, pp. 20 (form 114), 56, 75, fig. 24.

Nektaria Mavroudi

23 Bridge-Spouted Pithos with Lid

Late Minoan IA period (ca. 1600–1525/1500 B.C.)
Clay
H. (with lid) 0.417 m, max. diam. (with handles) 0.346 m,
diam. lid 0.24 m
Mochlos, Block A
Herakleion Archaeological Museum, HM 5465

Bridge-spouted pithos with barrel-shape body and several handles: two horizontal handles on the shoulders, and one vertical handle opposite the spout flanked by two smaller ones. Slanted papyrus-lilies decorate the lower part of the body, and a solid rock pattern ornaments the shoulder with dark reddish-brown and added white color. Mended and restored.

The circular lid has an arched handle at its center flanked by two smaller handles perpendicular to the large one. Its decoration consists of wide, hatched, interchanging zones. The selection and composition of themes recall fresco prototypes. Flowers, plants, and trees were very popular motifs in Minoan wall painting. In fact, the "Lily Fresco" from the Amnisos villa confirms the existence of planned, artificial gardens in the Minoan world. Specialists have identified three main species of lilies in Minoan art, namely the white lily (*Lilium candidum*), the red lily (*Lilium chalcedonicum*), and the maritime lily (*Pancratium maritimum*), which are often confused with papyrus flowers. The lily, papyrus, and crocus also occur in vase painting, particularly in the Neopalatial period, and on vases and vessels that are usually associated with the perfume industry.

Selected Bibliography

Evely 1999, pp. 100–101; Seager 1909, p. 280, pl. VI; Walberg 1992.

Christina Papadaki

24 Floral Style Conical Cup

Late Minoan IA period (ca. 1600–1525/1500 B.C.)
Clay
H. 0.118 m
Knossos, Palace, 1900
Herakleion Archaeological Museum, HM 3856

Conical cup with straight, thin walls and no handles. The preserved exterior wall is decorated with two oblique stems and elongated leaves contained within a wide band framed by two bands at the rim and base. Mended and restored.

The long, pointed leaves identify the plants as either grass, olive branches, or reeds, the last interpretation being the most prevalent, hence its adoption for this type of reed motif. Vertical, assymetrically parallel lines, which recall a pleated surface, or ripple pattern, decorate the interior. The association of these two motifs is characteristic of the vase painting of this period.

The reed motif is one of the most characteristic expressions of the so-called Floral Style, which introduced a new form of dark-on-light decoration and was a favorite motif of the Knossian workshop. This cup is usually identified as a drinking vessel, despite its large size. Some of the vases with reed decoration have particular morphological features, which may indicate a special use. A group of cups from the Knossian workshop generally identified as flower pots constitute a characteristic example. The size and refined rendering of the reeds suggest a possible alternative to its use as a drinking vessel, perhaps even as a palatial display vase.

Selected Bibliography
Marinatos–Hirmer 1959, p. 93, fig. 78; *PM* II, p. 472, figs. 276, 349; Popham 1967, p. 339.

Dimitris Sfakianakis

25 Conical Cup
Late Minoan I period (ca. 1600–1450 B.C.)
Clay
H. 0.05 m, base diam. 0.035 m, rim diam. 0.095 m
Kato Zakros, sector Γ, storeroom inside NW wall
Siteia Archaeological Museum, 8846

Cup with a flat base, conical body, and thin rim, decorated with a zone of ivy leaves with stalks framed by bands. Monochrome interior. Mended and restored.

The cup belongs to a large collection of such cups found stored in the West Wing of the palace at Kato Zakros.

Selected Bibliography
Platon 1962, pp. 158, 160; Platon 2002b, p. 150,pls. XLIV–XLVIIIc; Platon–Platon 1991, p. 394.

Evi Saliaka

26 Potter's Wheel

Late Minoan IB period (ca. 1525/1500–1450 B.C.)
Clay
H. 0.052 m, max. diam. 0.401 m, diam. of upper surface
0.37 m, wt. 8.38 kg.
Mochlos, Building B, Artisans' Quarter
Haghios Nikolaos Archaeological Museum, 14409

The upper side of the wheel has a channel around the circumference; the lip of the underside slopes inward to support the wooden frame. The interior of the underside has a central concavity, which is surrounded by five concentric incised circles and two relief rings. The incised circles create zones between them, two of which are decorated with small successively incised oblique lines. A large part of one side is restored with gypsum.

The upper surface preserves a noticeable amount of coarse red clay, which would have functioned to hold an object in place. The wheel was made of local clay and was probably used at some point in the studio of the potter of the Artisan's Quarter.

Excavations on the island of Mochlos and on the shore across from it began in 1908. Since 1989, new investigations have brought to light two Late Minoan IB buildings, which appear to have been industrial installations used for different activities, such as bronze working, ceramic production, and the manufacture of ivory objects. Each building, apart from its function as an industrial and storage area, was inhabited by the artisans' families and provides evidence for the existence of domestic shrines.

Selected Bibliography
Soles 2003, pp. 36–38, 48–50; Soles–Stos-Gale 2004, pp. 33–35, IC.158.

Maria Kyriakaki

27 Bridge-Spouted Jug

Late Minoan IB period (ca. 1525/1500–1450 B.C.)
Clay
H. 0.231 m
Knossos, Palace, north side of Royal Road
Herakleion Archaeological Museum, HM 15052

Ovoid wide-mouth vase with bridged spout, circular base, and a vertical strap handle with a deep groove along its ridge. Running spirals with stylized ivy leaves in the center cover most of the body. Below the spirals is an equal number of double arches. Painted lozenges fill the spaces between these motifs. A single row of leaves covers the shoulder; a dentate band covers the base of the neck and a zigzag the neck itself. The decoration is characterized by the precision and symmetry of the repeated motifs. Mended and restored.

The sherds that make up this vase had fallen from the upper story with other examples of the same decorative tradition. The product of a palatial workshop, this vase exemplifies the vase making and vase painting of the so-called Special Palatial Tradition, which flourished during this period for no more than five decades. These vases are characterized as outstanding examples of Cretan pottery, and the shape is distinguished by its symmetry and finesse. Several morphological and painted decorative elements indicate that the vase imitates a metal prototype. The decorative pattern of the vessel is an expressive variation of the so-called Abstract and Geometric Style.

Selected Bibliography

Betancourt 1985, pp. 140–44, pl. 22A, B, C, E; Hood 1961–1962, p. 27, fig. 37; Popham 1967, p. 341, pl. 80a.

Dimitris Sfakianakis

28 Bridge-Spouted Jar

Late Minoan IB period (ca. 1525/1500–1450 B.C.)
Clay
H. 0.29 m, max. diam. 0.343 m
Sklavokambos, Megaron
Herakleion Archaeological Museum, HM 8939

Bridge-spouted jar, with spherical, squat body; short neck; flat, everted rim; and ridged, S-shape vertical handle. Bands and coral motifs surround the base. On the body, multiple zigzag bands alternate with schematized sea urchins and solid discs. A one-sided foliate band occupies the shoulder, and a double row of reserved rosettes adorns the neck. Mended. Two-thirds of the shape and decoration restored.

A characteristic example of the Late Minoan IB Abstract Geometric Style, this jug from Sklavokambos also combines several other styles of the Special Palatial Tradition. The corals and stylized sea urchins, in particular, come from the Marine Style; the one-sided foliate band recalls the Floral Style, where it occurs on vases with spirals and arcades, whereas the reserved rosettes recall a stemmed cup in the Alternating Style from Phaistos. Similar, with the exception of the marine motifs, is the decoration of a rhyton from Gournia and two tall clay alabastra, one from Mochlos (Block B) and another from an Egyptian grave of the early 18th Dynasty, on which the zigzags may imitate the veins of their stone prototypes.

Selected Bibliography

Betancourt 1985, pp. 174, 205, pl. 22 H; Marinatos 1939–41, pp. 83–84, pl. 22; Pernier–Banti 1951, p. 533; Seager 1909, p. 282, fig. 5.

Christina Papadaki

29 Marine Style Ewer

Late Minoan IB period (ca. 1525/1500–1450 B.C.)
Clay
H. 0.29 m, rim diam. 0.017 m, base diam. 0.078 m,
max. diam. 0.21 m
Zakros, Palace, West Wing. Room III (probably fallen
from upper floor)
Herakleion Archaeological Museum, HM 32612

Ewer with a broad everted rim. Piriform body, gradually narrowing toward the discoid stepped base. High cylindrical neck. Vertical handle, slightly raised above the rim, with a bulge along its back, rectangular in section, and a button-shape knob where it meets the lip. Mended and restored.

The vase is decorated in the Marine Style with argonauts in a separate partition formed by bands of a scale pattern crossing each other diagonally. There are also argonauts arranged in a row on the neck, as well as seaweed and scale patterns. Rapidly painted scale pattern on the upper surface of the rim, as well as a row of foliate band on the edge, and chevrons on the angled lip. "Sponge" pattern where the neck merges into the shoulder. Rows of foliate bands high on the neck and on the shoulder, the handle (back and edges), and the point where it joins the body.

The ewer from the Zakros palace is one of the exceptional examples of pottery of the Special Palatial Tradition at the end of the Late Minoan IB period. The shape of the ewer is thought to be the sleekest example of the style, but only three exist in such a state that they can be restored in their entirety. Apart from the Zakros ewer, marvelous examples of the type include an ewer from a chamber tomb at Poros, Herakleion, and another in the Borély in Marseilles, which was probably found in Egypt. N. Platon thought that the latter example and the Zakros ewer were by the same artist. However, the discovery of the Poros ewer in 1986 shredded that hypothesis, which had in any case been brought into question earlier. The Poros ewer is unique, since extra sculptural decoration was added to fill the decorative fields. In terms of decoration and manufacture (e.g.,

the very similar treatment of the trefoil mouth), as well as its size, which is nearly the same as the Marseilles ewer (the Zakros ewer is taller than either of these), they establish criteria for the identification of the same potter, if not the same painter, as the individual who made these two examples. Furthermore, one may adopt as a working hypothesis the fact that the Marseilles ewer was exported from Crete to Egypt as a stolen grave good in the mid-nineteenth century A.D., because it later came to be bought by the city of Marseilles. At any rate, generally speaking, the three vessels in question seem to have been created in a specialized Knossian workshop of the mature Late Minoan IB period. Macroscopic examination of the clay of the ewer from the palace of Zakros supports this assumption.

With regard to the purpose of these magnificent vessels, it is reasonable to suggest that it was exclusively a ritual one. It is worth noting that a gold signet ring was found at Poros with the ewer, and this supports the hypothesis that the two objects were grave gifts of the burial of a priest or some other high-ranking individual. Even if it has not been absolutely verified that the entire corpus of Marine Style vases was manufactured to be used in ceremonies, it is certain that the sea had a particular religious significance for the Minoans. Moreover, there are many examples of depictions of ceremonial libation jugs on seal stones and signet rings. The most characteristic instance is that of jugs with S-shape handles, just like those on the Marine Style ewers, held by processional daemons depicted on the gold Tiryns ring. There also appears to be a depiction of a real ewer on the "Procession Fresco" in the West Wing of the palace at Knossos. The enormous artistic value of these vessels seems to be indisputable, even in their own era. It is sufficient to note that they are depicted among other objects brought as gifts to the pharaoh, supposedly by Cretans (Keftiu), on wall paintings of the tombs of Egyptian officials at Thebes.

Selected Bibliography

Betancourt 1985, p. 136, fig. 101; Dimopoulou-Rethemiotaki 1999a; Karetsou–Andreadaki-Vlazaki–Papadakis 2000, pp. 143–44 (Dimopoulou); Mountjoy 1985; Platon 1974, p. 92; Wachsmann 1987, pls. LIV–LVIII.

Lefteris Platon

30 Two-Handled Bucket Vase

Late Minoan IB period (ca. 1525/1500–1450 B.C.)
Clay
H. 0.183 m, rim diam. 0.162 m, base diam. 0.132 m
Nirou Chani
Herakleion Archaeological Museum, HM 7572

Cylindrical and spouted bucket vase with two horizontal handles. Below the rim, two projections that flank the spout and three cylindrical knobs, recalling rivet heads, may reflect a metal prototype. A horizontal groove defines the base and three horizontal ridges underlie the rim. Mended and restored.

The Marine Style decoration consists of four vertical triton shells alternating with three-stemmed seaweed motifs, which look as if they are swaying in water. Corals and anemones along the bottom also convey the feeling of a seascape. The artist arranged these motifs to harmonize with the vase's shape. The stripes and pointed projections on the triton shell demonstrate an attempt at naturalism.

Selected Bibliography

Betancourt 1985, pp. 196–203; *PM* II.1, 279–81; Xanthoudides 1922, p. 20.

Nektaria Mavroudi

31 Tall Alabastron

Late Minoan IB period (ca. 1525/1500–1450 B.C.)
Clay
H. 0.223 m, max. diam. 0.154 m, diam. base 0.135 m,
diam. rim 0.098 m
Knossos, Stratigraphical Museum Extension excavations,
North House, west of Unexplored Mansion
Herakleion Archaeological Museum, HM 24298

Tall Marine Style alabastron with askoid body; low, narrow neck with relief ring around its base; and broad, flaring rim. A curvilinear lozenge with two wavy lines crossing one another in its interior decorates the base. Ocular "starfish" or sun motifs, rocks, and seaweed cover the body. Mended.

This is a characteristic example of the Marine Style, which is found in artistic works of the Special Palatial Tradition. The sea, an integral part of the natural environment and economic life of Crete, was an important source of inspiration for Minoan artists. Marine subjects and motifs occur on a variety of Minoan artifacts and in different media: clay and stone vases, faience and ivory objects, and seal stones, and also in wall paintings, although less frequently than land flora and fauna. Marine Style vases depict a limited range of motifs, such as octopus and squids, nautilus/argonaut shells, tritons, and dolphins, all swimming in a seascape composed of rocks, corals, seaweed, and anemones. The highly stylized "starfish"—often described as a sun because it cannot be identified with any known marine species—is another popular motif.

Examples of the Marine Style have been found at several sites on the Greek mainland and in the Aegean islands. Scholars have distinguished several small subgroups, which may reflect the style of particular workshops, such as the Polyps Workshop, or even artists, such as the Marine Style Master, to whom the lentoid flask from Palaikastro and a stirrup jar from Zakros are attributed.

Selected Bibliography

Betancourt 1985, pp. 200–203; Catling 1979–80, p. 49, fig. 85; Evely 1999, pp. 113–14; Karetsou–Andreadaki-Vlazaki–Papadakis 2000, pp. 143–44 (Dimopoulou); Mountjoy 1984, p. 173; Popham 1978, pp. 181–82.

Christina Papadaki

32 Marine Style Stirrup Jar
    Late Minoan IB period (ca. 1525/1500–1450 B.C.)
    Clay
    Max. h. 0.198 m, max. w. 0.235 m, base diam. 0.09 m
    Gournia
    Herakleion Archaeological Museum, HM 2783

Squat globular stirrup jar with a short neck and three handles.
Mended and restored.

Two octopuses are painted on the front and back of the vase,
following its shape. They are depicted en face, their tentacles
curling around the neck and handles and meeting gracefully on
the sides. Triton shells, seaweed, and a sea urchin fill all the
empty spaces between the tentacles; *horror vacui* seems to be a
frequent approach on vases of this period. Corals frame the
main composition, emphasizing the naturalism of the seascape.
This naturalism is further emphasized by the lateral tilt of the
octopuses, which gives the impression that they are floating in
water, and by the dots in the center of each sucker.

This vase's decoration is an excellent example of the Marine
Style of the Late Minoan IB period. The artist has succeeded in
combining complementary marine motifs in a harmonious composition with aesthetic perfection on the vase's rounded surface.

Selected Bibliography
Betancourt 1985, pp. 200–203; Fotou 1993, p. 66; Hawes et al. 1908,
color pl. H; Mountjoy 1974; *PM* II.2, pp. 507–11; Popham 1967,
pp. 339–43.

Nektaria Mavroudi

33 Stirrup Jar with Stopper

Late Minoan IB period (ca. 1450 B.C.)
Clay
Pot: h. 0.46 m, body diam. 0.35 m, base diam. 0.14 m
Stopper: h. 0.034 m, diam. 0.049-0.046 m
Kastelli Hill, Khania, Plateia Haghia Aikaterini,
Greek-Swedish excavation, 1977
Khania Archaeological Museum, Π 4464-10350

Elongated ovoid body with narrow base. Two holes on the false spout's disc were used to secure the contents during transportation. The main decorative motif, which occupies the upper body and shoulder, consists of reeds rendered naturalistically and growing densely packed along the ground, which is indicated conventionally by four horizontal lines. Mended from several fragments. Traces of burning on the exterior.

This vase was found on the floor of Room M of the Late Minoan I Building I during the Greek-Swedish excavation (Plateia Haghia Aikaterini) on Kastelli Hill, Khania. The clay stopper that probably sealed the vase's spout was found in the same place. Handmade with unfired clay, the stopper was burned during the conflagration that destroyed the building. It has an irregular, truncated, conical shape and exhibits the fingerprints of its maker. This vase is an excellent example of the Floral Style. Its shape is suitable for the storage and transportation of liquids.

Selected Bibliography
Tzedakis–Martlew 1999, p. 31, no. 3 (Andreadaki-Vlazaki).

Eftychia Protopapadaki

34 Pithos

Late Minoan IB period (ca. 1450 B.C.)
Clay
H. 1.26 m, rim diam. 0.44 m, base diam. 0.30 m
Kato Zakros, House Z, Room Γ, Haghios Antonios Hill
Siteia Archaeological Museum, 9973

Flat base, elongated ovoid body with two rows of four vertical handles, cylindrical in section, and a high neck with an inverted rim. The decoration from top to bottom consists of four large double axes in relief with stems, four encircling bands of rope pattern, four groups of three parallel rope-pattern stripes placed obliquely, and three ridges near the base. Mended and restored with gypsum.

The Zakros region was an important production center of storage vessels. Its pithoi (storage jars) are set apart by the high quality of their manufacture and the ingenuity of their decoration. This pithos is a typical example decorated with relief double axes, the preeminent sacred symbol of the Minoans. Perhaps its contents were destined for religious use.

Selected Bibliography
Christakis 2005; Kopaka–Platon 1993, p. 100, figs. 32, 36, 38; Platon 1988, pp. 231–32, pls. 159, 160a; Platon 2002a, p. 11; Platon–Platon 1991, fig. 173.

Evi Saliaka

35 Four-Handled Pithoid Jar

Late Minoan IB period (ca. 1450 B.C.)
Clay
H. 0.93 m, base diam. 0.20 m, rim diam. 0.40 m
Kato Zakros, House Γ, Room Π
Siteia Archaeological Museum, 1057

Discoid base, piriform body, cylindrical neck, broad inverted rim, four horizontal handles on shoulder. The decoration consists of bands on base, body, shoulder, and neck: zones of reeds, revolving foliates, and branches; the usual running spirals on the body; and variegated stone pattern on the shoulder. The decoration is typical of eastern Crete with its combination of added white paint. Mended and restored with gypsum.

This pithoid jar belongs to a homogenous group of at least thirty-four pithoid jars whose decoration is organized in horizontal zones. The decorative motifs are repeated with variations, including imitations of conglomerate stones, spinning pairs of ivy leaves, spirals, foliate bands, double axes, wavy and vertical lines, and slanted reeds. This group of pithoid jars was found almost exclusively in the West Wing of the palace at Zakros. Their relatively high standard of manufacture, the execution of the decorative motifs, and the fact that a large number of them have been discovered, indicate that they were products of a palatial workshop at Zakros.

Selected Bibliography

Platon 1962, p. 160, pl. 156c; Platon 2002b, pp. 148–50, pls. XLIV–XLVIIIc.

Evi Saliaka

36 Palace Style Pithoid Jar

Late Minoan IB–Late Minoan II period (ca. 1450–1400 B.C.)
Clay
H. 0.58 m
Knossos, Unexplored Mansion, Pillar Room H, 1972
Herakleion Archaeological Museum, HM 21168

Piriform jar with discoid base, cylindrical neck, and protruding, flat, horizontal rim. The three vertical handles on the shoulders are deeply grooved. The vase's morphological features suggest a metal prototype. The decoration consists of three snakelike stems with large heart-shape ivy leaves. Between the leaves are irregular "sponge" motifs, which may represent rocks. A single-sided leafy band marks the base of the neck. The rim and base are decorated with solid color. Two reserved wavy bands adorn the neck. Mended and restored.

The sherds that compose this vase had fallen from the mansion's upper story, together with other vases and objects that suggest a ritual use (the excavator talks of a "domestic sanctuary"). This vase is one of the rare examples of the so-called Palace Style, which usually describes pithoid jars with handles. Most of these elaborate vases are attributed to Knossian workshops. The shape and quality of the decoration suggest that they were used not only for practical purposes, but also as display, or prestige, objects. The ivy is a favored plant motif, not only in vase painting, but also in other forms of art. The "sacral ivy" within a rocky landscape is usually considered a symbolic representation.

Selected Bibliography

Popham 1973, p. 58, fig. 32; Popham 1984, pp. 36, 171, fig. 68a, b; *PM* IV, pp. 318–22.

Dimitris Sfakianakis

37 Three-Handled Small Amphora

Late Helladic IIIA1 period (ca. 1400–1350 B.C.)
Plain, light-brown clay
H. 0.172 m, body diam. 0.130 m, base diam. 0.054 m
City of Khania, Greek-Swedish excavation, 1971, 1983
Khania Archaeological Museum, Π 10093

Elegant vase, Mycenaean import, with a pear-shape body, a tall foot with flat base, and three vertical strap handles. The short, wide neck ends in a spout with an almost horizontal rim. The vase is undecorated. Mended.

The amphora was found in pieces inside a wide refuse pit established in the ruined Late Minoan I Building I, in the Minoan settlement on the Kastelli Hill. It belongs to the time of the Mycenaean-Achaean rule of large parts of Crete, Kydonia in particular, a period of strong and varied influences in artistic production. This regime is associated with the establishment of a Mycenaean dynasty at Knossos, but evidence for some kind of palatial organization is also being gradually revealed in the Kydonia region.

A common type of vase, this small three-handled amphora frequently occurs inside the Kydonia cemetery's contemporary graves, together with copper-alloy weapons and other objects that illustrate political and cultural contacts.

Selected Bibliography

Hallager–Tzedakis 1984, pp. 1–2, 8–9; Pållson-Hallager 1986, p. 179; Tzedakis 1972, p. 390.

Sophia Preve

38 One-Handled Bowl

Late Cypriot II (ca. 1400–1300 B.C.)
Clay
H. 0.750 m, rim diam. 0.210 m
Kastelli Hill, Khania, 1965
Khania Archaeological Museum, Π 1959

Wide hemispherical bowl; horizontal wishbone handle with a small groove at the tip. Vertical brushstrokes decorate the rim, and a row of cross-hatched lozenges between two pairs of horizontal bands occupies the upper body. Cross-hatching and a row of dots decorate the top and bottom of the handle, respectively. The interior is left undecorated.

Largely restored with plaster, the bowl is recomposed from a few pottery sherds collected in a trial trench during the early years of the excavations on the Kastelli Hill that have uncovered a significant part of the Minoan settlement of Kydonia. More sherds from similar vessels were found during subsequent excavation campaigns at this site.

An identical vase comes from Kouklia in southwestern Cyprus. This suggests contacts between Cyprus and Kydonia in the fourteenth century B.C., a hypothesis further supported by the discovery of pottery products from the Kydonia workshop in Cyprus. The presence of cups, jugs, bowls, and other small vessels, as well as large storage jars, all of Cypriot origin, in the ports of Kommos and Poros and at Gournia demonstrates the broader commercial contacts between Cyprus and Mycenaean Crete.

Selected Bibliography
Stampolidis–Karetsou 1998, p. 62, no. 14 (Andreadaki-Vlazaki); Hallager–Hallager 2003, III:1, Text, p. 252.

Sophia Preve

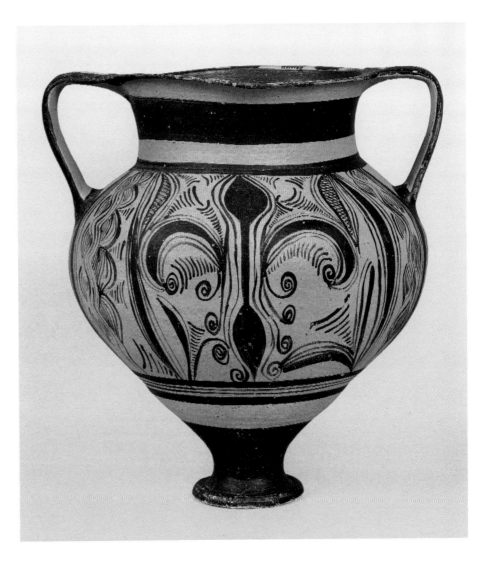

39 Krater

Late Minoan IIIA2–B period (ca. 1375–1200 B.C.)
Clay
H. 0.43 m, rim diam. 0.27 m
Episkopi, Hierapetra
Hierapetra Archaeological Collection, 555

Complete.

The main decoration, arranged in panels, includes a highly schematic hybrid palm tree-octopus and plant and linear motifs. Both the octopus and palm tree, which belongs to the so-called Nilotic repertoire, are particularly well-loved motifs in Minoan iconography, and the unrealistic combination of different motifs is found in the iconography of sarcophagi. The arrangement of the decorative motifs into panels is typical of the Late Minoan IIIA period. However, the placing of these motifs on a larger surface and the typology of the vase belong to a slightly later period.

This amphoroid krater is one of four, with many features in common, that were all found in two chamber tombs excavated at Episkopi, Hierapetra, a region where many tombs of the Late Minoan III period have come to light over the years. In one of these was discovered the famous Episkopi sarcophagus with its multitude of religious decorative elements. Parallels are to be found at Kritsa, Pharmokephalo, Sklavoi, and elsewhere.

Selected Bibliography

Επετηρίς Εταιρείας Κρητικών Σπουδών 1941, p. 273 (Platon); Kanta 1980, pp. 146–60, 275, pl. 103.7; *Κρητ. Χρονικά Α´* (1947): p. 638 (Platon); Popham 1967, pp. 347–49, fig. 87a.

Vasiliki Zographaki

40 **Multiple-Handled Flask**
   Late Minoan IIIA2–IIIB period (ca. 1375–1200 B.C.)
   Clay
   H. 0.263 m, body diam. (with handles) 0.248 m
   Knossos, Palace, corridor north of the Throne Room
   Herakleion Archaeological Museum, HM 2643

Biconvex body, flattened out (one side more than the other). Six handles along the periphery. Groups of concentric circles decorate both sides of the body. The rim and handle tops are also outlined with paint. Body complete. Two handles restored.

The morphological features (asymmetrically flattened body, several handles, and lack of foot) suggest that this was a pendant vase. On the basis of ethnographic parallels, such vessels are thought to have been used for carrying water or other liquids on journeys.

The flask was found in the corridor north of the Throne Room in the palace at Knossos, in its final destruction levels. Similar spherical flasks decorated with concentric circles and dating to the Late Minoan III period have been found at Zapher Papoura and Mouliana. An earlier (Late Minoan IB) flask of possible Cypriot origin from Pseira has a similar shape.

Selected Bibliography
Betancourt 1998; Palmer 1962; Palmer 1969, p. 64, fig. 9b; Popham 1964, pp. 7, 9, 16 and pl. 4f–g; Popham 1966, p. 19; Popham 1970, fig. 7 and pl. 10f; Warren 1989.

Deukalion Manidakis

41 **Stirrup Jar**
   Late Minoan IIIB period (ca. 1300–1200 B.C.)
   Clay
   H. 0.24 m, max. diam. 0.21 m
   Kritsa
   Haghios Nikolaos Archaeological Museum, 135

Decorated with a schematic octopus (a favorite motif on this type of vase), whose tentacles, in two rows, symmetrically cover the body of the vessel. Restored in gypsum at the lip.

Very fine stirrup jars are quite frequently found in Late Minoan III tombs and differ from their domestic counterparts found in settlements. The typological features—decoration and, above all, the clay and paint—point to a production workshop in the Khania region of western Crete. Other Khaniote vases were recovered in the same tomb where this stirrup jar was found, as well as in other tombs excavated later in the region of Kritsa.

Apart from the local East Cretan vases, and those linked to the Khania workshop, some were either imported from mainland Greece or imitated Mycenaean originals.

The quantity and quality of vases from tombs at Kritsa, as well as the fact that some were imported from other workshops within and outside Crete, indicate the existence of an economically robust community that would have had a relationship with both western Crete and mainland Greece, probably through Khania.

Selected Bibliography
Davaras n.d., n. 61; Demakopoulou 1988, pp. 150–51; Kanta 1980, pp. 134–39, 244, 252–56; Platon 1951a; Tsipopoulou–Vagnetti 2006, figs. 1e, 2e.

Vasiliki Zographaki

42 **Krater**
Late Minoan IIIC period (ca. 1200–1150 B.C.)
Clay
H. 0.195 m, rim diam. 0.26 m
Khamalevri, Arismari, rubbish pit, 1997
Rethymnon Archaeological Museum, Π 23708

Exquisite vase with horizontal handles and a ring base. The interior is entirely painted with a reserved disc in the bottom. The main decorative panels between the handles contain two heraldic birds on either side of Minoan sacred symbols: two big spirals recalling the shape of horns of consecration, with a double axe and two biconcave altars in between. Another, smaller bird sits above each handle. The birds' bodies and the composition's empty spaces are filled with various motifs, including wavy lines, curvilinear motifs, dots, and hatching, which suggest an imaginary landscape. Mended and restored.

The stylized scene is finely executed in a highly decorative way. This stylistic trend, in which living creatures are rendered as lifeless, decorative motifs, often in a Mycenaean-type antithetical composition, is characteristic of the twelfth century B.C. and is common throughout Crete. Kraters were the second most common type of vase, after the skyphos (deep bowl), in the Late Minoan IIIC period and provide the best examples for the development of pictorial representations. Kraters with similar decoration are known from Phaistos and Kastelli, Pediada.

Selected Bibliography
Andreadaki-Vlazaki–Papadopoulou 2005, pp. 381–82, n. 36, fig. 45.

Eleni Papadopoulou

As early as the Prepalatial period, Minoan craftsmen and specialized lapidary workshops indulged in mastering techniques of working with stone, which resulted in an impressive quantity and quality of production. Small vases made of veined marbles and local conglomerate stones, such as saucers, bowls, and bottles, some of them relatively sophisticated, have been found in the tombs of central and eastern Crete dating from about 2600 B.C. and later. These labor-intensive objects were produced through the use of drills and other tools, along with abrasives for smoothing and polishing surfaces.

From the Protopalatial period, and especially during the Neopalatial (ca. 1900–1450 B.C.), stone vases were considered luxury items, and the most elaborate pieces, such as the bull's-head rhyta from the palaces at Knossos and Zakros and the lioness of Knossos, were reserved for palatial ceremonies. Local steatite and serpentine rocks were worked, but stones were also imported from the surrounding regions, including dotted diorite, snow-white alabaster, and translucent rock crystal from Egypt; grayish-green Spartan basalt and purple-red *antico rosso* from the Peloponnese; and hard dotted obsidian from Nisiros. Even utilitarian pieces of equipment, such as porphyry lamps from Knossos and Palaikastro, were transformed into works of art through the use of fine materials and the application of elaborate relief decoration.

After the destruction of the palaces about 1350–1250 B.C., when the urban population and palatial clientele no longer demanded the creation of stone vessels, the importation of raw materials ceased and the lapidary craft eventually diminished.

43 **"Teapot"**
Early Minoan II period (ca. 2600–2300 B.C.)
Breccia
H. 0.086, rim diam. 0.062, base diam. 0.047 m
Mochlos, found behind destroyed wall of Tomb VI and
transferred to Herakleion Museum in 1949
Herakleion Archaeological Museum, HM 2395

Teapot-shape jug of light-colored alabaster. Prominent rim, vertical handle, and beaked spout flanked by small knobs. Mended.

The stone was cut to be translucent in places, and the veining
was used to maximum effect to form concentric circular motifs
on one side and wavy patterns surrounding an ovoid hub on the
other. The method of execution reflects ceramic prototypes,
especially Early Minoan II Vasiliki Ware "teapots."

Selected Bibliography
Κρητ. Χρονικά 2 (1948): 589 (Platon); Warren 1969b, pp. 98–99,
P 558.

Nektaria Mavroudi

44 **Sauceboat**

Early Minoan II period (ca. 2600–2300 B.C.)
Gray marble
Max. h. 0.064 m, rim diam. 0.116 m, max. base diam.
0.062 m
Mochlos, Tomb VI
Herakleion Archaeological Museum, HM 1204

Sauceboat of gray marble. Long trough spout with a triangular tip. Conical body and horizontal handle, directly below the rim, with a groove on the exterior. The horizontal veining, in various shades of gray, follows the vase's form, adding a decorative touch. Mended from two pieces.

Sauceboat-shape clay vases also occur in the Cyclades and on the Greek mainland. A Cretan variation appears in the Early Minoan II period and continues into Middle Minoan I. Sauceboats come from various sites in central and northern Crete, Mochlos having yielded some of the most elegant examples.

Selected Bibliography

Gerontakou 2003, pp. 320–21; Marinatos–Hirmer 1960, p. 68, pl. II; Seager 1912, p. 51, fig. 22 (VI 3); Warren 1969b, pp. 94–95, P 538.

Nektaria Mavroudi

45 Miniature Globular Vase

Early Minoan II period (ca. 2600–2300 B.C.)
Green steatite
H. 0.037 m, rim diam. 0.038 m
Mochlos, Tomb VI
Herakleion Archaeological Museum, 1246

Miniature handleless complete vase of high-quality opaque steatite. Squat, globular body and flat, everted rim. The exterior surface is smooth and shiny, whereas there are drill marks on the interior in the form of horizontal scratches. This shape is thought to reflect contemporary Egyptian models.

This vase is one of the earliest examples of its type. It comes from Tomb VI, which is one of the earliest and least disturbed graves of the Mochlos cemetery. The other three examples from Mochlos and those from the Mesara tombs date to the Early Minoan III and Middle Minoan I periods.

Selected Bibliography

Phillips 1991, pp. 68–71, figs. 299–300, 302, 307; Seager 1912, p. 52, fig. 22 (VI 9), pl. V; Warren 1969b, pp. 91–92, P 503–6.

Nektaria Mavroudi

46 Small Cylindrical Pyxis
   Early Minoan II–III period (ca. 2600–2100 B.C.)
   Greenish steatite
   H. (with lid) 0.084 m, rim diam. 0.021 m, base diam. 0.027 m
   Mochlos, Tomb II
   Herakleion Archaeological Museum, 1237

Slender cylindrical pyxis in excellent condition, made of high-quality, opaque, greenish steatite. The cylindrical body gradually tapers toward the top. The circular lid has a circular knob with a triangular ridge at its base. The exterior surface is smooth and shiny; traces of the carving process are visible on the interior. Complete.

This is a new shape in Prepalatial Crete. The choice of a green-colored stone for this type of vase may reflect a wish to imitate bronze and could be related to demand for that metal.

Small stone vases were originally manufactured primarily as grave gifts. They are found by the dozens in Early Minoan cemeteries, such as those at Mochlos, Pseira, and Palaikastro in eastern Crete, but also in central Crete, in Mesara, and the Asterousia mountains to the south. This small pyxis is a grave gift from Tomb II, one of the most opulent graves in the Mochlos cemetery; it may have contained an offering for the deceased.

Selected Bibliography
Seager 1912, p. 25, fig. 7 (IIe), pl. II; Warren 1969b, pp. 92–93, P 526; Warren 1992, pp. 153–54.

Nektaria Mavroudi

47 Bowl (Sauceboat)

Early Minoan IIB–Middle Minoan I period
(ca. 2400–1800 B.C.)
Stone
H. 0.065 m, l. 0.185 m
Mochlos
Haghios Nikolaos Archaeological Museum, 280

Bowl with horizontal open mouth ending in a heart-shape spout. Horizontal handle, circular in section, opposite the spout and three short stub feet on the base. Made of veined polychrome tuff.

The bowl is a surface find from the island of Mochlos, where there is a Minoan settlement and cemetery; it probably came from a destroyed tomb in the cemetery.

The shape has many parallels in Crete. The material is also very common for the Early Minoan IIB–Middle Minoan I period, particularly on Mochlos, where it was used for a great number of vessels in the cemetery. Although the precise provenance of the raw material remains unknown, it is certainly Cretan in origin. The attraction of this material appears to be the veins, which are red-brown and off-white to gray, as well as the stone's softness, which allowed it to be worked with elaborate shapes and details. In order to manufacture such vessels, numerous skills and craftsmanship were needed, as well as the use of drills and abrasive materials, such as emery.

Stone vessels are a frequent find in cemeteries of the late Prepalatial period throughout Crete, although they were substantially fewer and less elaborate in settlements. Stone vessels were objects with a particular significance but of limited functional value, either deposited as grave gifts inside tombs or used in the funeral rites that took place in cemeteries.

Selected Bibliography

Branigan 1993, pp. 68–70; Platon–Davaras 1960, p. 527; Sakellarakis–Sapouna-Sakellaraki 1997, pp. 568–73; Soles 1992, p. 41; Warren 1969b, pp. 94–96, 126–27, 157–60.

Yiannis Papadatos

48 Miniature "Bird's-Nest" Vase

Middle Minoan I period (ca. 2100–1800 B.C.)
Grayish-white marble
H. 0.031 m, rim diam. 0.036 m, base diam. 0.031 m
Mochlos, Tomb III
Herakleion Archaeological Museum, 1255

Miniature "bird's-nest" vase, complete and in excellent condition. It has been combined with a circular, knobbed lid. Squat, globular body with inset rim. Polished exterior with horizontal ring marks on the interior from drilling during its manufacture.

The white vein that crosses the body of the vase indicates that the artisan intended to use the stone's natural characteristics to achieve a decorative effect. Originally, the lid probably belonged to a different vase; it has deep red veins and does not fit the rim properly.

Bird's-nest vases are probably the most common type of Minoan stone vase. They appear from the Early Minoan III to the Middle Minoan I–II period in small sizes and made from a variety of stones. The value they had is apparent from the way in which some were handed down from one generation to another, either as functional vessels or as grave gifts, so that they are found in funerary contexts as late as Late Minoan I. This vase, however, is probably later than the construction of Tomb III, which was looted and reused. It was at this time that the vessel was used as a pyxis in connection with offerings to the dead.

Selected Bibliography
Seager 1912, pp. 37–39, fig. 46 (IIIb); Warren 1969b, pp. 7–11.

Nektaria Mavroudi

49 Pedestaled Lamp

Late Minoan I period (ca. 1600–1450 B.C.)
Rosso antico stone
H. 0.455 m, max. diam. of bowl 0.20 m
Palaikastro
Herakleion Archaeological Museum, HM 616

Complete, slightly restored.

This is a luxury version of a common type of lamp of the Neopalatial period. It comprises a shallow basin at the top for the inflammable liquid; two "spouts," or narrow channels, opposite each other and across the width of the basin's lip to hold a wick; and a high pedestal, which rests on a discoid base. The handles hanging down from the edge of the rim were used to carry the lamp.

An essential part of any Bronze Age household, lamps were made in different materials (clay, stone, bronze), different sizes (small as a man's hand, medium-size, heavy, and awkward to move) and many variants (high or low, with one or more spouts, with a variety of handles, lips, bases, etc.).

The Palaikastro example was manufactured from a deep red stone from the Peloponnese called *rosso antico*, which was rarely worked on Crete and is mainly found in lamps of this kind. The singular material of which the lamp is made and the relief decoration of a row of ivy leaves at the rim and in a zone that is about the midpoint of the pedestal make it exceptional. The lamp's provenance, however, in the town of Palaikastro, whose busy harbor attracted a multitude of exotic and semi-precious materials throughout the Late Bronze Age, indicates that it blended well into the cosmopolitan environment of an urban center of the period.

Selected Bibliography

Bosanquet–Dawkins 1923, pp. 139–40; Warren 1969b, p. 58.

Emmanouela Apostolaki

50 **Lamp**
Late Minoan I period (ca. 1600–1450 B.C.)
Porphyry
H. 0.042 m, int. diam. 0.065 m
Pseira, Minoan settlement
Siteia Archaeological Museum, 3161

Single-spout lamp with a long handle. Relief band of vertical incisions around lip and three incised rings at the end of the handle, which is mended.

It was found in the excavation of the Minoan settlement on Pseira in 1907 and demonstrates the use of the object in a domestic context. A similar example was found in a tomb at Mochlos.

Selected Bibliography
Seager 1910, p. 37, fig. 18; Warren 1969b, P 316, 60.

Chrysa Sophianou

51 **Lamp**
Late Minoan IB period (ca. 1450 B.C.)
Serpentine
H. 0.13 m, diam. 0.27 m
Mochlos, Building C7, Artisans' Quarter
Siteia Archaeological Museum, 9943

Large, double-spout lamp, with a low foot, conical body, and two solid horizontal handles below the broad, flat rim. Complete.

It was located in Building C7 in the so-called Artisans' Quarter of the Minoan town on Mochlos and is a local product. The stone vases of Mochlos are considered very well made and some of the most important of the Minoan era. They are found in a variety of shapes and sizes. For their manufacture, stones such as steatite, serpentine, chlorite, marble, and alabaster of various colors were used. The working of the stone was carried out in such a way that the veins in the stone showed, and this called for great expertise on the part of the craftsmen.

During the Late Minoan period, many stone vases were elaborate, with engraved and relief decoration that imitated flowers or foliage; some were designed to stand on the floor and had a high foot or pedestal.

Selected Bibliography
Soles–Davaras 1996, p. 201, pl. 57b.

Chrysa Sophianou

52 **Bowl**
Late Minoan II–IIIA1 period (ca. 1450–1375 B.C.)
Egyptian porphyry
H. 0.13 m, max. diam. of body 0.28 m
Knossos, Royal Tomb at Isopata
Herakleion Archaeological Museum, HM 611

Mended and restored in places, this bowl has a carinated shape, a broad mouth, and a lightly defined base.

The material used for the manufacture of this bowl, a dark-colored rock with white inclusions, imparts an almost artistic feel. It is one of the many splendid rocks of Egypt, where this particular vessel may well have come from. At diametrically opposed points at the level of the carination, the bowl has a pair of perforations probably used for attaching handles, which may have been made of a different material. In other Egyptian imports found at the palace at Zakros, bronze rings were used for handles rather than for hanging up the vessel, as its excavator first suggested.

This bowl was found in the Isopata Royal Tomb in the Knossos region, where an interesting number of Egyptian vases of different periods were discovered, along with other opulent contents. These, combined with fact that the burial complex was large and elaborately constructed, led to its being interpreted as and named "royal." That deposit sheds light on the close ties between Egypt and Crete over a long period of time, on an economic or mercantile and thus diplomatic level, with gift exchanges of the sort represented by the stone vessels of Isopata. However, the bowl also indirectly reflects the cultural value of a material that was transported by sea during this period, whether it was imported to Crete ready-made or was manufactured on the island using imported stone, In any case, the bowl was found to be eminently suitable as a grave gift in a "royal" tomb.

Selected Bibliography
Evans 1906, pp. 141, 146; Warren 1969b, p. 111, P 602.

Emmanouela Apostolaki

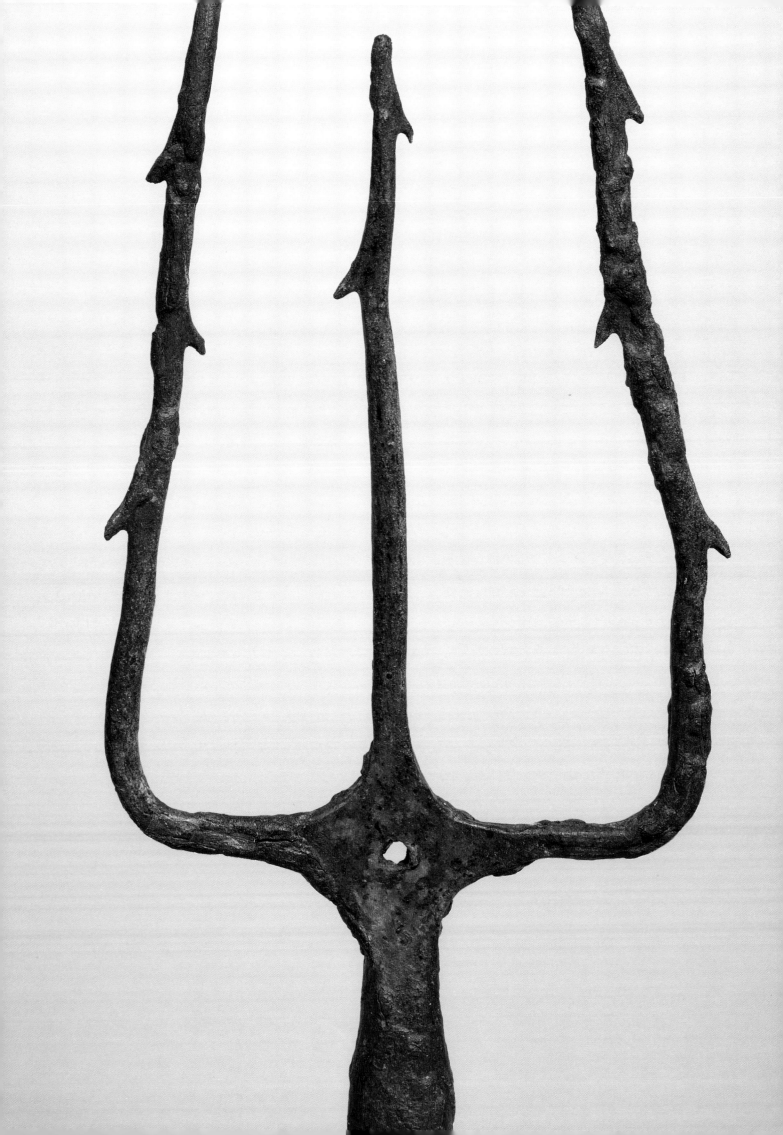

The extent and quality of material culture in Crete relied on workshop production and the specialized labor offered by guilds of artisans and craftsmen, not only in terms of production but also in setting social boundaries and displaying prestige and identity.

Tools made of obsidian, a hard volcanic glass resembling stone that was imported from the island of Melos, were produced in vast quantities and widely distributed from about 3000 B.C. on. The driving force of technology and craftsmanship, however, gradually turned to the acquisition, processing, and circulation of metals. The earliest metallurgical remains were found at Poros, the harbor town of Knossos, and Chrysokamino in eastern Crete, and date back to about 3000 B.C. Poros hosted extensive workshop installations, which were active continuously until about 1350–1300 B.C. Smelting took place in furnaces and resulted in the production of a copper alloy with tin or zinc. Tuyeres of clay bellows that fanned the fire, crucibles for carrying molten metal and molds for making tools and weapons have been found. Metallurgical remains came as well from Mochlos, Palaikastro, Knossos, and Kommos.

The importance of copper for the central administration is demonstrated by the presence of stocks of copper ingots (blocks of cast copper) in palatial storage areas. These ingots were produced at the mines of Cyprus and Lavrion and transported on commercial boats to ore-poor Crete, where the copper was remelted and cast into objects. Various bronze tools were cast, as attested by the existence of stone molds for knives, hammers, sledgehammers, pickaxes, drills, awls, chisels, saws, hooks, and a unique trident from Mochlos. These bronze tools, as simple and functional as their modern iron equivalents, were used along with bone implements by professionals, specialized craftsmen, and manual workers, who practiced their skills to fulfill the daily material needs of the Minoan society—from farmers who cultivated the land and fishermen to harpoon fish to carpenters, tanners, and stone masons. Bronze and silver vessels were also manufactured through more complex casting methods, which included the hammering and soldering of metal plates with rivets or special glues.

Other workshops specialized in the production of personal items and luxurious objects, such as jewelry, seals, miniature artwork, and inlays for implements and furniture. A superb example is the magnificent chessboard from Knossos, a masterpiece of technical achievement and artistic expression. These workshops operated within urban environments with ready markets, such as those at Knossos, Poros, Malia, and Zakros. Their craftsmen worked with gold, ivory, amethyst, sard, onyx, and lapis lazuli from Egypt and the Levant, as well as crushed quartz, a glassy paste for the manufacture of jewelry cast in molds.

After the destruction of palatial centers about 1300 B.C., very few precious raw materials reached the island. The workshops declined in prosperity, and luxurious objects became rare. A limited number of bronze tools and cheap jewels made of glass constitute the last material remains of their activity.

53A–E **Tools**
Gerani Cave, 1969

In the Neolithic period, before the use of metal, humans used stone, wood, and bone to manufacture the tools necessary for survival. Bone tools, such as awls, made from the polished long bones of sheep and goats and chisels and spatulas made from ribs are present already in pre-ceramic levels.

Located seven kilometers west of Rethymnon, the Gerani Cave was identified by chance during the construction of the Rethymnon-Khania highway. Its entrance was blocked by stone tumble at the end of the Final Neolithic period, thus providing a *terminus ante quem* for the cave's use. Trapped inside the cave were three humans, whose skeletons provided important anthropological information.

Excavation inside the cave revealed hearths, pottery, and bone and stone tools of the Early Neolithic II, Middle, and Final Neolithic periods. The zoo-archaeological study of the bone tools indicated the presence of pigs, sheep, goats, and hares, while chemical analyses of the remains inside clay vases revealed the presence of grease from marine species. The cave is thought to have been used occasionally for activities related to animal husbandry and fishing and for the manufacture of tools.

53 A **Awl**
Bone
Preserved l. 0.078 m
Rethymnon Archaeological Museum, O 330

Long and slightly concave spindle-shape tool. Angle at one end; the other end wider and rounded. Upper surface polished. Almost complete.

53 B **Awl**
Bone
L. 0.057 m
Excavation no. 241
Rethymnon Archaeological Museum, O 361

Two chips on the narrow end. Long, crescent-shape, concave tool with rounded and polished ends. Similar tools were found during trial excavations in the central court of the palace at Knossos. They were probably used for removing meat from the bone.

53 C **Awl**
Bone
L. 0.07 m
Corridor. Excavation no. 333
Rethymnon Archaeological Museum, O 376

Long, pointed tool with a roughly polished trapezoidal handle. Similar tools were found in a Late Neolithic level, during trial excavations in the Central Court of the palace at Knossos. Like catalogue number 53b, this was probably used for removing meat from the bone. Complete.

Selected Bibliography
Evans 1994, p. 18, pl. 5f.

C   E   B   D   A

53 D **Awl**
    Bone
    Preserved l. 0.086 m
    Entrance. Excavation no. 62
    Rethymnon Archaeological Museum, O 557

Chips along the edges. Tongue-shape tool with an angular outline and a polished upper surface. Almost complete.

Tools like this were made from the splinters of small bones. Their size varies according to their use, which was probably for piercing and sewing animal hides. Similar tools were found during trial excavations in the central court of the Knossos palace. This handy type of tool was used over a long period of time, as demonstrated by a bronze example found at Troy dating to the Middle Bronze Age.

Selected Bibliography
Chatzoudi 2002, drawing 1: a–d, h; Evans 1994, p. 18, pl. 5d; Sampson 1987, pp. 53–54, pls. 72–73: 901, 903 (layer 9–15) and 156–63; Treuil 1983, p. 181, note.

53 E **Spatula**
    Bone
    L. 0.06 m
    Corridor. Excavation no. 304
    Rethymnon Archaeological Museum, O 384

Fine oblique scratches from use at one end; other end possibly broken. Oblong tool with one concave surface and the other curved. Wide and thinner at one end.

This comparatively rare type of tool with one wide end was probably used for scraping animal hides. At Knossos, three bone spatulas were used for cleaning grinding stones after use. Similar tools from pre-ceramic levels in the central court of the Knossos palace were probably used for removing meat from the bone. Comparable examples have been found on Rhodes.

Selected Bibliography
Evans 1994, p. 18, pl. 5f; Sampson 1987, p. 54, pls. 73: 918, 927; Zois 1973, p. 173.

Irini Gavrilaki

54 Five Blades

End of Early Minoan I–beginning of Early Minoan IIA
period (ca. 2700–2600 B.C.)
Obsidian
L. 0.108; 0.108; 0.123; 0.123; 0.112 m, w. 0.015; 0.010;
0.018; 0.012; 0.017 m
Early Minoan cemetery of Haghia Photia, Siteia, Tombs
74, 90, 135, 140
Haghios Nikolaos Archaeological Museum, 4142ξ, 2682ιβ,
2673ιη, 332ατ, 3523ε

Long narrow blades of Melian obsidian, prismatic and triangular in section. Although particularly fragile, they have two very
sharp parallel blades suitable for light work, such as shaving or
cutting up small quantities of food. Complete.

These blades are the final product of a difficult technical process
that includes the initial cleaning of the raw material, the removal
of flakes and preliminary blades, and the preparation of the
core, so that, at the end, a thin but very sharp blade could be
produced with only a single pressure blow at the appropriate
point.

The raw material came from the Cyclades (Melos), and
their deposition inside tombs is a practice also rooted in the
Cyclades. For all that, both obsidian and this particular practice
were very prolific in Crete, as the relatively large quantities of
blades found in numerous cemeteries indicate. The absence of
waste products from obsidian preparation (debritage and flakes)
at Haghia Photia and in nearly all Cycladic and Cretan cemeteries indicates that the preparation of cores took place in the settlement. However, the blades found in cemeteries have no traces
of use, which suggests that their production took place shortly
before or during the funeral, perhaps next to the tomb at the
time of the interment of the deceased. Therefore, they were not
deposited in the tomb because they were the personal property
of the deceased but had some symbolic character not yet under-
stood.

Selected Bibliography

Alexiou 1951, fig. 7; Carter 1994; Carter 1998; Davaras 1971;
Davaras–Betancourt 2004, pp. 74, 86, 119, 126; Galanaki 2006,
pl. V:2; Marangou 1990, pp. 76–77; Papadatos 2005, p. 46,
figs. 27–28; Xanthoudides 1918a, fig. 15.

Yiannis Papadatos

55 Hammer

Middle Minoan II period (ca. 1800–1700 B.C.)
Bronze
L. 0.099 m, w. 0.018 m, th. 0.017 m
Malia Quartier Mu, North Court (M 78/B 1)
Haghios Nikolaos Archaeological Museum, 13445

Asymmetrical ends and pierced hole for the wooden handle. Ends are worn and damaged through use. Complete.

The hammer was not found in situ but in the North Court of Quartier Mu, in an area that had already been excavated in 1956 and back filled, south of the Potter's Workshop and very close to the Bronze Smith's Workshop, to which it probably belongs. It can be dated to the Middle Minoan II or Middle Minoan III period. The latter date is supposed by the shape and the circular hole for the handle—on later hammers the hole is square—as well as the discovery in the Bronze Smith's Workshop of a fragment of a mold for the manufacture of similar hammers, dated to the Middle Minoan II period. Comparable hammers in Crete have been found at Saba, Pediada, and at Rogdia, Malevyzi.

Selected Bibliography
Poursat 1996b, pp. 118, 125, pl. 43k.

Vili Apostolakou

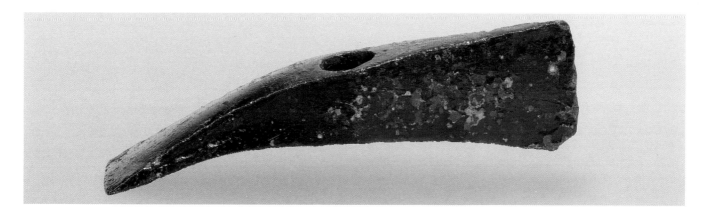

56 Axe-Adze

Middle Minoan II period (ca. 1800–1700 B.C.)
Bronze
L. 0.167 m, th. 0.026 m, w. 0.046 m
Malia Quartier Mu, Building A, Corridor I 9
Haghios Nikolaos Archaeological Museum, 14380

Small abrasions at the ends caused by use. Made of an alloy, chiefly copper and tin. Complete.

This tool first appears in the Cyclades in Early Cycladic II. The earliest example in Crete comes from Chamezi and is dated to Middle Minoan I or II. Although Cyprus is well known for producing and exporting great quantities of copper, a large amount of the copper that reached Crete appears to have come from elsewhere, and lead isotope analyses indicate that Lavrion was the source. Chemical analyses indicate that the tin came from the east. Both materials reached Crete in the form of ingots and were processed and cupelled there.

Selected Bibliography
Branigan 1968, p. 31; Huot–Yot–Calvet 1985, pp. 120 ff., no. A 1, abb. 1–2.

Vili Apostolakou

57 Double Axe

Middle Minoan II period (ca. 1800–1700 B.C.)
Bronze
L. 0.137 m, w. 0.058 m, max. th. 0.026 m
Malia Quartier Mu, Building B, Corridor I 9
Haghios Nikolaos Archaeological Museum, 14381 (3066)

The axe is almost rectangular in outline with a central circular socket. Complete.

The small chips off the sharp ends show that it was used over a long period for hard work. It belongs to a common type of double axe that appeared in Early Minoan II in many regions of Crete. As a functional tool, the axe was used for felling trees, stone cutting, and woodworking, and some researchers include it among weapons of war. At the same time, it was one of the most important and commonly found symbols of Minoan religion and ritual, probably linked with bull sacrifice. The shape of the double axe occurs as a mason's mark carved on important Minoan buildings, and models of double axes were commonly included among the offerings at shrines.

Selected Bibliography
Branigan 1968, pp. 30–31; Huot–Yot–Calvet 1985, pp. 120 ff., no. B 1, abb. 1–2.

Vili Apostolakou

58 Double-Ended Pick

Late Minoan IB period (ca. 1450 B.C.)
Bronze
L. 0.255 m, max. w. 0.062 m, min. w. 0.043 m, th. 0.006-0.032 m, diam. of shaft hole 0.03 m, wt. 1.12 kg.
Mochlos, Hoard in the House of the Metal Merchant, House 3
Haghios Nikolaos Archaeological Museum, 14397

Two flat heads curving slightly downward, nearly equal in length and breadth. A circular shaft hole for the wooden handle with a distinctly raised edge around it on both sides of the pick. The pick has some marks from use in the form of cuts and traces of damage at both cutting ends. Complete.

The double-ended pick seems to have developed in the Aegean region, with many parallels for the basic shape. The history of the pick is linked with that of the axe, although the pick worked in such a way as to split the material rather than to chop it. It was mainly used for agricultural activities as a hand pick and for breaking soft stone, such as sandstone, during quarrying.

Selected Bibliography
AE (1910): 181 (Keramopoullos); *AE* (1924): 12 (Soteriou); Deshayes 1960, p. 109; Evely 1993–2000, 1 (1993), p. 63.

Maria Kyriakaki

B

A

59 A–B Two Chisels
Late Minoan IB period (ca. 1450 B.C.)
Bronze
59a: L. l. 0.24 m, max. w. 0.028 m, th. 0.007 m, wt. 200 g
59b: L. 0.16 m, max. w. 0.047 m, th. 0.01 m, wt. 300 g
Mochlos, Hoard in the House of the Metal Merchant,
House C3
Haghios Nikolaos Archaeological Museum,
14395 and 14396

Chisel 59a is thin and shaped like a wedge, with a broad cutting edge and narrow handle. The end of the chisel is damaged through use. Chisel 59b is also a wedge-shape chisel with a broad, curved cutting edge and a narrower percussion end, worn through use. Both preserve traces of cloth, probably the linen bag in which they were kept. Both complete.

Minoan chisels like these were used chiefly for working with wood, although they may have been used for cutting soft stone or giving finishing touches to bronze tools.

Selected Bibliography
Branigan 1968, p. 32; Evely 1993–2000, 1 (1993), pp. 7–13; Hazzidakis 1934, p. 96, pl. 27.Ic; Orlandos 1958, pp. 118–22; Soles–Davaras 1996, pp. 192–94, pls. 56a,d,e.

Maria Kyriakaki

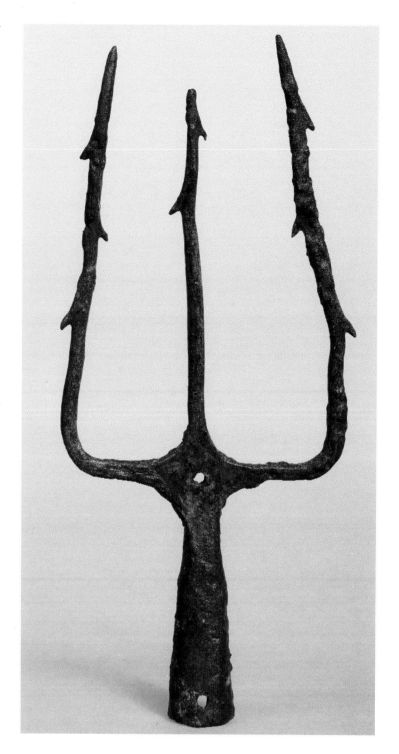

60 Trident

Late Minoan IB period (ca. 1450 B.C.)
Bronze
L. 0.24 m, max. w. 0.101 m, handle diam. 0.007-0.021 m,
wt. 136.5 g.
Mochlos, foundation deposit in Cult Building B2
Haghios Nikolaos Archaeological Museum, 14399

Three prongs and a narrow, cylindrical socket for the handle. Each exterior prong has three barbs and the central one has two. The socket for the shaft has a small hole (diam. 0.004 m) for the nail that would attach the wooden shaft. Complete.

The trident is shaped so that its exterior prongs incline inward at a slight angle toward the central prong, which appears to be slightly shorter than the exterior ones. The balance of the whole object is almost centered on the base of the central prong. A wooden shaft would have been inserted into the socket of the base and nailed in place. There are no traces of damage, and it may never have been used.

Selected Bibliography
Soles 2005, pl. 99e; Soles (in press); Soles 2007.

Maria Kyriakaki

61A–B Two Tongs

Late Minoan IB period (ca. 1450 B.C.)

Bronze

61a: L. 0.29 m, w. 0.011 m, th. 0.004 m, wt. 134.5 g

61b: L. 0.35 m, w. 0.009 m, th. 0.003 m, wt. 182 g.

Mochlos, Hoard in the House of the Metal Merchant, House C3

Haghios Nikolaos Archaeological Museum, 14400 and 14401

Each tong has a rectangular section bent into a U-shape to create a loop and straight prongs. One complete, the other mended.

The tongs were used in furnaces and hearths, mostly in metal working, for moving the full crucible, the mold, the liquid or the cast, and the hot object. The prototype for this kind of object seems to be found in Egypt, where tongs appear in very early contexts and in large numbers. Crete may have adopted this type of tong from the Cyclades, where it is found in Early Cycladic II contexts.

Selected Bibliography

Branigan 1968, p. 33; Dimopoulou-Rethemiotaki 2005, p. 88; Evely 1993–2000, 2 (2000), p. 365.

Maria Kyriakaki

62 Knife Axe

Late Minoan IIIA–B period (ca. 1400–1200 B.C.)

Bronze.

L. 0.20 m, max. w. 0.07 m

Lasithi area

Haghios Nikolaos Archaeological Museum, 1866

Broad blade, trapezoidal in shape with a slight curve toward the handle. Two double-headed rivets served to fix a handle of some perishable material, probably wood. Mended and restored.

This bronze tool was definitely used for a particular purpose, although we do not know exactly what that purpose was. It could have been used for chopping meat or processing wood in order to produce wooden artifacts. Similar bronze items found in Late Minoan tombs are considered razors and are characteristic of male burials.

Selected Bibliography

Alexiou 1967, p. 55; Evans 1906, p. 87; *Μινωικός και Ελληνικός Πολιτισμός*, p. 230; Tzedakis–Martlew 1999, no. 256 (Protopapadaki).

Chrysa Sophianou

63 **Saw**

Late Minoan IIIA–B period (ca. 1400–1200 B.C.)
Bronze
L. 0.422 m, w. 0.023–0.055 m
Armenoi, Late Minoan cemetery, Tomb 115 (X. III)
Rethymnon Archaeological Museum, M 452

The saw has a long, narrow, thin blade with a straight sawing edge and back and with three holes for attaching the hilt plates.

This is a typical Minoan tool that was used in construction and shipbuilding. Four fragments of medium to large saws come from the Unexplored Mansion at Knossos. Saws three times the size of the Armenoi example have been found at Knossos, Zakros, Malia, Gournia, and Haghia Triada, all dating to Late Minoan I. Their occurrence was not so significant on mainland Greece.

Selected Bibliography
Catling–Catling 1984; Shaw 1971; Tzedakis–Martlew 1999, p. 257, no. 254 (Protopapadaki).

Irini Gavrilaki

64 Ingot

Late Minoan IB period (ca. 1450 B.C.)

Copper

L. 0.45–0.46 m, w. 0.273–0.365 m, th. 0.045 m, wt. 29.9 kg

Mochlos, Cult Building, Pillar Basement

Haghios Nikolaos Archaeological Museum, 14388

The ingot is shaped like an ox hide, perhaps to facilitate transport, with one surface smooth and the other rough and lumpy. The corners have been blunted; the long sides are curved, and the short ones are straight, with a ridge running around the upper edge. The ingot was manufactured in an open mold with the smooth surface face down. The lumpy side was created by air bubbling to its surface. The ridge seems to be the result of the initial fast solidification of the molten metal against the cold walls of the mold. Complete.

The "ox-hide" ingots found at Mochlos originated in Cyprus. Ingots also dated to the Late Minoan IB period have been found in other regions of Crete (Haghia Triada, Zakros, Tylissos, Gournia, etc.). Apart from Crete, copper ox-hide ingots are found throughout most of the Mediterranean dating from the sixteenth to the twelfth century B.C., and perhaps even later.

Of interest here are the wall paintings found in the Tomb (T.100) of Rekh-mi-re, an officer of the royal court, in Egyptian Thebes (18th Dynasty and the reigns of Tuthmosis III and Amenhotep II: 1490–1412 B.C., where foreigners are depicted rendering tribute to the pharaoh. Among the tribute bearers are "Keftiu" (Cretans), who are wearing Aegean costumes and bearing Aegean products. Ingots are included among the gifts.

Selected Bibliography

Karetsou–Andreadaki-Vlazaki–Papadakis 2000, pp. 64, 67, 90–92, figs. 64, 67 (Betancourt); Pulak 1988; Soles–Stos-Gale 2004, pp. 45–46, table 6; Stampolidis 2003, pp. 416, 668; Stampolidis–Karetsou–Kanta 1998, pp. 52–53, 105; Tylecote 1976, p. 31.

Maria Kyriakaki

65 Ingot

Late Minoan IB period (ca. 1450 B.C.)

Copper

Max. l. 0.24 m, max. w. 0.335 m, w. at center 0.235 m,
th. 0.051 m, wt. 15 kg

Mochlos, Hoard in the House of the Metal Merchant,
House C3

Haghios Nikolaos Archaeological Museum, 14389

Half only extant, lightly curved on the underside and with angular edges.

The upper side of this "ox-hide" ingot is lumpy, with a smoother border along the long edges. A sign on it closely resembles one from the Ulu Burun shipwreck, which Pulak describes as "a quarter rudder." Ingots with inscribed signs of Linear script have been found in other regions of Crete, such as Haghia Triada.

Selected Bibliography

Dimopoulou-Rethemiotaki 2005, pp. 210–11; Pulak 2000, p. 146, fig. 4d; Soles (in press), pl. 100b.

Maria Kyiakaki

66 Crucible

Late Minoan IIIA2–B period (ca. 1350–1200 B.C.)
Clay
L. 0.222 m, w. 0.112 m, h. 0.08 m
Malia Quartier Nu
Haghios Nikolaos Archaeological Museum, 13113

Coarse clay crucible, handmade and ovoid in shape, with a semicircular edge at one end and no discernible spout. At the opposite end is a short cylindrical socket, probably for the handle. The exterior surface is covered with densely packed relief circles. The interior bears traces of metal that was poured into it in order to be transferred to molds for making vessels, weapons, and tools. Mended and restored in gypsum.

Fragments of molds for rings came from the same findspot as this crucible. It is therefore likely that a metallurgical workshop was active in the area.

Selected Bibliography
Branigan 1974; Catling–Catling 1984.

Vili Apostolakou

67 Tool Mold

Middle Minoan II period (ca. 1800–1700 B.C.)
Grayish-green schist
L. 0.35 m, w. 0.159 m, w. 0.05 m
Malia Quartier Mu, Bronze Smith's Workshop (B 81/C 15)
Haghios Nikolaos Archaeological Museum, 13420

It belongs to the category of multiple open molds. One surface has three cuttings, for casting different sizes of bronze chisels, while the other one has only one indentation, for casting a bronze tool with two sharp ends. Three small holes along the length of one long side were probably caused by an attempt to repair the mold. Mended.

Two metallurgical workshops—the Bronze Smith's Workshop, where this mold was found, and House C—were located in the Protopalatial Quartier Mu at the archaeological site of Malia and were identified as such on the basis of the stone molds found there.

This mold has many points of comparison with similar examples from Troy, where they were also used for manufacturing flat chisels.

Selected Bibliography
Poursat 1996b, pp. 55, 116, pl. 52d.

Vili Apostolakou

68A–B Double-Axe Molds

Third–second millennium B.C.
Stone
H. 0.045 m, w. 0.198 m, th. 0.09 m
Lasithi area
Hierapetra Archaeological Museum, 103

One surface has an almost rectangular cutting in the shape of the double axe. One part is slightly restored in gypsum.

As with most tools and weapons, the process of cupellation was used for the manufacture of double axes. Most molds of bronze weapons were made of stone or fireproof clay. Since axes were rather thick in section, the molds were made in two pieces joined by strips of copper, after which the liquid metal was poured into the cavity with the help of a crucible.

Apart from being the most characteristic Minoan religious symbol, the double axe was also the most typical Minoan tool used in heavy jobs such as felling trees, woodworking, and boat building.

The earliest example of a two-piece double axe mold comes from Vasiliki; it is made of metal and dates to Early Minoan IIB. Quite a few stone double-axe molds have been found at Malia.

Selected Bibliography

Branigan 1968, pp. 30–31, 43–44; Bucholz 1959; Davaras 1992; Deshayes 1960, pp. 253–61; Evely 1993–2000, 1 (1993), pp. 41–55; Poursat 1996a, p. 16.

Vasiliki Zographaki

69A–B **Two Molds for Handles of Bronze Vessels**
Late Minoan IB period (ca. 1450 B.C.)
Clay
69a: H. 0.067 m, max. w. 0.075 m, diam. of cavity
0.029 m, filling hole 0.007-0.014 m
69b: H. 0.073 m, max. w. 0.076 m, diam. of cavity
0.023 m, diam. filling hole 0.003 m
Mochlos, Artisans' Quarter, Building A
Haghios Nikolaos Archaeological Museum, 14392 and
14393

Made of fine clay with a layer of coarse black clay, these molds are shaped like a horseshoe and have a filling hole that protrudes slightly and leads to the internal narrow channel. One mold is complete, the other mended.

These two molds were used to manufacture a pair of handles for a large bronze vessel such as catalogue number 70, with vertical basket handles that were circular in section. The molds are semicircular or shaped like a horseshoe, with a similar circular section and a maximum width of 0.076 m. Each has an interior channel roughly 0.01 m in diameter and has been shaped around the wax model of a handle that had a piercing for a rivet at each end. The wax model was first totally covered with a layer of fine clay (clay lining) about 0.001 m thick, which when dried was covered by a thicker layer of coarse clay (clay covering) used to strengthen specific points of the mold, particularly the ends and lower parts. The molds were fired in a kiln before use, and the initial wax model was melted away through the perforations, probably during the course of the firing. Once the molds had been fired and were ready for use, the molten metal was poured in through the two holes and left to solidify. The molds were then broken, and the bronze handles were popped out. The molds could be used only once and then had to be discarded. The finished handles may have been altered slightly in width but were otherwise designed with slots, in order to be applied to the same surface as the rim of the vessel and riveted to its sides with a minimum of extra work.

Selected Bibliography

Soles 2003, pp. 19–22, fig. 12, pl. 9c; Soles–Stos-Gale 2004, p. 22, IC.30–31, fig. 6, pl. 4.

Maria Kyriakaki

70 **Basin**
   Late Minoan IB period (ca. 1450 B.C.)
   Bronze
   H. without handles 0.077 m, diam. ca. 0.29 m, w. of handles
   0.077 m, handle section 0.009 m, wt. 986 g.
   Mochlos, Cult Building, House B2. Found with cat. no. 72
   Haghios Nikolaos Archaeological Museum, 14391

The underside is concave and has two vertical basket handles,
circular in section, each of which has been attached to the rim
by two small rivets. Mended and restored.

The vase is made of a single sheet of hammered bronze, whereas
the handles were made with molds like catalogue numbers 69a
and 69b. They were all probably manufactured in the Industrial
Quarter of Mochlos.

Selected Bibliography
Soles–Davaras 1996, pp. 192–94.

Maria Kyriakaki

71 **Cup**
Late Minoan IB period (ca. 1450 B.C.)
Bronze
H. 0.076 m, max. rim diam. 0.141 m, base diam. 0.066 m,
th. 0.003 m, w. of handle 0.069 m, diam. of section 0.005
m, wt. 240 g.
Mochlos, Hoard in the House of the Metal Merchant,
House C3
Haghios Nikolaos Archaeological Museum, 14394

Mended and restored. It has a straight rim and a flat base. A
horizontal handle, circular in section, was applied to the rim of
the vessel with two silver-headed bronze rivets. The cup is of
hammered bronze, whereas the handle was mold-made. The silver was attached to the rivet heads by hammering.

Selected Bibliography
Branigan 1968, p. 91, fig. 9,6; Seager 1912, p. 56, fig. 26, VII.c.

Maria Kyriakaki

72 **Basin**

Late Minoan IB period (ca. 1450 B.C.)
Bronze
H. without handle 0.071 m, h. with handle 0.15 m, rim
diam. 0.364 m, base diam. 0.18 m, w. of handle 0.039–0.075
m, wt. 2.53 kg
Mochlos, Cult Building, House B2. Found with cat. no. 70
Haghios Nikolaos Archaeological Museum, 14390

The vase has a flat, raised base and a vertical loop handle. The
rim band is decorated with foliates and beadings executed in
high relief. The handle is joined to the wall of the basin by three
rivets and is decorated in the center with a row of beadings
flanked by foliate bands. The basin was hammered out from a
single sheet of metal, whereas the decorative band on the rim
and the handle were manufactured in separate molds. The rim
of the basin inclines sharply outward, and the decorative band
was secured by means of eight small rivets. Mended and restored.

The basin was probably imported to Mochlos from Knossos.

Selected Bibliography
Dimopoulou-Rethemiotaki 2005, p. 349; Soles–Davaras 1996,
pp. 192–94.

Maria Kyriakaki

The military weapon in Crete was a prestigious and highly respected object. Daggers were personal weapons and utilitarian tools, which men proudly wore at the waist, as seen in clay figurines from peak sanctuaries of the Protopalatial period (ca. 1900–1700 B.C.). The earliest daggers made of copper and silver have been found in the tombs of the Prepalatial period (ca. 3000–1900 B.C.), where they had apparently been deposited to indicate the identity and the high social status of the deceased. Long, elaborate swords with gold-covered hilts appear for the first time in the Protopalatial period (ca. 1900–1700 B.C.); two examples found near the Royal Quarters of the Palace at Malia suggest that they served as status symbols and as attributes of palatial authority. Replicas of swords and daggers made of thin metal plates were discovered in a great hoard of metals of the Neopalatial period (ca. 1700–1600 B.C.) in the Cave of Arkalochori, which suggests that these objects also had a votive ritual function.

There did, however, exist an actual military elite, a group of warriors who used weaponry to mark and display their identity in the Neopalatial harbor town of Poros (ca. 1700–1450 B.C.), attested by the fragmentary swords and dirks and the remains of boar's-tusk helmets that were found in the settlement's communal tombs. This kind of material evidence is consistent with the powerful, expansionary character of the Minoan thalassocracy during the Neopalatial period, not only in supporting overseas trade by military means but also in defending the homeland and maintaining internal stability throughout the Minoan state.

Burials in individual tombs that contained weapons and armor along with other precious metals and jewelry are evidence that a proud and ostentatious military class developed in Crete after the appearance of the Mycenaeans, from about 1450 to 1300 B.C. Swords were lavishly decorated with gold-plated rivets and with ivory hilts and pommels, and sumptuous helmets were covered with boar's tusks—all of them true works of art. Heavy spears, arrowheads, and various lengths of swords with blades of different widths indicate the tactics of warriors who specialized in fighting from a distance in columns and in hand-to-hand combat. Linear B tablets record bronze weapons and also mention the existence of a two-wheeled chariot.

After about 1300 B.C., few bronze weapons are found in individual burials, reflecting the collapse of a weakened palatial authority that no longer had need of a powerful army.

73 Dagger

Early Minoan I/IIA–Middle Minoan I period
(ca. 3000–2000 B.C.)
Bronze
Max. l. 0.21 m
Mesara, Koumasa, Tomb B, 1904
Herakleion Archaeological Museum, HM 1187

Long, bronze dagger blade with a reinforcing midrib. Four holes and part of a fifth are visible along the edge of the heel; two holes preserve the rivets used for securing the handle. The blade is complete; there is some damage at the heel.

Whether triangular or elongated, bronze daggers form an important group of early Cretan metallurgical products, since the dagger was the earliest and most common type of weapon in use before the creation of the first palaces. The great variety in their shape and features illustrates advances in metalworking, as well as influence from the Cyclades, the northeastern Aegean, and the East. Crete's limited copper sources led its early inhabitants to import the raw materials, which were subsequently worked in local workshops in the widely known techniques of casting and hammering. Metal daggers exemplify the most advanced technology of that period and demonstrate increasing specialization in production. Most of them, including the Koumasa dagger, come from the Mesara tholos tombs. Wear marks and repairs, visible in the fragile area where the blade joined the handle, demonstrate the significance of these daggers for their owners.

Selected Bibliography

Branigan 1974, p. 9, pl. 4, no. 164; Nakou 1995; Stos-Gale–Macdonald 1991; Xanthoudides 1924, pp. 25–27, pl. XXIV.

Eirini Galli

74 **Dagger**
Early Minoan IIA/III–Middle Minoan IA period
(ca. 2600–1900 B.C.)
Silver
Max. l. 0.153 m
Mesara, Koumasa, Tomb Γ, 1904
Herakleion Archaeological Museum, HM 213

Triangular silver dagger with a strong central midrib. The flat base has three holes and parts of at least two others, used for securing the handle with rivets. Three silver double-headed rivets were found in situ. The dagger is complete, with some damage.

This is one of the three silver daggers found in Tomb Γ at Koumasa. Because of its elongated blade, reinforced back, and rectilinear sides, it is considered a predecessor of the long sword that appeared during the Protopalatial period.

    Daggers are the only type of metal weapon used in Early Bronze Age Crete. Silver daggers probably had a symbolic function rather than any use as a weapon. The significance of the dagger as a sign of its owner's social identity is particularly apparent in Middle Minoan clay figurines from peak sanctuaries, which represent male worshipers with daggers attached at their sides. Having originally been weapons with a number of functions, the daggers became symbols of their owners' gender and social status. The silver dagger from the Koumasa group/family tomb is a characteristic example of this semiotic symbolism. The rarity of the imported silver and the specialized labor necessary for its manufacture are closely related to its use as a grave gift and reflect its owner's place within his family and community.

Selected Bibliography
Branigan 1974, p. 11; Peatfield 1999, p. 68; Xanthoudides 1924, pp. 46–47, pl. XXIX, b.213.

                                          Eirini Galli

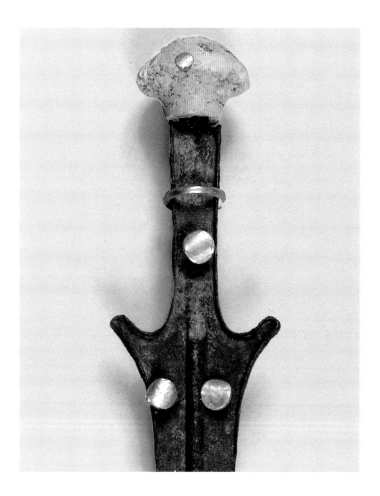

75 Long Sword

Late Minoan IIIA1 period (ca. 1400–1375 B.C.)
Bronze, gold, and ivory
L. 0.830 m, max. w. 0.065 m
City of Khania, Kouklakis plot, 2004, Tomb 46
(Late Minoan cemetery of Kydonia)
Khania Archaeological Museum, M 862

Long blade with a central strengthening rib along its entire length. Ivory pommel with a gold two-headed rivet and two projecting handle guards. Made of the same piece of metal as the blade, the handle had a wooden casing attached with four two-headed gilt bronze rivets. Mended.

Chronologically this type of sword belongs to the Late Minoan II–IIIA period (ca. 1450–1350 B.C.) and may be attributed to a Knossian workshop. The sword is the warrior's symbol par excellence, as much in battle as in status. This type of sword requires skilled fighters of high social status, well trained in this particular type of combat. Such swords appear in the so-called warrior graves together with other bronze weapons, vases, and jewelry, as in the case of this particular find. The almost identical picture presented by these burials indicates exactly the same costume, armor, and decoration for the living warrior and suggests a type of soldier with a particular ideology and lifestyle, perhaps analogous to that of the Japanese samurai or the medieval knight.

Although much later, Tomb 46 of the Kydonia cemetery is a unique and excellent example of the shaft grave type best known from Mycenae's Grave Circle B. Both its architecture and its contents stress Kydonia's direct relationship with the Peloponnesian Achaean centers, Mycenae and Argos in particular.

Fifty new graves were discovered in the Late Minoan Kydonia cemetery in 2004, a very important milestone for the archaeology of Crete. Such a concentration of shaft graves and pit caves with single warrior burials dating from Late Minoan II and particularly the Late Minoan IIIA1 period, was unprecedented in Khania. These graves recall those at Zapher Papoura, near Knossos, unique in Crete until 2004. The presence of Late Minoan II burials pushes back the date for the beginning of this particular burial practice at Kydonia and inevitably associates it with the arrival of new Achaean population that assumed an important place in local society. Among the newly discovered graves are also family chamber tombs, mostly of the Late Minoan IIIA2 and Late Minoan IIIB1 periods, which typify the funerary architecture of the Final Palatial period.

Selected Bibliography

Driessen–Macdonald 1984; Peatfield 1999; Sandars 1963 (Type C1).

Maria Andreadaki-Vlazaki

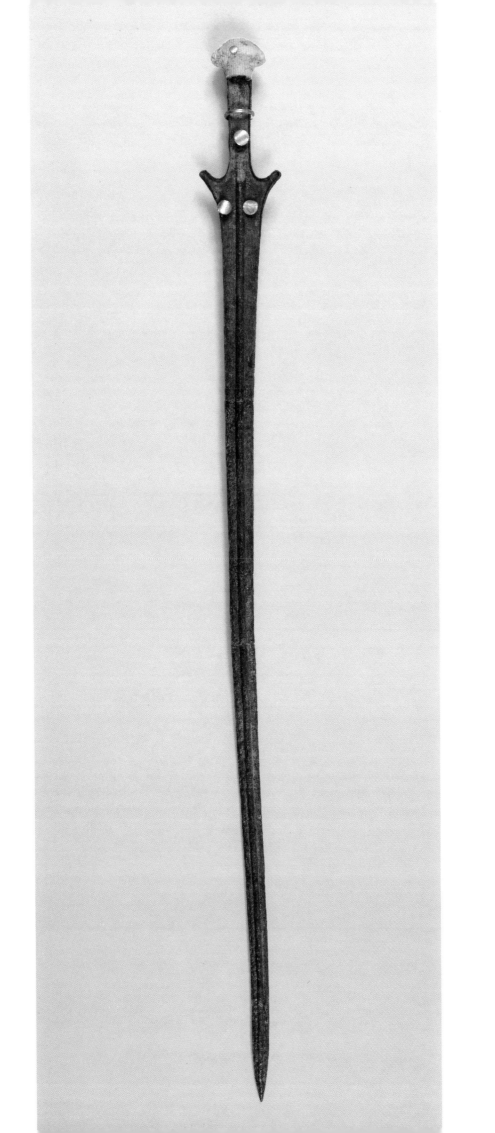

76 Sword

Late Minoan IIIA period (ca. 1400–1300 B.C.)
Bronze
Max. preserved l. 0.46 m, hand guard w. 0.072 m,
blade w. 0.044 m, th. 0.026 m
Armenoi, Late Minoan cemetery, Tomb 200 (M1)
Rethymnon Archaeological Museum, M 1201

The blade tapers gradually to a sharp point with a pair of parallel grooves on each side. Spindle-shape section with no central midrib. The handle has a flange with a pair of relief lines where it joins the cruciform hand guard and three holes for attaching the hilt plates. One rivet, the organic material for the hilt plates, and the rectangular protuberance that supported the pommel are not preserved.

This sword is part of a particular group of shorter swords (0.40–0.50 m) without the central midrib. The large swords that appeared about 1500 B.C. in Crete and mainland Greece belong to this type, which seems to be linked with the development of a military aristocracy. This kind of sword is deposited in warrior burials, together with bronze daggers and spears, bronze tools, and vessels, as well as seal stones, underlining the standing of the deceased in Mycenaean Crete. However, about 1350 B.C., there was clearly a major change in metalworking, since weapons gradually became simpler and more functional. This trend was probably the result of a series of changes that took place in the socioeconomic structure of Crete and are likely to have originated with the destruction of the palace at Knossos.

Selected Bibliography

Andreadaki-Vlazaki, 1997, p. 504, pl. 14; Driessen–Macdonald 1984; Papadopoulou 1997, pp. 331–33, pl. 17; Popham 1980; Popham–Catling–Catling 1974; Sandars 1963 (Type Di).

Irini Gavrilaki

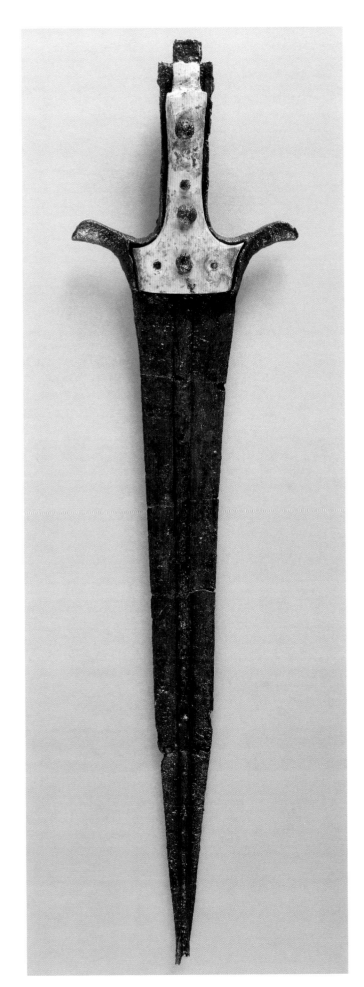

77 **Dirk**
   Late Minoan IIIA–B period (ca. 1400–1200 B.C.)
   Bronze, ivory hilt plates
   L. 0.39 m, max. w. 0.035 m
   Chamezi, Siteia, Phatsi, Tomb V
   Haghios Nikolaos Archaeological Museum, 3099

The triangular blade has a central rib, and its shoulders are strengthened with downward curving "horns" that protected the hand of the user. Four double-headed rivets secure the ivory hilt plates. Mended and restored.

This is a fairly short weapon, but it is strong and easy to handle. Made for war, this type first appeared in the thirteenth century B.C. The rapid development of weaponry mirrors the political instability of the age and the increase in military requirements.

The object was found in a small rectangular tholos tomb, which was in use during the Subminoan and Protogeometric periods. The tomb, although disturbed, contained bronze and iron daggers, a bird-shape vase, and necklaces of glass paste and rock crystal.

The Mycenaean type of sword and its presence among grave gifts, a burial habit encountered in the grave gifts of Helladic tombs, are indicative of the lineage of the deceased and his high social standing. It is likely that the dirk was handed down from previous generations and, as a valuable object with its handle of a rare and costly material, was deposited in the tomb of a ruler of the local community.

Selected Bibliography
Kilian-Dirlmeier 1993, p. 84; Sandars 1963 (Type G).

Chrysa Sophianou

78 Dirk

Late Minoan IIIC period (ca. 1200–1100 B.C.)
Bronze, ivory hilt plates
L. 0.40 m, max. w. 0.10 m
Lasithi area
Haghios Nikolaos Archaeological Museum, 1865

The hilt is ornamented with ivory hilt plates, held in place by four rivets, with two more in the shoulders of the blade. The pommel is part of the handle forming a T shape so that the entire weapon is a single piece and consequently stronger. Mended and restored.

From the mid-fifteenth century B.C., a change in the manufacture of weapons can be observed, owing to the settlement of Achaeans in Crete. The long and slender Minoan sword was no longer of any use, and the broader, short Mycenaean types prevailed as more suitable for war. This dirk belongs to a type that appeared in Crete during the thirteenth century B.C. and is considered a Mycenaean product, particularly successful in battle because of its one-piece handle and short length. The handles of these weapons are usually decorated or had an attachment of some valuable material, which would have been worked exclusively in palatial workshops in either the Minoan or Mycenaean era.

The ivory embellishment of the handle indicates that its owner was an important person with a distinguished social and economic standing.

Selected Bibliography
Sandars 1963 (Type F).

Chrysa Sophianou

79 **Spearhead**
  Late Minoan IIIA–B period (ca. 1400–1200 B.C.)
  Bronze
  Preserved l. 0.397 m, socket diam. 0.032 m,
  max. w. of blade 0.035 m
  Armenoi, Late Minoan cemetery, Tomb 205 (M. 1), 1989
  Rethymnon Archaeological Museum, M 590

Conical socket, without a strengthening ring; two holes opposite each other near the lip to attach the shaft. Long, leaf-shape blade with a flat midrib and sharp point. Complete. Blade chipped.

The conical socket and long, leaf-shape blade with broad midrib are found on corresponding examples from Mochlos and Haghios Ioannis, Knossos. The broad midrib is also found on examples from Elis, Ialysos, and Eretria.

Selected Bibliography
Avila 1983, pp. 131–34; Hood 1956, fig. 4: 8, pl. 15a; Sandars 1963, pl. 23: 14.

Irini Gavrilaki

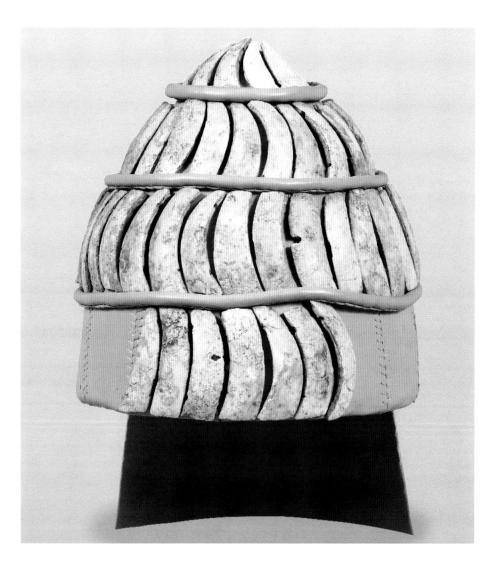

80 Helmet
Late Minoan IIIA2–B1 period (ca. 1375–1250 B.C.)
Boar's tusk
Estimated h. 0.23–0.25 m
Armenoi, Late Minoan cemetery, Tomb 167
Rethymnon Archaeological Museum, O 266

This helmet was restored from fifty-nine plaques made from boar's tusks, found during the excavation of Tomb 167 at the Armenoi cemetery. Tomb 167, a rock-cut chamber tomb, a type common in this cemetery, contained at least six burials, the last of which had been placed inside a clay sarcophagus. The grave gifts included pottery, beads of semiprecious stones, glass-paste jewelry, seal stones, and fragments of bronze knives.

Plaques of three different shapes were used for this helmet: triangular pointed plaques (five), rectangular (four) and rectangular with curved sides (fifty). All of the plaques have three pairs of holes on the reverse, except for the rectangular plaques, which have two. The holes, which were opened along the width at the top, middle, and bottom, were used for sewing the plaques onto the helmet.

The helmet's reconstruction is based on ancient representations, but also on Homer's description of Meriones's helmet. According to Homer (*Iliad* K, 266–271), the plaques protected the κυνέη, a leather cap with a woolen lining, on which they were placed in antithetical rows (ένθα και ένθα). The four rectangular, straight-sided plaques make up the nape guard.

The find is of exceptional importance since the Armenoi helmet is the second boar's-tusk helmet to have been discovered in a tomb of the Mycenaean period in Crete. The first example came from a grave at Zapher Papoura, Knossos. Poros, Herakleion has also yielded tusks of the Neopalatial period, but in small numbers. There are many representations of boar's-tusk helmets from Crete as early as the Middle Minoan III–Late Minoan periods (ca. 1700–1450 B.C.).

Selected Bibliography
Banou 1990; Borchardt 1972.

Panagiota Karamaliki

81 Head of Helmeted Warrior

Late Minoan IIIA–B period (ca. 1350–1250 B.C.)
Bone
H. 0.046 m, max. w. 0.036 m
City of Khania, Rovithaki Plot, Tomb 2, 1996
(Late Minoan cemetery of Kydonia)
Khania Archaeological Museum, K 114

Bone plaque representing the head of a helmeted warrior *en face*. A beardless youth is depicted with an ovoid face, large, almond-shaped eyes, and long, well-defined eyebrows. The ears are large and prominent, the nose markedly protruding, and the cheeks accentuated. A smile forms faintly on thin lips. The haircut is indicated by incised lines and serrations on a stepped surface. In accordance with the custom of the time, he wears a bell-shape helmet that ends in a discoid knob at the top and a broad band at the brim. The main part of the helmet is made up of densely spaced parallel incisions in three vertical rows, slanting in opposite directions, which depict, in the most schematic manner, boar's tusks. The reverse of the plaque has two circular dowel holes for bone rivets.

The plaque was part of the applied relief decoration of a wooden box that had been placed as a grave gift in an important burial. The rest of the plaques found in the same burial were also works of exceptional skill, depicting flower-bearing female figures, helmeted heads in profile, heraldic lions, columns, and rosettes. Most of the plaques are made of hippopotamus tusk, a material that appears to have been more widely used than elephant tusk. Favorite subjects of these works of art were the helmeted warrior heads, but in profile not *en face*. The plaque discussed here is a rare example, along with a comparable one from Spata, Attica.

The monumental chamber tomb at Kydonia, where the plaque group was found, had been plundered but the remaining grave goods were sufficient to indicate the wealth of the deceased (jewelry of faience, rock crystal, and gold leaf and stone and clay vessels, including the fragment of a Canaanite jar) and Kydonia's foreign contacts with the East during the fourteenth and thirteenth centuries B.C.

Selected Bibliography

AΔ 52 B (1997): 1008–10 (Andreadaki-Vlazaki); Krzyszkowska 1990; Poursat 1999; Sakellarakis 1979; Varvaregos 1981.

Maria Andreadaki-Vlazaki

82 Head of a Helmeted Warrior

Late Minoan IIIA2–B period (ca. 1375–1250 B.C.)
Hippopotamus tusk
H. 0.060 m, max. w. 0.040 m, max. th. 0.012 m
Phylaki, Apokoronas, Tholos Tomb, 1980
Khania Archaeological Museum, K 29

Ivory plaque in the form of the helmeted head of a warrior, in profile. Complete, with small chips missing from the nose and tip of helmet. The plaque shows a beardless youth without detailed features. He has a broad forehead, almond-shape eye, large ear, protruding cheekbone, and a gentle smile on his very thin lips. The bell-shape helmet consists of two horizontal rows of scales, which represent boar's tusks, and a knob on top. The lower part of the hair is arranged in two levels. Two superimposed pegs are carved on the plaque's flat reverse side.

The plaque forms part of the inlaid relief decoration of a wooden chest, like the one from the city of Khania (cat. no. 81), which was deposited as a grave gift in the tomb of the local governor for whom the outstanding tholos tomb at Phylaki, Apokoronas, was built. The other plaques that adorned the chest bear a variety of representations: sphinxes, columns, figure-of-eight shields, rosettes, and flowers. This particular representation of a warrior's head in profile was a popular subject in

Mycenaean ivory work, with examples from mainland Greece and Crete (Spata, Mycenae, Delos, Knossos, Archanes, and Kydonia). The nearest iconographic parallel is the example from Delos. Tusks from a real boar's-tusk helmet were found in a tomb at the Armenoi cemetery, Rethymnon (cat. no. 80).

The Phylaki tholos tomb has a rectangular chamber and is the third to be excavated (1980) in the Khania prefecture, joining those at Maleme and Stylos. Because it was looted by grave robbers, numerous precious artifacts were lost to science. Both the tomb's construction and the recovered grave gifts demonstrate Mycenaean influence in the Phylaki/Dramia, Apokoronas, region at the Khania-Rethymnon border and indicate the existence of a powerful center there.

Selected Bibliography

ΑΔ 36 B1 (1981): 398–99 (Tzedakis); Demakopoulou 1988b, p. 152, no. 104 (Andreadaki-Vlazaki) but also p. 240, no. 238 (Demakopoulou); Poursat 1977a, pl. VII; Stampolidis–Karetsou 1998, p. 90, no. 63 (Andreadaki-Vlazaki); Xenaki-Sakellariou 1985, p. 98, pl. 22.

Maria Andreadaki-Vlazaki

83 Pithoid Jar

Late Minoan II period (ca. 1450–1400 B.C.)
Clay
H. 0.473 m, max. diam. 0.365 m
Katsambas, Tomb Z
Herakleion Archaeological Museum, HM 10058

Piriform pithoid jar with low, wide neck and concave sides; broad, horizontal rim; and three ridged vertical handles. Helmets set on their side, surrounded by "sponge" patterns, decorate the body. A foliate band and a cut braid adorn the shoulder. Mended and restored.

The helmets have cheek pieces and a knob to hold the crest and are decorated with horizontal rows of rosettes and stylized boar's tusks. The rendering is unrealistic and highly decorative. Besides its obvious practical use, the helmet, an important part of protective military attire, had a significant symbolic dimension as sign of valor, prestige, social identity, and superiority. Its impressive decoration reinforced the warrior's morale and frightened opponents. Boar's-tusk helmets, in particular, were prestigious luxury items intended for the elite. They were made with at least thirty-three boars' tusks, which were cut, pierced, and sewn in dense rows onto a cap of perishable material, such as leather or fabric. Influenced by Homeric descriptions and the

wealth of representations and finds from the Greek mainland, scholars once considered them to be of Mycenaean origin. However, recent discoveries from Crete (boar's tusks from helmets in graves at Poros) and Thera (wall paintings depicting boar's-tusk helmets from Xeste 4 and the West House) indicate that these helmets were in use long before the Mycenaean expansion into the Aegean. This raises questions about the connections between the Aegean islands and the Greek mainland at the beginning of the Late Bronze Age and about the existence of organized military groups that helped establish and safeguard the Minoan palatial system.

Selected Bibliography

Akrivaki 2003; Alexiou 1967, p. 51; Betancourt 1985, pp. 216, 218; Borchardt 1972, pp. 48–49; Dimopoulou-Rethemiotaki 1999b, pp. 35–36, figs. 11–13, Table 7:5; Dimopoulou-Rethemiotaki 2005, pp. 199–200; Hencken 1971; Niemeier 1990; Popham 1970, p. 59, pls. 26a, 47; Popham 1978, pp. 179–80, fig. 1a, pl. 22 (a); Schiering 1960, pp. 26, 27; Televantou 1994; Varvaregos 1981.

Christina Papadaki

84 Plaque with Sphinx

Late Minoan IIIA2–B period (ca. 1375–1250 B.C.)
Hippopotamus tusk
H. 0.070 m, w. 0.043 m
Phylaki, Apokoronas, Tholos Tomb, 1980
Khania Archaeological Museum, K 36

Rectangular ivory plaque, complete, with relief representation of a standing sphinx facing left. The reverse side is eroded. The entire figure is heavily proportioned. The features are schematically rendered on the disproportionately large head: almond-shape eye, long nose, large ear, and fleshy lips. A long lock of hair ends at the shoulder. A diadem ornamented with interlocking triangles ending in double lobes and a wavy crest adorns the head. A similarly ornamented necklace covers the neck. Schematic toes are rendered on short and stubby legs. The short lion's tail rises in a curve, and the large elaborate wings rise upright to the rear. The beast stands on a wide band decorated with a series of closely set hatched arches.

This plaque adorned the same wooden chest as catalogue number 82. The sphinx motif, Near Eastern and Egyptian in origin, was popular in the Mycenaean world, but it appeared rarely in Minoan art. By contrast with the Minoans, who had the bull as the preeminent symbol of their power, the Mycenaeans tended to display their power with the image of a lion, so the sphinx figure—the hybrid of a lion and a fantastic creature—was appropriate here. Similar relief ivory inlays with sphinxes occur in compositions that decorated wooden chests from Mycenae and Spata. This plaque is closest stylistically to that from Spata. The material (hippopotamus tusk) may come from either the Nile valley or the Syro-Palestinian coast.

Selected Bibliography
Stampolidis–Karetsou 1998, pp. 90–91, no. 64 (Andreadaki-Vlazaki); Tilmann–Pöhling 1990, no. 5 (Papadopoulou).

Maria Andreadaki-Vlazaki

The Minoans based their nutrition on cereals, pulses, wild greens, herbs, and olive oil, which were basic agricultural products of the Mediterranean region. They made bread from wheat or barley flour and sweets with grape sugar, figs, honey, and almonds, remains of which have been traced in clay vessels. Several types of meat were also consumed, including pork, goat, lamb, beef, and, more rarely, deer, wild goat, and hare. Secondary animal products, such as milk and cheese, became especially common. Evidence of fish bones and shells indicate that fish and seafood provided nourishment in coastal settlements. Broad beans, lentils, and peas seem to have been the preferred species of pulses. Alcohol consumption was dominated by wine, but judging from residue analyses, other liquors were also produced, such as retsina flavored with pine-tree resin, malt beer made from the fermentation of barley, and even a cocktail of wine, beer, and hydromel (a combination of water and honey); this last drink was used primarily in ceremonial rituals.

Food was prepared with a variety of clay vessels and utensils. Cooking was generally done in tripods and plain, footless cooking pots, and the food was served in clay dishes, trays, and other forms of tableware. Amphorae, jugs, and different types of cups were used for transferring and serving liquids. Wealthy households certainly possessed luxurious dishware made of copper, silver, and gold, although only a few examples survive today. These would have been reserved for formal occasions and feasts.

Alongside the production of foodstuffs was the systematic collection of herbs and aromatic plants for the production of perfumed olive oil, an industry that seems to have played an important role in the economy as well as in rituals and personal grooming, according to relevant finds and records in Linear B tablets. Crete then, as now, was famous for its variety of aromatic herbs, which were used as extracts or as pharmaceuticals until late antiquity. Some Minoan clay vessels with pierced walls may have been used to dry and store flowers and plants for making perfume. A perfumery workshop dating to about 1900–1800 B.C. was excavated at Khamalevri, Rethymnon, where chemical analyses indicated that perfumed olive oil was produced with iris oil, resin, and wax.

Detail of cat. no. 95

85 **Grater**
Middle Minoan IIB period (ca. 1750–1700 B.C.)
Clay
Max. h. 0.061 m, l. 0.288 m, max. w. 0.156 m
Phaistos, Palace, Room LX, 1955
Herakleion Archaeological Museum, HM 10620

This mended and restored clay grater has an elliptical body, a pulled-out spout, and a vertical handle. Its use is indicated by the raised, oblong segment in the middle of its interior, where eight parallel horizontal relief ridges, scored with crosswise cuttings, served to grate food, perhaps juicy fruits or vegetables. Much like vessels with similar uses today, this clay grater was essential for food preparation.

The grater was found on a bench in a room of the palace at Phaistos. In addition to Phaistos, similar vessels have been found at Monastiraki in the Amari.

Selected Bibliography
Levi 1976, pp. 56, 133, pl. 140 d; Tzedakis–Martlew 1999, pp. 96–97, nos. 68, 69 (Kanta, and Karetsou–Kavoulaki).

Katerina Athanasaki

86 **Beekeeping Vessel (Smoker)**
Late Minoan IB period (ca. 1525/1500–1450 B.C.)
Clay
Max. h. 0.185 m, l. 0.345 m, diam. base 0.14 m
Zakros, House I, Room XIV, 1901
Herakleion Archaeological Museum, HM 2113

Mended and restored clay vessel with cylindrical body shaped in
the form of a gun shell, with a large elliptical opening near the
one end and four protruding feet for horizontal support. On top
are two arched handles; underneath is a small channel that runs
along the surface to allow a moving part to be inserted, perhaps
a wooden rod. The ramlike end is domed and irregularly perforated; another pair of holes have been pierced near the flat,
cylindrical end, presumably the bottom. Traces of burning,
probably through use, can be seen on both interior and exterior,
mainly on the bottom.

The function of this vessel has long been the subject of debate.
Initially its use was unknown, but later it was associated with
metalworking and beekeeping; it has even been identified with the
beehive itself.

The morphological features of the vessel, along with relevant
ethno-archaeological evidence, suggest that it may have served
as a *kapnodochi*, or smoker, the most useful piece of equipment
for a beekeeper and one that is still used today in traditional
beekeeping. Some kind of smoke-producing material is placed in
the bottom of the vessel, where two pairs of holes allow the air
in and keep the embers alive. As smoke is produced, it is spewed
out from the perforation in the domed end in the direction of the
bees, lulling them so that the honey can be collected.

This piece of beekeeping equipment was found in Room
XIV in House I at Zakros, where it was probably stored. Similar
vessels are attested in the Zakros region, which is well known
today for producing honey. Less pertinent parallels of the same
period come from Knossos and Phaistos and other areas of
mainland Greece.

Revealing evidence for the importance of the Zakros beekeeping vessel comes from ancient Greek sources, which mention
"unsmoked" or "smokeless" or "unheated" honey, apparently
to distinguish it from honey that has been smoked by means of
a beekeeping smoker of the Zakros type.

The importance of honey in Minoan Crete is noted in the
Linear B tablets. Reference is made to its sweetening properties
and probably its therapeutic qualities, which is also recorded in
classical texts, and to its economic importance. Noteworthy also
are the references to honey and bees in Cretan mythology, where
Glaukos, son of Minos and Pasiphae, drowned in a pithos filled
with honey and where the bees of the Diktaion Cave were the
wet nurses of Cretan-born Zeus.

Selected Bibliography
Chouliara-Raios 1989, p. 108; Davaras 1989; Evely 1993–2000, 2
(2000), p. 365; Georgiou 1981, p. 87; Hogarth 1900–1901, p. 141;
Melas 1999; Montelius 1924, pp. 88–92, fig. 253; Mosso 1910,
pp. 222–23, fig.146; Platon 1962, p. 166; Strabo IX, 1, 23, 13.

Katerina Athanasaki

87 **Wine Press**
Late Minoan IB period (ca. 1450 B.C.)
Clay
H. 0.30 m, base diam. 0.58 m, ext. rim diam. 0.67 m, int. rim
diam. 0.61 m, ext. spout diam. 0.15 m, handle th. 0.030 m
Kato Zakros, House B, Antechamber N
Siteia Archaeological Museum, 13316

Flat base and a cylindrical body that opens slightly upward. A
large spout protrudes from the lower part. Mended and
restored.

This is a *lenos*, a vessel for pressing grapes, which is combined
with a receptacle for collecting the must, called an *ypolenio* in
Greek. Wine-making installations have been found at farming
settlements, such as the Early Minoan settlement at Phournou
Koryphi, Myrtos, and in villas and farmsteads, such as
Vathypetro, Prophitis Ilias Tourtouloi, Ano Zakros, the site of
"Koukou to Kephali" at Azokeramo, Siteia, as well as in town
houses, such as those at Palaikastro, Petras, Gournia, Malia,
and Kommos. Zakros may be the only settlement in Crete where
such a large concentration of wine-producing installations has
been observed, namely in eight houses. In five of these, the
presses were of clay and set on platforms, whereas in the other
three, the floors were lined so that they could function as wine
presses. The numerous grape-pressing installations found in the
town houses confirm the evidence of the Linear A tablets—that
the Zakros region may have specialized in wine.

Selected Bibliography
Kopaka–Platon 1993, pp. 39, 46–59, 64–65; Platon 1961, p. 221,
fig. 2, pl. 174b; Platon 1962, pp. 148–49; Platon 1963, p. 168, fig. 2,
pl. 143b; Platon 2002a, pp. 9–10.

Evi Saliaka

88 **Vat**
Late Minoan IB period (ca. 1450 B.C.)
Clay
H. 0.295 m, base diam. 0.33 m, rim diam. 0.455 m
Kato Zakros, Palace, Strong Building, Kitchen
Siteia Archaeological Museum, 2462

Flat base, conical body. Two vertical handles, cylindrical in section, are placed directly below the rim. The decoration consists
of a rope-pattern band immediately above the base and another
one below the rim. Mended and restored with gypsum

These vessels have a capacity of 40 to 60 liters. They were used
for storage, for funerary purposes, and as collecting tanks suitable for stirring and soaking materials. It has been suggested
that the rope-pattern decoration was inspired by ropes that were
bound around the mouth of the vessel, either to ease transportation or to protect it from becoming deformed in the drying
process before firing. A good parallel for this type can be found
from the Minoan farmhouse of Prophitis Ilias Tourtouloi dating
to the Middle Minoan III period.

Selected Bibliography
Christakis 2005, table 1: forms 118–22; Platon 1960, pl. 239; Platon
1971, p. 245, pl. 334a.

Evi Saliaka

87

88

89 **Cooking Pot**
   Late Minoan I period (ca. 1600–1450 B.C.)
   Clay
   H. 0.34 m, diam. 0.30 m
   Makrygialos, Siteia, Minoan villa
   Haghios Nikolaos Archaeological Museum, 8627

Flat base, ovoid body, and three legs. Two handles preserved beneath the rim. A small pulled-out spout on the rim of the vessel, between the two handles. Mended and restored in gypsum.

This particular form of cooking pot is considered typical for Middle Minoan III and Late Minoan I. Similar Neopalatial tripod cooking pots have been found at many Minoan sites throughout Crete, notable at Mochlos, Pseira, Gournia, Palaikastro, Malia, and Khania. Chemical analyses carried out on some of them have shown that those vessels were often used to boil meat and vegetables with added olive oil.

Selected Bibliography
Barnard–Brogan 2003, pp. 80–82, figs. 47, 48; Betancourt 1980, p. 3 (Type A); Tzedakis–Martlew 1999, p. 103 (Martlew).

Chrysa Sophianou

90A–B **Cooking Pot and Stand**

Late Minoan IIIC early period (ca. 1200–1150 B.C.)

Clay

Cooking pot: h. 0.210 m, rim diam. 0.193 m

Brazier: h. 0.195 m, rim diam. 0.225 m, base diam. 0.215 m

Khania, Kastelli Hill, Greek-Swedish Excavation, 1977, House I, Room O

Khania Archaeological Museum, Π 4485 and Π 4486

The cooking pot has a squat globular body, two vertical strap handles, a tall rim, and a flat base. It is heavily burned inside and out. It fits the cylindrical stand that held it over the burning charcoal. The stand has a circular piercing (perhaps an air hole) in the wall and a wide rectangular opening with a relief border. It shows heavy traces of burning on the inside. Both objects are unpainted, mended, and restored.

These two objects were found in situ in the center of a room, together with a storage jar and a grinding stone. The room belonged to a Late Minoan IIIC building that was erected over the remains of the Late Minoan IB, Late Minoan IIIA, and Late Minoan IIIB structures of Haghia Aikaterini Square. Like the entire settlement on Kastelli hill, this building was abandoned before the middle of the Late Minoan IIIC period.

Selected Bibliography
Hallager–Hallager 1997–2000, pp. 131–34 (E. Hallager), pp. 159–60, 162 (B. P. Hallager); Tzedakis–Martlew 1999, pp. 99, 102 (Andreadaki-Vlazaki).

Sophia Preve

91 **Sea Shells**
   Middle Minoan IB period (ca. 1900–1800 B.C.)
   Khamalevri, Tzabakas House, 1996
   Rethymnon Archaeological Museum

92 **Carbonized Grass Peas**
   End of Late Minoan IB period (ca. 1450 B.C.)
   Kastelli Hill, Khania, Plateia Haghia Aikaterini, Greek-
   Swedish excavation, 1977
   Khania Archaeological Museum

A group of approximately sixty limpet shells was discovered inside the Minoan building at Khamalevri, in an occupation level dating shortly before the building's final destruction. They were the remains of a meal and belong to three species: *Patella rustica*, *Patella caerulea*, and *Patella ulyssiponensis*, which are still common on Mediterranean shores.

   Shellfish was a very popular and important dietary supplement for the inhabitants of Khamalevri in the Protopalatial period. Limpets still cluster and cling to the upper surfaces of the rocky coastline and were probably easily found and collected by the Minoans of Khamalevri.

These carbonized grass peas (*Lathyrus cicera/sativus*), mixed with broad beans (*Vicia faba*) and lentils (*Lens asculentus L.*), were found inside a large tripod cooking vessel in a storeroom of the Late Minoan I Building I during the Greek-Swedish excavation at Kastelli (Plateia Haghia Aikaterini), Khania. They were probably the remains of the last meal cooked in the pot shortly before the building's destruction. The find is particularly interesting because it illustrates the dietary habits of the building's occupants. Overconsumption of grass peas may cause poisoning and, in extreme cases, lathyrism, a neurological disease characterized by a crippling paralysis of the legs.

Selected Bibliography
Tzedakis–Martlew 1999, pp. 70–73 (Baltzinger).

Eleni Papadopoulou

Selected Bibliography
Tzedakis–Martlew 1999, pp. 100 (Arnott), 101 (Sarpaki).

Eftychia Protopapadaki

93 Carbonized Figs

Late Minoan IIIB period (ca. 1300–1200 B.C.)
Sternes, Akrotiri, Khania 1972, Amygdalokephali site,
Minoan Farmstead
Khania Archaeological Museum

This relatively large quantity of figs (*Ficus carica*), which were dried before carbonization, were discovered during the excavation of a Minoan farmstead on Amygdalokephali Hill, south of the village of Sternes. The building had at least two rooms. One room contained a small dilapidated oven, inside which the figs were found. The site also yielded two large storage jars (pithoi) and a bronze axe.

Figs have been widely consumed in their natural state since prehistoric times. Like many other species (edible or not), they are preserved today only as carbonized remains. In this particular case, archaeo-botanical analysis provided proof of the earliest instance of drying as a method of preserving foodstuffs, a technique that was applied to the figs before they were burned.

Selected Bibliography
ΑΔ 28 (1973): 582 (Tzedakis); *Im Labyrinth des Minos*, pp. 172–73 (Andreadaki-Vlazaki); Sarpaki 2000, pp. 92, 102.

Sophia Preve

94 Miniature Cup

Middle Minoan IA period (ca. 2100–1900 B.C.)
Clay
H. 0.039 m, rim diam. 0.039 m, base diam. 0.031 m
Khamalevri, Bolanis Workshop, 1992
Rethymnon Archaeological Museum, Π 15307

Plain handmade cup with deep conical profile, flat base, and crude spout. It is burned both inside and out. Almost complete, slightly restored.

This vase comes from an important archaeological site, where the extensive remains of an open-air workshop for aromatic compounds were revealed. The cup's miniature size and its clearly utilitarian character indicate that it was used for measuring the ingredients used in the preparation of aromatic oils. This hypothesis was confirmed through chemical analyses of the clay, which revealed traces of iris oil, resin, beeswax, and grains. It appears that the inhabitants of Khamalevri were involved in perfume production on a community and collective scale as early as 2000 B.C., shortly before the first Minoan palaces were founded.

Selected Bibliography
Momigliano 1991, p. 249, figs. 11:4, 30:3 (Footless Goblet Type 3); Tzedakis–Martlew 1999, pp. 45–46, 51, no. 19 (Andreadaki-Vlazaki).

Eleni Papadopoulou

95 Strainer Pyxis

Late Minoan II period (ca.1450–1400 B.C.)

Clay

H. 0.311/0.408 (with lid) m, body diam. 0.260 m,

lid diam. 0.171 m

Stavromenos-Khamalevri, Rock-cut tomb, 1980

Rethymnon Archaeological Museum, Π 2337

Pyxis with short rim, elongated globular body with pierced base, and tall, splayed foot. Two strap handles with central ridge are attached horizontally directly below the rim. The rounded conical lid has a basket strap handle. Petrographic analysis of the fine-grained brown clay points to a workshop in central Crete. Complete. The lid is mended.

The vase's exterior is painted throughout with vegetal motifs, and the rendering suggests an early stage of stylization. Running spirals with alternating antithetical papyrus flowers occupy the shoulder. Below these are groups of lilies (*Lilium candidum*), crocuses (*Crocus cartwrightianus* or *sativus*), and possibly caper leaves. Rows of lily heads, spirals, and double semicircles decorate the lid. Leaflike motifs adorn the foot.

Strainer pyxides were a popular ceramic form in the Minoan world, and in the Aegean generally, of the Neopalatial and Final Palatial periods. They are usually decorated with impressive floral motifs, best exemplified by the exquisite examples from Thera. Both this vase's form and its decoration suggest its use in the perfume industry, which flourished at that time. The vase was probably used for storing and preserving dried plants and flowers.

The most important Minoan center of the north coast of the Rethymnon prefecture lies in the Khamalevri-Pangalochori region. This center might be identified with the town *da-22*-to* mentioned frequently in Linear B tablets from Knossos, whose life begins in the Prepalatial period. The region's inhabitants were involved in aromatic oil manufacture since the beginning of the second millennium B.C., as suggested by the discovery of traces of related activities during excavation on the Tsikouriana Hill, Khamalevri, south of Stavromenos (cat. no. 94).

Selected Bibliography
Andreadaki-Vlazaki 1987; Andreadaki-Vlazaki 1997; Tzedakis–Martlew 1999, pp. 45–46, 48–49, 54, no. 27 (Andreadaki-Vlazaki).

Maria Andreadaki-Vlazaki

96 Cooking Pot with Fire-Box Lid

Late Minoan II period (ca. 1450–1400 B.C.)
Clay
H. 0.113–0.141 (with lid) m, base diam. 0.170 m
Stavromenos-Khamalevri, Rock-cut tomb, 1980
Rethymnon Archaeological Museum, Π 2338

The cooking pot has a cylindrical body with flat base, a short vertical rim, and two cylindrical, horizontal handles placed high on the shoulder. The collar rim facilitates the fitting of the lid, which belongs to the flanged type. The body of the pot is decorated with bands and labiate flowers (stylized crocuses) in a horizontal row. Complete, except for the diaphragm of the fire-box.

This vase and the strainer pyxis (cat. no. 95) were found and handed in by a private individual. They come from the same context, an almost completely destroyed grave cut into the marl limestone. The vase's shape and its association with the strainer pyxis relate it to the manufacture and use of aromatic oils at Stavromenos. Similar Late Minoan IB cooking pots (ca. 1525/1500–1450 B.C.) were found during excavations in a space identified as a workshop for the production of aromatic oils at the palace of Kato Zakros.

Selected Bibliography

Andreadaki-Vlazaki 1987; Tzedakis–Martlew 1999, pp. 54–55, no. 28 (Andreadaki-Vlazaki).

Maria Andreadaki-Vlazaki

97 Stirrup Jar

Late Minoan IIIB (ca. 1300–1200 B.C.)
Fine yellowish clay
H. 0.180 m, max. diam. 0.195 m
City of Khania, Courthouse area, 1928
Khania Archaeological Museum, Π 726

Conical body with flat top and base. Three slender strap handles on the shoulder. Carefully painted linear and plant decoration, stylized and architecturally arranged. Bands define two decorative zones. The wider one bears two sides of equal size. On one side six panels contain voluted flowers with dotted or fringed outline, as well as palms with a double central eye. On the other side, sea anemones are bordered by semicircles and quadrants or mixed into a background of dense chevrons. The sea anemone motif is repeated on the more confined shoulder zone. Complete.

In the extensive area of the "Courthouse–Mazali plot" lies the most important part of the Late Minoan cemetery of Kydonia, where large clusters of tombs come to light every now and again during rebuilding, from 1900 to the present day. The vase in question, a product of the local workshop, was in all likelihood filled with precious aromatic oil. Like many others of a similar shape, it was a common grave gift in tombs of the period. The local Kydonian workshop of the Mycenaean period produced a large number of stirrup jars for aromatic oil, as well as a larger trading variety for the transport of oil or wine.

Selected Bibliography

Jantzen 1951, p. 74, pls. 49: 2, 59; Mackeprang 1938, p. 549, pl. XXVIII: 4; Tzedakis 1969a.

Sophia Preve

The effective administration of a political state is based on the use of written records and the development of methods to guarantee the distribution of products and the accurate measurement of quantities in transacting trade.

The earliest form of writing attested in Crete is a script in which syllables are represented by symbols or hieroglyphs; this script, which dates to about 2000 B.C., is found primarily on clay bars and roundels. A more highly developed system, with a corresponding number of more simplified "linear" symbols, was the so-called Linear A script, the principal Minoan writing system from about 1700 to 1450 B.C. Linear A symbols, which have not yet been deciphered, were written mainly on rectangular clay tablets and sealings for administrative purposes, but they are also found on storage vessels indicating their contents, on stone offering tables, and on other ritual objects, perhaps as verses, mottos, or prayers. Such an example was found on a silver pin, a grave gift from the Mavrospelio cemetery at Knossos. Occasionally Linear A symbols are accompanied by explanatory ideograms that enable scholars to identify the content of the recordings, mainly agricultural products, such as cereals, olive oil, and wine, as well as the names of administrative personnel.

From the Protopalatial (ca. 1800 B.C.) to the Neopalatial and the Final Palatial periods (ca. 1700–1250 B.C.), the use of clay sealings, or impressions of seals and signet rings on raw clay, guaranteed the safe transport of goods through a complex network of central and regional bureaucratic systems. Sealings were attached to or hung from wooden boxes, papyri, and leather wrapping materials for products that were conveyed across the length and breadth of the Minoan state.

With the advent of the Mycenaeans in Crete after about 1450 B.C., the first Greek script, known as Linear B, appeared; it survives in abundance of documents provided by the extensive archive of the palace at Knossos, in recently discovered tablets from Kydonia in western Crete, and in inscriptions on commercial clay stirrup jars. Linear B documents testify to the operation of a centrally administered bureaucratic system that controlled a wide area, using officials as intermediate regulators or inspectors in towns and sanctuaries that are mentioned by name. Particular care was taken in recording the production of wool, which was supplied by a hundred thousand goats and sheep in the region of Knossos, as well as recording the textile industry, the production of olive oil and aromatic herbs, and the manufacture of weaponry, such as swords, spears, armor, and chariots. The tablets report numbers and quantities per unit in a decimal system with relevant symbols and even fractional subdivisions.

In addition to the numeric system, there existed a metric system for weighing products. Its smallest unit was about 60 grams, and its largest can be identified as the weight of one copper ingot, about 30 kilograms, with many subdivisions in between. Weights made of stone and lead have been found in various settlements in and outside Crete, providing evidence for commercial exchange throughout the Minoan state. Bronze scales have also been found, obviously intended for weighing smaller quantities of relatively precious products or raw materials.

© CMS Archive, Marburg

98 Seal with Hieroglyphic Signs

Middle Minoan II–III period (ca. 1800–1650 B.C.)
Sardonyx
Max. l. 0.019 m
Malia, area of the Early Christian basilica, surface find, 1958
Herakleion Archaeological Museum, HM 1883

Half-cylindrical seal made of brownish-red sardonyx with dark spots, with a pierced circular hole along the long axis. The convex side is decorated with three tongue-shape leaves in relief; the flat side is inscribed with hieroglyphic signs. Mended from two pieces.

Hieroglyphs constitute the earliest organized script in Crete, and its appearance coincides with the establishment of the first palaces at the beginning of the Middle Minoan period.

The seals with hieroglyphic inscriptions are usually prismatic, three-sided, or four-sided. These shapes provide larger surfaces for incising one large or several smaller inscriptions. Toward the end of the Protopalatial period, seal engravers began to use hard, semiprecious, often imported stones, such as amethyst and sardonyx, which required new manufacturing techniques. Like this Malia seal, hieroglyphic seals made of semiprecious stones are usually small with short inscriptions, possibly reflecting the small available quantities of the imported raw material.

It is uncertain whether hieroglyphic seals had a different use than those with representational or geometric decoration. It is possible that hieroglyphic signs were also used for decorative purposes. The existence, however, of sealing archives with hieroglyphic inscriptions demonstrates that many of these seals were used in administration for certifying the contents or quantity of a product, as with later Linear A and B sealings.

Selected Bibliography

CMS II, 2, no. 227; Evans 1909, pp. 181–231, fig. 103; Krzyszkowska 2005a, pp. 95–97; Olivier 1995; Olivier–Godart–Poursat 1996, pp. 224–25; Younger 1993, pp. 44–45, 184.

Eirini Galli

99 Inscribed Heart-Shape Vessel

Middle Minoan III–Late Minoan IA period
(ca. 1700–1525/1500 B.C.)
Marble
Max. preserved l. 0.088 m, w. 0.069 m
Archanes. Troullos
Herakleion Archaeological Museum, HM 1545

Complete, slightly damaged.

This small, marble heart-shape vessel with a shallow interior bowl is often referred to as a "ladle" because of its shape. Comparable to similar types of vessels found at places of worship inside and outside Crete (peak sanctuary of Jouktas, Knossos, Palaikastro, etc.), the ladle has been considered a religious object.

An engraved inscription in the Linear A script runs around its rim (TL Za 1) with twenty-two preserved signs, to be read from left to right. As the inscription unfolds, some of these signs are repeated in a similar order, demonstrating a kind of regularity. Owing to the supposed ritual function of the vessel, it has been suggested that the inscription has a religious content, specifically as a kind of saying or prayer, because of the repetition of certain signs.

Selected Bibliography
GORILA 4, pp. 58–59 (TL Za 1); Sakellarakis–Sapouna-Sakellaraki 1997, pp. 335–37, 537; Warren 1969b, p. 48; Xanthoudides 1909.
Emmanouela Apostolaki

100 Inscribed Table of Offerings

Middle Minoan III–Late Minoan I period (ca. 1700–1450 B.C.)
Serpentine
H. 0.183 m, max. w. 0.145 m
Palaikastro, probably peak sanctuary of Petsophas
Herakleion Archaeological Museum, HM 1341

Complete but chipped.

Like many other vessels of its kind, this probably came from an area of worship, the peak sanctuary of Petsophas at Palaikastro; two similar inscribed tables and a large number of votive figurines also came from there. The table is rectangular with a circular hollow in the "table" surface, defined by a relief ring for placing the offerings; a high foot, rectangular in section, ends in a step. At the front there is a carved Linear A inscription, probably religious, a feature often found on tables of offerings of the period.

During the Neopalatial period, tables of offerings were made in a large variety of materials, sizes, and types. They were intended to display the offerings of worshipers or votaries in liquid or solid form in open-air shrines, palaces, and caves. This example from Palaikastro is typical of its kind.

Selected Bibliography
Brice 1961, p. 13 (no. 14); GORILA 4, pp. 32–35 (PK Za 11); Warren 1969b, p. 66 (P342).
Emmanouela Apostolaki

101A

101A–B **Two Linear A Tablets**
  End of Late Minoan IB period (ca. 1450 B.C.)
  Clay
  101A: L. 0.080 m, max. w. 0.057 max. th. 0.008 m
  101B: L. 0.105 m, w. 0.053 m, max. th. 0.013 m
  Palace at Kato Zakros, Archive
  Siteia Archaeological Museum, 1619 and 1627

101A: Completely preserved. Mended. Side A has six lines that contain sign groups followed by numbers—one or two units and fractions. In addition, two double axe signs (no. 52 on the table of syllabograms) may be an ideogram. The content of the text is related to the distribution of materials. Side B is uninscribed.

101B: Almost completely preserved. Inscribed on both sides. Mended. Side A has seven lines that contain signs followed by numerics. Side B has two lines divided by a horizontal line. The first line includes the wine ideogram 82 and a number. The second line consists of a group of syllabograms, the ideogram 82, and the number 78. The group of syllabograms means "all" or "total," whereas 78 refers to the total number of the citations on the list that precedes it.

The text of the tablet involves a transaction with quantities of wine and some other commodity, which is indicated by sign 44. These may describe the distribution of commodities controlled by the palace administration. The content of these texts seems to be connected with accounting, since almost all contain numerical signs.

Selected Bibliography
Platon 1974; Platon–Brice 1975.

Evi Saliaka

101B

102A–B **Two Inscribed Tablets**

End of Late Minoan IB period (ca. 1450 B.C.)
Clay
102A (KH 5): 0.097 x 0.081 x 0.012 m
102B (KH 7): 0.111 x 0.089 x 0.014 m
City of Khania, Kastelli Hill, 1973, Archive of
10 Katre Street
Khania Archaeological Museum, KH 5 and KH 7

Mended. Marked traces of burning.

The two rectangular tablets with text in the Linear A script were written by the same scribe and belong to the group of seventy-two tablets found in the Minoan Archive at 10 Katre Street in Kastelli, Khania.

Catalogue number 102A bears a complete text in four lines. The ideograms for wine, figs, and wheat, among others, are recognizable.

Incomplete tablet (cat. no. 102B) is a rare Khania example of a tablet inscribed on both sides. The text is developed along six lines on the main side and two on the reverse. There are ideograms for wheat and human beings, among others.

The ideograms tell us that the archive contains records of individuals, animal husbandry, and agricultural products, which provide important evidence for understanding both the administration and the economy of the building complex that extended over the Kastelli hill at the end of the Late Minoan IB period.

Like all documents of this sort, these tablets were originally made of unbaked clay. They were preserved by chance, baked during the conflagration that destroyed the settlement where they were found in about 1450 B.C., when similar fires destroyed the island's palatial centers and signaled the establishment of the Achaeans in places like Kydonia (Khania).

Selected Bibliography

GORILA 3, pp. 24, 25, 28–31; Papapostolou–Godart–Olivier 1976.

Eftychia Protopapadaki

103 Inscribed Roundel

End of Late Minoan IB period (ca. 1450 B.C.)
Clay
Diam. 0.047 m, th. 0.016 m
City of Khania, Kastelli Hill, 1973, 10 Katre Street
Archive
Khania Archaeological Museum, KH 2055

Complete, but cracked from burning. Linear A signs L 88+76 are inscribed on the upper surface. Along the periphery are six impressions of the same ovoid seal or signet ring.

The seal depicts a worship scene with a central female figure dressed in a long garment. The body is rendered frontally. The head with long hair tilts to her right. The figure places her right hand on her chest and reaches out with her left hand toward the tree that grows inside a stepped structure crowned with horns of consecration.

Selected Bibliography

CMS V, 1A, p. 179, no. 176; *GORILA*.3, p. 134; Hallager 1996, II, p. 93; Papapostolou 1977, pp. 17, 73–77; Papapostolou–Godart–Olivier 1976, p. 145.

Eftychia Protopapadaki

104 Inscribed Roundel
    End of Late Minoan IB period (ca. 1450 B.C.)
    Clay
    Diam. 0.048 m, th. 0.014 m
    City of Khania, Kastelli Hill, Plateia Haghia Aikaterini,
    Greek-Swedish Excavation
    Khania Archaeological Museum, KH 2002

Circular roundel with clear indications of the maker's fingers. Linear A sign L 80 is inscribed on one flat side. Along the periphery impressions of the same amygdaloid (almond-shape) seal stone, engraved with a seated lion in profile facing left. The antithetical head and bent forelimbs of a second lion emerge behind the main lion's back. The heads are shapeless, the manes linear and schematic. The eyes and ears are rendered with spots. An additional line marks the belly's outline. The legs connect clumsily to the body. The strongly linear representation departs from the naturalistic style. Complete.

Impressions of the same seal stone occur on fifteen roundels from the Minoan Archive at 10 Katre Street, as well as on another example from the Greek-Swedish Excavation in Plateia Haghia Aikaterini. Clay roundels functioned as receipts for imported goods in the Minoan bureaucratic system.

Selected Bibliography
CMS V, no. 236; GORILA 3, p. 114; Hallager 1996, II, p. 40; Papapostolou 1977, pp. 15, 56–57.

Eftychia Protopapadaki

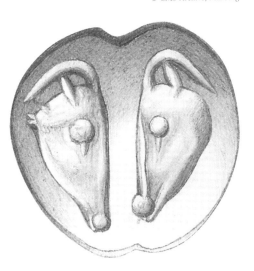

105 Inscribed Roundel

End of Late Minoan IB period (ca. 1450 B.C.)

Clay

Diam. 0.044 m, th. 0.015 m

City of Khania, Kastelli Hill, 1978, Archive at 10 Katre Street

Khania Archaeological Museum, KH 2030

Circular outline with obvious indications of the maker's fingers. The Linear A ideogram Lc 55 for *human being* is inscribed on one flat surface. Along the periphery are three impressions of the same lentoid seal stone. The seal impressions depict two antithetical bovine heads in profile and in low relief. Dots denote the eyes and muzzle, and two short vertical lines below the horns, which curve backward along the seal's outline, denote the ears. This motif has religious significance. The same ideogram and seal impression occur in two more roundels from the archive. Complete.

Selected Bibliography

GORILA 3, p. 125; Hallager 1996, II, p. 68; Papapostolou 1977, pp. 15, 64–66; Papapostolou–Godart–Olivier 1976.

Eftychia Protopapadaki

106 Roundel Fragment

End of Late Minoan IB period (ca. 1450 B.C.)
Clay
Diam. 0.058 m, th. 0.012 m
City of Khania, Kastelli Hill, Plateia Haghia Aikaterini,
Greek-Swedish Excavation, 1982
Khania Archaeological Museum, KH 2117

Less than half preserved. The surface on the obverse is smooth, whereas the reverse is fairly worn. There are no traces of fingerprints. An unclear Linear A sign, possibly L1, L32, or L99, is incised on the obverse. Another sign, identified as L36, appears on the reverse. Along the periphery are three complete and one fragmentary impression of the same almond-shape seal.

The seal impressions depict a female figure with long hair and large breasts standing in profile, her head tilted forward toward her hand, which holds an oar. Her posture is thoroughly naturalistic. The edge of a boat is rendered schematically in the scene's lower right. This is a religious scene.

This unusual roundel was found by chance on the floor of a Late Minoan IIIA (ca. 1400–1300 B.C.) courtyard during the Greek-Swedish Excavation at Haghia Aikaterini. It belongs, however, to the same group as the Late Minoan IB documents discovered in Khania's Minoan archives.

Selected Bibliography

Boulotis 1989, p. 72, figs. 1a–b; *CMS* V, 1A, p. 146, no. 143; *GORILA* 5, p. 47; Hallager 1996, II, p. 150; Hallager–Andreadaki-Vlazaki 1984.

Eftychia Protopapadaki

107A–B **Two Linear B tablets**

Late Minoan IIIA2 period (1375–1300 B.C.)

Clay

107A: max. l. 0.203 m, max. w. 0.043 m

107B: max. l. 0.133 m, max. w. 0.031 m

Knossos, Palace

Herakleion Archaeological Museum, HM 107 and 115

These two tablets, which are complete, come from the extensive archive of the palace of Knossos. They are shaped like leaves (a palm-leaf type) and are of exceptional importance, as are all the tablets, for the information they contain concerning the economy and administration during the Mycenaean period on Crete.

Catalogue number 107A belongs to a series of tablets that were written by the same scribe and contain lists of flocks of animals from regions far from Knossos, whose produce and transport is checked by an overseer for the palace accounts. The location of the flocks in this particular tablet is in western Crete (Kydonia), and the animals counted include 952 sheep, 365 goats, 81 pigs, and 12 oxen. The numbers are further refined according to the gender of the animals and are registered in descending order according to the type of flock, from the largest to the smallest.

Catalogue number 107B is part of a series of tablets that contains records of grain. In this particular tablet, amounts of wheat are given according to place names: 30 units or portions correspond to someone from Lato, 261 to someone from Tylissos, and 246 to someone from a place whose location is unknown, although it is probably in the vicinity of Lato and Tylissos. According to one interpretation, the amounts denote portions of wheat in the context of a monthly transaction between the palace at Knossos and a particular number of men from the regions mentioned. However, another interpretation suggests that the tablet measures the amounts of wheat that could be produced by the tilling of one animal (ox) in each of the stated regions, within the context of a kind of local tax system.

Selected Bibliography

Bennett 1985, pp. 240, 246; Chadwick et al. 1986, pp. 252 (E 668), 370 (Co 907); Palmer 1963, p. 233.

Emmanouela Apostolaki

108 **Inscribed Stirrup Jar**
Early in Late Minoan IIIB period (ca. 1300–1250 B.C.)
Clay
H. 0.390 m, body diam. 0.250 m
City of Khania, Kastelli Hill, Building 2, Greek-Swedish
Excavation, 2005
Khania Archaeological Museum, Π 10344

Pear-shape stirrup jar with a distinctive belly, narrow base, short false spout, and handles of ovoid section. Mended and restored. The brownish-red clay with white inclusions is probably local.

The Linear B inscription occupying the belly consists of three syllabograms, a separation mark, and a fourth syllabogram. These read *ze-ta-ro*, probably the personal name of the content's producer, and possibly part of the syllabogram *wa* (from the word *wa-na-ka-te-ro* = royal).

The jar was found inside Building 2 (the "Linear B House"), probably in the entrance area. For some unknown reason, it had been placed inside a pit sealed by an early Late Minoan IIIB floor. Chemical analyses of inscribed stirrup-jar fabrics from Crete and the Greek mainland suggest that Kydonia was a production center for commercial jars of this sort at that time. Filled with oil, often perfumed, or wine, they traveled to the Mycenaean palaces at Mycenae, Thebes, Orchomenos, and Eleusis. The word *wa-na-ka-te-ro* written on some of these jars may confirm a Kydonian ruler who controlled exports to the Greek mainland after the final destruction of the palace at Knossos.

Selected Bibliography
Andreadaki-Vlazaki–Hallager 2007; Tzedakis–Martlew 1999, pp. 136–37 (Godart-French).

Sophia Preve

109A

109B

109A–B **Balance Discs**
Late Minoan IB period (ca. 1450 B.C.)
Bronze
Diam. 0.113 m and 0.11 m, th. 0.002 m, combined wt.
215.3 g
Mochlos, Hoard in House of the Metal Merchant,
House C3
Haghios Nikolaos Archaeological Museum, 14407 and
14408

Two slightly concave discs bent at the edge to form a small lip. Four small holes, one in each quarter, were used to attach the suspension chain. The discs were hammered from a sheet of metal. Suspended at the ends of a pivot, which was balanced on a central vertical axis, they were used to measure the weight of goods such as wool, linen, perfumes, wax, ivory, or precious metals, including fragments of bronze, tin, and lead. The discs are now stuck together, and one is mended from three pieces.

Scales, a product of Eastern inspiration, were probably imported to the Aegean from Egypt. The weighing discs are more common as grave goods on mainland Greece than in Crete and are found throughout the Late Minoan/Early Helladic period. All published examples come from tombs.

Weighing involves comparing the weight of two different objects. The invention of standard weights was derived from the measuring of gold in Egypt. Balances and standard weights have been found in houses, palaces, and tombs in both the Aegean and Egypt. The discoid stone or lead standard weights, which predominated in the Neopalatial period in Crete, were used for the so-called Minoan system, with a basic unit of weight being 61 to 65.5 grams. At the same time, in 18th Dynasty Egypt, the *deben* unit of 91 grams predominated.

Weighing provides an instant method of two amounts—two objects as well as two values, material or not. Since it functioned automatically and objectively, the scale enjoyed a dominant role both in economic life and in the ideology of the people of the Aegean and Egypt.

Selected Bibliography
Brogan 2006; Karetsou–Andreadaki-Vlazaki–Papadakis 2000, pp. 132–33 (Michailidou), 134 (Markoulaki).

Maria Kyriakaki

110 A–E **Standard Weights**

Late Minoan IB period (ca. 1450 B.C.)

Lead

110A (Pb 42): diam. 0.115 m, th. 0.012 m, wt. 1142.5 g

Mochlos, House A, House of the *Telestas*

110B (Pb 70): diam. 0.595 m, th. 0.75 m, wt. 239.4 g

Mochlos, E45142.1

110C (Pb 27): diam. 0.445 m, th. 0.75 m, wt. 97.6 g

Mochlos, Room 3.3

110D (Pb 28): diam. 0.280 m, th. 0.60 m, wt. 34.9 g

Mochlos, Room 3.3

110E (Pb 61): diam. 0.02 m, th. 0.004 m, wt. 6.6 g.

Mochlos, Building C7, Sector C

Haghios Nikolaos Archaeological Museum,

14402–14406

Complete. Lead weight Pb 42 (cat. no. 110A) has three incised rectangles and two small protuberances on one side, and Pb 61 (cat. no. 110E), a small incised "X" on one side, which indicates that the weight fits into the Minoan system of weights.

More than twenty-five discoid lead weights have been found in the Mochlos excavations, often in the company of the bronze weighing discs with which they would have been used. Most of these are securely dated to the Late Minoan IB period, and the one example found in a Late Minoan IIIA context had probably been reused. Lead isotope analyses of ten of the weights show that the lead came from the mines of Lavrion in Attica. Two groups of weights seems to have been used at Mochlos and elsewhere in Crete, one lighter at 60 grams and one heavier at 65 grams.

Standard weights have been found at different sites on Crete. The most important aspect of the standard weights is that they were economic tools, which go hand in hand with commercial agents. This explains the presence of standard weights from different measuring systems in shipwrecks of the Bronze Age, as well as at commercial harbors. Evans, in *The Palace of Minos*, linked the weight of the standards to the incised signs they bore and suggested a metric unit with a value of 65.5 grams. The same unit has also been recognized in the standards from Kea in the Cyclades. The so-called Minoan unit is 61 to 65.5 grams and is a duodecimal system that predominated in the Aegean throughout the Late Bronze Age. This system appears to be a metric language current in the settlements of Crete and the Cyclades, known in the Mycenaean world and reaching as far as Samothrace.

The discovery of standard weights at a site indicates that the people of the society in question had an appreciation of measurement, conceived the relationship between mass and weight, and discovered the idea of the modular unit, which is repeated with a standard ratio.

Standard weights are one step away from the invention of coinage, since their production aims at the manufacture of objects of a desired, predetermined, and classified weight.

Selected Bibliography

Brogan 2006, fig. 2, table 1; Karetsou–Andreadaki-Vlazaki–Papadakis 2000, pp. 132–33 (Michailidou).

Maria Kyriakaki

B   C   D   A   E

Seals used for sealing clay or worn as amulets and jewelry were made in a variety of materials and shapes. The earliest seals, which date to the Prepalatial period (ca. 2600–1900 B.C.), are made of local soft stone, mainly steatite, and of bone, ivory, and hippopotamus tusk. Seals in the form of animals, carved in the round, were of particular interest in this early glyptic phase, but by the Protopalatial period (ca. 1900–1700 B.C.), another category became popular, that of three-sided prisms bearing representations of human figures and animals. It is believed that depictions of boats, men with bows, weaving looms with loom weights, and pottery were intended to reflect the professional occupation of their owners—sailors, hunters, weavers, and potters.

During the Neopalatial and the Final Palatial periods (ca. 1700-1250 B.C.), lentoid, or lens-shape, seals became the predominant type; they were made of semiprecious stones, such as agate, sard, onyx, amethyst, and lapis lazuli imported from Egypt or the Levant. (Some seals, such as Levantine cylinder seals and Egyptian scarabs, were also imported.) Images on the seals include animals (mainly bulls; but also wild goats, lions, and imaginary creatures, such as griffins and sphinxes) and religious scenes, such as rituals of offerings to the goddess, animal sacrifice, bull-leaping, and the use of ceremonial vessels.

Gold signet rings constitute a special category of objects that were used for sealing. They depict religious and athletic events, especially the appearance of the goddess, the tree cult, the worship of baetyl (a type of venerated stone), and bull-leaping. The impressions of these images on clay demonstrate that both seals and signet rings were used to mark lumps of clay attached to parcels and documents, apparently the sender's guarantee of the commodities being traded.

Minoan seal carving was of very high quality; indeed, the art and craft of miniature work reached its peak on sealing surfaces that were no larger than a few centimeters in length or diameter. Images were painstakingly engraved with fine implements, and it is likely that special lenses were used to create details that cannot be seen with the naked eye. In spite of their small size, the mobility of the figures and their contorted positions convey the sense of a whirling space in which the limitations of weight, volume, and gravity have been overcome. Seal engraving declined after 1250 B.C. during the Postpalatial period, when semiprecious stones became rare.

Detail of cat. no. 120

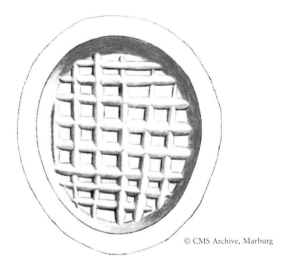

111 Zoomorphic Seal

Early Minoan II period (ca. 2600–2300 B.C.)
Bone
H. 0.02 m, signet surface 0.014–0.019 m
Haghia Triada, Tholos Tomb A, 1904
Herakleion Archaeological Museum, HM 444

An almost complete seal carved in the shape of an animal's head, with a net pattern on the sealing surface. It comes from Tholos Tomb A at Haghia Triada, where it had been deposited as a grave gift, together with many other objects.

The eyes of the animal are rendered with circular depressions, and the ears and snout are also shown. A horizontal string hole behind the head indicates that, apart from its practical use as a seal, this object was probably used as an ornament or amulet.

A large number of Prepalatial seals were found in tholos tombs containing many burials. In most cases when tombs were used repeatedly, it is difficult to assign a seal to a specific burial and consequently to relate it to the social status of its owner in terms of gender, age, or occupation.

Seals of the Prepalatial period were made of bone, hippopotamus teeth, or soft stones, such as steatite and chlorite, manipulated with the use of stone hand tools and drills.

Carved seals, both anthropomorphic and zoomorphic, belong to a particular category of Prepalatial seals and illustrate the imagination and the creative ingenuity of the Minoan craftsman in his attempt to perceive forms and to transform an object of practical use into a work of art.

Selected Bibliography
Banti 1930–31, pp. 216, 247, fig. 120d; CMS II, 1, pp. 17, 44; Krzyskowska 2005a, pp. 57–69; Sakellarakis–Sapouna-Sakellaraki 1997, pp. 686–89; Sbonias 1995, pp. 44, 165; Yule 1981, pp. 91–100.

Katerina Athanasaki

112 **Cylindrical Seal**

Early Minoan III–Middle Minoan IA period
(ca. 2300–1900 B.C.)
Hippopotamus tusk
Max. h. 0.02 m, diam.: (124a) 0.014 m; (124b) 0.019 m
Mesara, Drakones, Tholos Tomb Δ, 1907
Herakleion Archaeological Museum, HM 680

Cylindrical hippopotamus-tusk seal, discolored by fire, with concave sides and three string holes arranged in a triangle for suspension. Complete, with cracks.

This seal has two sealing surfaces of different diameters at each end of the cylinder. The larger sealing surface depicts four stylized lions walking in a circle toward the right. In the center, two opposing leaf-shape motifs end in spirals. Four figure-of-eight spirals sprout from a leaf-shape motif on the smaller sealing surface.

The seal was placed as a grave gift in a communal tholos tomb at Drakones, in the Mesara Plain. Its shape and material and the layout of the sealing surfaces make it one of the most characteristic examples of Early Minoan seal carving.

The iconographical theme belongs to the "parading lions/ spirals group," which reflects Eastern influences. All known examples are found on two-sided hippopotamus-tusk seals, of which some particularly characteristic pieces were found inside graves at Archanes and Platanos. The rendering of the lions' fur with a net motif on a surface less than 1 square centimeter is characteristic of the Minoans' mastery of miniature art. The lions are depicted in a continuous circle in association with leaf-shape spiral motifs. In addition to their possible practical use, Prepalatial seals also had a high artistic value and thus contributed to the demonstration of their owner's social status.

Selected Bibliography

CMS II, 1, p. 3, inv. no. 680; Krzyszkowska 2005a, pp. 57–68; Sakellarakis–Sapouna-Sakellaraki 1997, p. 678; Xanthoudides 1924, p. 80, pl. VIII, no. 680; Yule 1981, pp. 208–9.

Eirini Galli

113 Cylinder Seal

Middle Minoan IB period (ca. 1900–1800 B.C.)
Hematite
L. 0.024 m, diam. 0.011 m
Mochlos, Tomb Λ
Siteia Archaeological Museum, 8540

This complete seal, imported from northern Syria, was revealed in a tomb that had been greatly disturbed. The latest pottery found in the same context must be dated to the nineteenth century B.C., and the seal does not seem to have been much used before it was deposited in the tomb, unlike many cylinder seals found in the Aegean that circulated for centuries before their final deposition.

The tombs that have been investigated on the island of Mochlos belong to the house tomb category, including Tomb Λ, where this Syrian cylinder seal was found. It is large in size, lies near the top of the hill of the island, and is built on top of earlier burials. The pottery that came from the tomb is dated to Early Minoan II, Early Minoan III, and Middle Minoan I.

The scene on the seal shows a beardless god seated on a throne of a typical form, his feet resting on a small footstool, also a typical, probably wooden structure. He is holding up an alabastron-shape vessel and wears a foot-length robe twisted around the body in six zones; on his head he wears a conical hat. In seal engraving, this robe is said to identify the wearer as divine, regardless of gender. The vessel symbolizes the gift of water from the goddess of vegetation to the faithful. Life-giving water was considered the most precious offering in regions such as Mesopotamia that were encircled by deserts.

A beardless male figure approaches the god and raises one hand in worship in front of his face as he holds an offering or sacrifice of a huge hare, which is held by its hind legs. The heads of the two human figures, even though one is seated, follow the "rule of heads on the same level." Between them and suspended in mid-air is depicted the usual combination of cosmic symbols—the sun disc with an inscribed cross and the half moon. Behind the enthroned divinity, the decorative zone of the seal is split into two strips divided by a horizontal interlace, a design characteristic of Syrian cylinder seals. In each frieze, a series of worshipers is represented in miniature moving in opposite directions, thereby giving a sense of movement to the whole scene. The worshipers are differentiated in each row by their gestures, and it looks as if men are depicted in the upper zone and women below.

This cylinder seal was probably of great value to the Minoans as an amulet, since Cretan seal engraving of this period, made of necessity in soft materials, was still in its infancy on a technical as well as an artistic level. The cylinder can be placed chronologically in Frankfort's first Syrian group, known later as the Old Syrian style. The influence of contemporary Mesopotamian seal-stone engraving of the first Babylonian Dynasty is apparent in the main figures and the central theme.

© CMS Archive, Marburg

The subject matter and the countless details of the cylinder seal from Mochlos appear to come from the old Mesopotamian repertoire, although the seal is undoubtedly a northern Syrian creation. Another important detail that points to the Syrian origin of this cylinder seal is the material of which it was made, namely hematite. Almost all hematite cylinder seals come from Syria.

Selected Bibliography
CMS V, 1B, no. 332; Davaras–Soles 1992; Davaras–Soles 1995.

Maria Kyriakaki

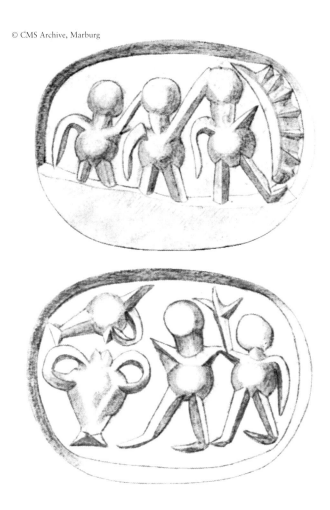

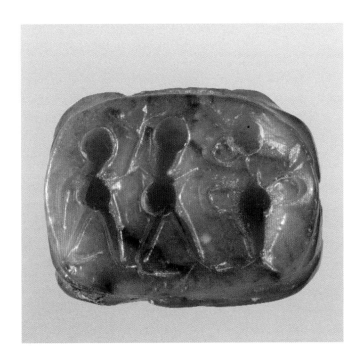

114 Three-Sided Seal (Human Figures and Vases)

Middle Minoan II period (ca. 1800–1700 B.C.)
Gray-green steatite
L. 0.016 m, max. preserved w. 0.011 m
Malia, Seal Engraver's Workshop
Herakleion Archaeological Museum, HM 1831

One side complete, second side half missing, and third ruined.

A typical example of Protopalatial Cretan seal carving in terms of its shape and material, this steatite prism is one of about six hundred examples of the same date discovered so far, and one of over a hundred with the same provenance, the so-called Seal Engraver's Workshop at Malia. The products of this workshop, which took its name from the discovery of a great number of seals in different states of manufacture, as well as raw materials and associated tools, all in the same place—a building in the town of Malia—are distinguished by their rather crudely engraved iconographic motifs, which appear naïve to the modern eye. The stylistic homogeneity of the representations on the Malia seals suggests that they were made by the same craftsman.

The best preserved side of the prism depicts two human figures walking left, one with a raised arm, along with an amphora with large handles and a jug with an upright spout. The second, partly preserved side shows three human figures, each with one arm raised and walking to the right, and a curved linear motif at the edge of the composition. The third side is destroyed. The figures are depicted in a linear style, with geometric shapes for the main parts of the body: spheres for the heads and torsos, cylinders for the necks, and triangles for the weakly rendered arms, in the case of two of the figures, and so on.

A series of prisms depicting daily or occupational activities have come from Malia. Examples include the fisherman (figure with fish), the hunter (figure with bow) and the weaver (figure with "loom"). The simultaneous depiction of vases and human figures on this prism, like the depiction of single vases on other seals from the same workshop, has been linked to the occupation of vase making. It may not be a coincidence that next to the Seal Engraver's Workshop was a ceramic production workshop. Furthermore, clay impressions made by this kind of prism were discovered in a neighboring part of the industrial sector of the town of Malia, indicating the use of the prisms for both adornment and sealing purposes.

Selected Bibliography

CMS II, 2, pp. 213–14 (no. 159); Effenterre 1980, pp. 551–61; Krzyszkowska 2005a, pp. 93–95; Poursat 1996b, pp. 7–22; Poursat–Papatsarouha 2000.

Emmanouela Apostolaki

A

B

115A–B **Sealings**

Middle Minoan II period (ca. 1800–1700 B.C.)
Clay
115A (Π 7577): max. l. 0.055 m, max. w. 0.038 m
115B (Π 7581): max. l. 0.078 m, max. w. 0.062 m
Monastiraki palatial center
Rethymnon Archaeological Museum, Π 7577 and
Π 7581

115A: Elongated, almost semicylindrical piece of clay. Traces of rope or another fine cylindrical object, to which the sealing was attached, are visible on the reverse. Ten impressions made with the same circular seal are visible on the main surface. The impressed motif consists of two double lines crossing each other diagonally within a double square.

115B: Elongated, irregularly shaped piece of clay with curved section. Traces of the rim of the vase, probably a pithos or a basket to which the piece of clay was attached, are visible on the reverse. Eleven impressions made with the same circular seal are visible on the main surface. The impression comprises an S-shape motif flanked by hatched triangles.

Excavations at Monastiraki revealed a large complex of Proto-palatial buildings (ca. 1900–1700 B.C.), whose architectural characteristics recall the Cretan palatial centers. The discovery of large numbers of sealings in three different areas within the complex confirms its palatial character. The need to control supplies (agricultural produce and artifacts) in the Protopalatial period led to the creation of an administrative system in which sealing was the main bureaucratic device. Pieces of unbaked clay were used to secure doors, vases, and other containers in various materials. The clay was subsequently stamped with the seals of those who were responsible for the protection and redistribution of these goods. These clay sealings were preserved by chance when the clay was baked during the fires that destroyed the island's early palaces at the end of the Middle Minoan IIB period, in approximately 1700 B.C.

The discovery of sealings at Monastiraki confirms the existence of a centralized administration that controlled access to and redistribution of produce at the center. It has been suggested that the Monastiraki palatial center depended on Phaistos, in the Mesara plain. This is confirmed by the center's position on the route that links the fertile plain with the north coast of Rethymnon and the affinities in the pottery of these two sites. Further proof is provided by the use of the same seal for two sealings, one from Monastiraki and the other from Phaistos.

Selected Bibliography

Godart–Kanta–Tzigounaki 1996; Kanta 2006; Tzigounaki 2006; Tzedakis–Martlew 1999, pp. 94–95 (Kanta).

Panagiota Karamaliki

© CMS Archive, Marburg

116 Seal Stone

End of Late Minoan IB period (ca. 1450 B.C.)
Amethyst
L. 0.016 m, w. 0.011 m, max. th. 0.004 m
Zakros
Siteia Archaeological Museum, 4509

Elliptical in shape with curved upper surface. A groove runs around the sides with a perforation through the long transverse axis. Complete.

A lion or lioness with an open mouth is rushing toward the left into a schematically rendered rocky landscape with reeds. The animal's body is naturalistically depicted, and the violent movement is portrayed in a lively and realistic manner. The Neopalatial period (Middle Minoan IIIB–Late Minoan IB), to which this work of art belongs, saw the peak of seal-stone carving.

Selected Bibliography

CMS V, S. 1B, no. 331; Krzyszkowska 2005b; Papadakis 1984, p. 137; Papatsarouha 1998, pp. 94–99, 328, 341–44, 352–53.

Evi Saliaka

117 Sealing

End of Late Minoan IB period (ca. 1450 B.C.)
Clay
L. 0.0225 m, w. 0.0185 m, th. 0.007 m
City of Khania, Kastelli Hill, 1973, 10 Katre Street Archive
Khania Archaeological Museum, KH 1547

Small piece of clay with four-sided cutting on the lower side with the imprint of the string by which the sealing was attached to the sealed object. The upper surface displays a bull-leaping scene, which occurs on nine other simple sealings from the same archive. The sealing was probably made with a gold signet ring with ovoid bezel. Complete.

The bull strides to the right at a gallop, its head thrust backward. The wavy horns occupy the empty space above the beast's body, and the tail swings upward. Behind the galloping bull hovers the leaper shortly before he reaches the ground, his body and open limbs rendered frontally and his left arm extended toward the bull. Except for the belt, no other detail of a garment is visible. A simple horizontal line denotes the ground below.

In terms of style, this representation is an exquisite example of realism in its most powerful pictorial expression. It belongs to a group of sealings that are well known through examples from Gournia, Haghia Triada, and Sklavokampos, which depict bull-leaping and were impressed by metal rings. The similarity between these rings suggests that they were made by the same goldsmith or in the same workshop.

Selected Bibliography
CMS V, 1A, p. 174, no. 171; Papapostolou 1977, pp. 33–43, pl. 1a.

Eftychia Protopapadaki

118 **Prismatic Sealing**

    End of Late Minoan IB period (ca. 1450 B.C.)
    Clay
    L. 0.024 m, w. 0.017 m
    City of Khania, Kastelli Hill, Plateia Haghia Aikaterini,
    Greek-Swedish Excavation
    Khania Archaeological Museum, KH 1561

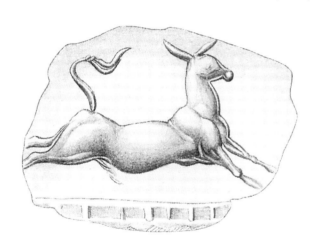

Complete. Fingerprints on the surface. The impression of a signet ring with ovoid bezel occupies the obverse. The sealing depicts with remarkable naturalism a bull in a "flying gallop" over a paved area, a possible reference to bull-leaping.

Prismatic sealings were autonomous documents, which probably enveloped the ropes that secured boxes or cupboards, like a kind of proof or label. This find comes from the floor of Room D of the Late Minoan I Building I. It was found near a cupboard together with other precious objects.

Selected Bibliography
CMS V, 1A, p. 148, no. 145; Papapostolou 1977, p. 20.

Eftychia Protopapadaki

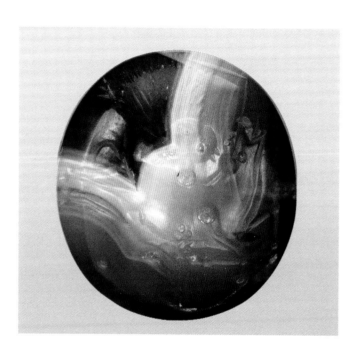

© CMS Archive, Marburg

119 **Seal Stone (Lion Attacking a Bull)**
   Late Minoan II period (ca. 1450–1400 B.C.)
   Onyx with white veins
   Diam. 0.023–0.025 m
   Knossos, Haghios Ioannis, Gold Cup Tomb
   Herakleion Archaeological Museum, HM 1712

Complete, slightly restored.

The Haghios Ioannis seal depicts a lion with a body that has been elongated to follow the border of the circular seal surface in a most unnatural way as it savages a bull, biting its back. The bull has been carved on an axis perpendicular to the attacking animal. This conventional composition owes much to the effect created by the circular impressions that have been engraved in depth by a drill.

Compositions with animals simply arranged, attacking or fighting one another, are favorite subjects for seal engraving, primarily during the Neopalatial period and later. The subject of a lion mauling a bull has as many parallels in Crete as it has in mainland Greece during the Mycenaean period. The theme occurs mostly on seals from the so-called warrior graves, accompanied by a plethora of weapons, jewelry, and luxury items, as in the case of the Haghios Ioannis tomb. As a result, some scholars have suggested that the subject matter of the seals was chosen for its symbolism, i.e., the valor or military prowess of the deceased. In Crete, particularly in the area of Knossos, the fact that many seals of very good quality have been found in wealthy tombs of the period is indicative of the established order of ownership or use. The seal's shape (lentoid), its large diameter, and the style of rendering belong to the early Mycenaean period.

Selected Bibliography
CMS II, 3, p. 71 (no. 60); Hood 1956, pp. 93–94; Krzyszkowska 2005a, pp. 203, 325; Laffineur 1990; Niemeier 1997; Younger 1985, pp. 67–68.

Emmanouela Apostolaki

© CMS Archive, Marburg

© CMS Archive, Marburg

120 Three-Sided Seal Stone (Bull and Lion)
> Late Minoan II period (ca. 1450–1400 B.C.)
> Carnelian with gold granulation
> L. with granulation 0.024 m, diam. 0.019–0.02 m
> Knossos, Sanatorium, Tomb III
> Herakleion Archaeological Museum, HM 1658

Complete. Three-sided prismatic seal with rounded and curved surfaces, two of which have seal engravings, the third left uncarved. The edges of the string hole—the perforation for the chain or string from which the seal stone was suspended or by which it was held—are ornamented with groups of gold granules.

One side of the seal depicts a bull running to the left and a tree with branches at the seal's border. The bull is depicted in some detail. On the other side and perpendicular to the string-hole axis, a lion is depicted seated on the ground, head turned backward, wounded in the side by a javelin and in the chest by a smaller shaft, perhaps an arrow. The way in which this animal is depicted is more schematic than the bull.

As a shape, the prism, which was used from the inception of seal-stone carving in Crete and was widespread in earlier periods, appears only rarely in the Mycenaean period. It is even rarer in the entire Late Minoan period to find a gold "setting" with the granulation technique, which this Sanitorium seal has. Its closest parallel is a three-sided seal of sard from the Neopalatial cemetery at Poros, Herakleion.

The rarity of the prism seems to be consistent with its discovery in a rich tomb in one of the wealthiest cemeteries of the period, where the dissemination of seals appears to be restricted now, indirectly giving some indication of the social status of its owners.

Selected Bibliography
CMS II, 3, p. 75 (no. 64); Hood–de Jong 1952, p. 273; Krzyszkowska 2005a, pp. 203, 325; Laffineur 1990; Niemeier 1997; Younger 1985, pp. 65–66.

Emmanouela Apostolaki

121 **Egyptian Scarab**

New Kingdom, 18th dynasty (ca. 1390–1353 B.C.)
Faience
W. 0.039 m, th. 0.028 m, h. 0.017 m
City of Khania, Kastelli Hill, Lionakis/Vlamakis plot, 1967
Khania Archaeological Museum, Π 6182

This complete scarab of Egyptian pharaoh Amenhotep III is made of gray-brown faience blackened by fire. Five hieroglyphic signs occupy the sealing surface: 1 and 4, solar disc symbolizing the god Re; 2, open wicker basket *nebet*; 3, seated goddess of justice and order *Maat*; 5, agricultural tool *meri* with the same phonetic value as the epithet "beloved." The first three make up Amenhotep III's throne name—that is, the name that he took when he ascended to the throne: "Neb (2) Maat (3) Re (1)." The other two constitute the epithet that accompanies the throne name: "Meri (5) Re (1)," that is, "beloved of the sun god Re."

This scarab with Amenhotep III's cartouche, found in the excavations on Kastelli Hill, Khania (prehistoric Kydonia), stresses the overall atmosphere of close relationship between Egypt and Crete at the beginning of the fourteenth century B.C., when the island was under Achaean rule. Another scarab with the same pharaoh's cartouche was found in a chamber tomb at Sellopoulo, Knossos, and a scarab with the name of his wife, Queen Tiyi, was found in a tomb at Haghia Triada.

It is worth mentioning that the names of well-known Cretan and Greek cities, including Kydonia, are inscribed on the base of Amenhotep III's funerary monument. This list of cities may refer to an official journey of the Egyptian pharaonic court, and possibly of the pharaoh himself, in Crete and the Greek mainland.

Selected Bibliography

AΔ 22 B2 (1967): 501 (Tzedakis); Karetsou–Andreadaki-Vlazaki–Papadakis 2000, p. 320, no. 329 (Keel–Kyriakides).

Maria Andreadaki-Vlazaki

122 **Seal Stone (Bull-Leaping, Two Bulls)**

Late Minoan II–IIIA 1 period (ca. 1450–1375 B.C.)
Basalt (*Lapis lacedaemonius*)
Diam. 0.022 m
Maroulas cemetery, 2001, Chamber Tomb 3 (Late Minoan IIIA2 context [1375–1300 B.C.])
Rethymnon Archaeological Museum, Σ 217

Large lentoid seal with depictions on both sides. One side shows a male figure with a belt and a codpiece kneeling before a bull, which he holds by the horns. An astral symbol with ten rays is depicted between the man's legs. The other side has two antithetical bulls on either side of an impaled triangle, a well-known sign of the Linear B script.

A similar scene of a man wrestling a bull, although in a different style, occurs on a seal stone from Grave 7 at Kalyvia, near Phaistos; a few more examples were found at Knossos, Mycenae, and Pylos. Although unrelated to each other and limited in number, these scenes were probably part of the broader bull-leaping cycle and were directly related to the promotion of Knossian palatial rule. The heliacal disc is probably not a mere decorative motif, but may be, according to some scholars, a means of indicating a particular time period during which certain related rituals took place.

Lapis lacedaemonius, a hard green stone encountered only at Krokees in Lakonia, was rarely used in seal carving. In Crete it only appears in the Neopalatial period, unlike other hard stones that were in use as early as the Protopalatial period. Seal stones in *Lapis lacedaemonius* are rare in the Aegean, and very few have a known provenance. All of them, including this Maroulas example, are distinguished by the high quality of craftsmanship and are usually associated with palatial workshops.

Selected Bibliography
CMS III, p. 1, 16; Gill 1966, pp. 11–16, figs. 6: 1–10; Hallager 1996; MacGillivray 2004; Marinatos 1986, pp. 61–64; Niemeier 1997, p. 298; Papadopoulou (in press); Younger 1995, p. 510, pls. LX d–g.

Eleni Papadopoulou

© CMS Archive, Marburg

123 Seal Stone (Bull-Leaping Scene)
    Late Minoan IIIA2–B period (ca. 1350–1200 B.C.)
    Basalt (*Lapis lacedaemonius*)
    Diam. 0.0196–0.0199 m
    Malia, Quartier Nu
    Haghios Nikolaos Archaeological Museum, 13944

Complete. The scene on one side of this lentoid seal stone depicts a bull running to the left with its head raised. Above its back, a naked male figure with open legs and his head in an unnatural position seems to be trying to vault as he holds the bull's head with his hands. The lentoid shape of the seal stone lends itself to the arrangement of the subject matter, which fills the pictorial surface.

The sport of bull-leaping, popular in the context of religious affairs, appears in Minoan iconography as early as 2000 B.C. and is frequently depicted, because of its particular religious significance, on seals, vases, rhyta, figurines, and wall paintings.

Two seal stones of similar shape, of the same material and with a comparable bull-leaping scene, come from Gournes, Herakleion, and Maroulas, Rethymnon (cat. no. 122).

Selected Bibliography
CMS I, no. 408, II, 4, no. 157, VII, no. 108, X, no. 141; *CMS* V, suppl. 3, no. 33; Driessen–Farnoux 1994, p. 474, fig. 4; Younger 1986, pp. 136–37, 1.

Vili Apostolakou

© CMS Archive, Marburg

124 Seal Stone (Bull-Leaping Scene)
Late Minoan IIIA period (ca. 1400–1300 B.C.)
Agate with white veining
Diam. 0.024–0.026 m
Praisos, Tomb D
Herakleion Archaeological Museum, HM 185

Complete, with a little damage.

This seal depicts a dramatic moment in the popular Minoan sport of bull-leaping. A huge bull, its strength made clear by the depiction of its anatomy, appears to be sitting on the ground, as a male athlete, his belt around his hips, executes an acrobatic leap above its back, having grabbed hold of the animal's horns. Other elements are depicted conventionally, namely the ground with four horizontal lines and a small tuft of grass at the right. The Praisos seal is somewhat removed from the more realistic representations of the Neopalatial period, when naturalism dictated that the springing of the acrobats and the forward movement of the bulls gave a sense of urgency to the modeling of the muscular bulk. What interested the craftsman here was the depiction of the subject in a schematic way rather than an analytically detailed narrative.

The choice by the seal engraver or his agent of bull-leaping as a subject at a time when the sport may no longer have been practiced reflects its popularity, which is also evident from the large number of similar representations dating to different periods of the Bronze Age on the island.

The subject of bull-leaping appears to be a recognizable and clear image in Minoan Crete, a kind of sign or symbol that, during the acme of the island, was deemed suitable for validating economic and administrative relationships between trading centers. This is reflected in the bull-leaping scenes on clay sealings produced by gold signet rings, which accompanied negotiable or exchangeable products both within Crete (e.g., Haghia Triada, Zakros, Sklavokambos) and beyond, notably Akrotiri on Thera.

Selected Bibliography
Bosanquet 1901–2b; *CMS* II, 3, p. 322 (no. 271); Krzyszkowska 2005a.

Emmanouela Apostolaki

© CMS Archive, Marburg

© CMS Archive, Marburg

125 **Seal Stone (Caprids, Lioness)**
Late Minoan IIIA period (ca. 1400–1300 B.C.)
Agate
Diam. 0.0156–0.0163 m
Armenoi, Late Minoan cemetery, Chamber tomb 167
Rethymnon Archaeological Museum, Σ 131

Complete lentoid seal with two sealing surfaces. The string hole is horizontal in relation to Face A and vertical in relation to Face B. Face A depicts two caprids in a circle. One gallops toward the right, its horned head turned back, while the second, smaller animal is shown upside down, its body and legs contracted. Face B has a left-facing lioness, her head bowed toward her nursing cub, which stands on its rear legs. Short lines denote her stylized mane, and an arrow, directly above her back, may refer to hunting. In both scenes, circles mark the eyes and joints. Despite their naturalistic postures, the figures are rendered in a stylized manner.

Animals, particularly deer, caprids, cattle, wild boars, and pigs, singly or in pairs, stationary or in action, were often depicted up to about 1300 B.C. In the late Mycenaean period, these figures became highly stylized to the point of abstraction. Forms were simplified, and legs were engraved separately as lines with dots in the place of the joints; compositions were formal and not natural as seen in the earlier seals.

Selected Bibliography
CMS V, 1B, no. 276, p. 271.

Epameinondas Kapranos

© CMS Archive, Marburg

126 **Seal Stone (Griffin)**
Late Minoan IIIA period (ca. 1400–1300 B.C.)
Serpentinite
Diam. 0.0178–0.0185 m
Armenoi, Late Minoan cemetery, Chamber Tomb 87
Rethymnon Archaeological Museum, Σ 76

This complete lentoid seal with vertical piercing depicts a griffin galloping toward the left, its head turned back. The front legs are contracted, the wings are sickle shape, and the tail is raised.

Similar representations of griffins occur on other serpentinite seal stones from Armenoi, but also on steatite seal stones from the Late Minoan cemetery at Metochi Kalou, near Herakleion. The sickle-shape wings also occur on a seal stone from a chamber tomb at Maroulas, near Rethymnon.

The origin of the griffin motif on seal stones is Minoan. It often occurs in Mycenaean times, since it is a popular motif of Creto-Mycenaean iconography, and usually appears in religious scenes.

Selected Bibliography
CMS V, 1B, p. 241, no. 222.

Epameinondas Kapranos

127 **Seal Stone**

Late Minoan IIIA2 period (ca. 1375–1300 B.C.)
Blue glass paste
Diam. 0.020 m
Maroulas cemetery, 2001, Chamber Tomb 2
Rethymnon Archaeological Museum, Σ 218

Mold-made lentoid seal with conical back. The obverse depicts two upright intersecting wild goats, with palm fronds between their heads. The same scene occurs on six other glass-paste seal stones from the Mycenaean cemetery at Medeon, in Phocis. Despite the iconographic similarities, the representations are not identical, showing that the seal stones were not made in the same mold.

Mold-made glass-paste seal stones appeared in the Aegean in about 1400 B.C. Stylistically they are related to the so-called International Style. Unlike contemporary glass-paste beads, they are hard to find.

Most glass-paste seal stones come from the Greek mainland, particularly central Greece, where there may have been a workshop. A very few have been found in Crete, in graves in the city of Khania and the Late Minoan cemetery at Armenoi, near Rethymnon. A unique mold associated with the production of glass-paste seal stones was discovered at Katsambas, the port of Knossos.

Glass paste was a precious material imported from the East in the form of ingots, as demonstrated by the Ulu-Burun shipwreck on Turkey's south coast and dated to about 1300 B.C.

Selected Bibliography
Bass 1986, pp. 281–82; Krzyszkowska 2005a, pp. 198, 267–70; Müller-Celka 2003, pp. 87–88, 90–91; Papadopoulou (in press); Pini 1999, p. 332; Younger 1999, pp. 955–56.

Eleni Papadopoulou

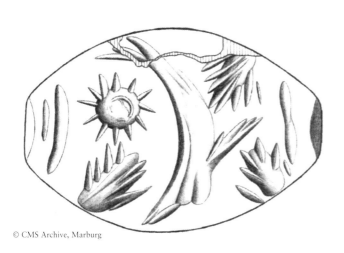

© CMS Archive, Marburg

128 **Seal Stone (Dolphin)**
　　Late Minoan IIIA period (ca. 1400–1300 B.C.)
　　Jasper
　　L. 0.0192 m, w. 0.0129 m, th. 0.007 m
　　Armenoi, Late Minoan cemetery, Chamber Tomb 188
　　Rethymnon Archaeological Museum, Σ148

Cracked amygdaloid (almond-shape) seal depicting a dolphin with its head placed down across the sealing surface and a sea urchin at the right. Three highly stylized plant motifs ornament the background of the composition.

Scenes inspired by the marine world may indicate the interests of those who lived near the sea or engaged in maritime travel. Like catalogue number 125, this seal belongs to the category of talismanic seals, which developed from the Middle Minoan III period (ca. 1700 B.C. onward) and were thought to have magical properties for their owners.

Selected Bibliography
CMS V, 1B, no. 300, p. 285.

Epameinondas Kapranos

129 Seal Stone (Amphora on Altar)

Late Minoan IIIA period (ca. 1400–1300 B.C.)
Carnelian
L. 0.0186 m, w. 0.0147 m, th. 0.0076 m
Armenoi, Late Minoan cemetery, Chamber Tomb 167
Rethymnon Archaeological Museum, Σ 130

This complete, amygdaloid (almond-shape) seal with vertical piercing depicts an amphora on top of an altar, a subject with apotropaic properties. Above the central motif is a grid with two horizontal and several vertical lines. The space between the amphora handles and body is filled by a grid-shape ornament. Stylized vegetal motifs occupy the border.

This seal belongs to the so-called talismanic (apotropaic) seal stones, a group that developed in the Middle Minoan III period (ca. 1700 B.C. and later). These seal stones were thought to have magical properties and were used as talismans. Most of them are amygdaloid and are characterized by highly stylized motifs. They occur more frequently in Crete than on the Greek mainland and in the Cyclades. The correlation between ritual vessels, such as the amphora and the jug, with vegetal motifs, as in this case, is thought to attribute the aspect of fertility to the rite.

Selected Bibliography
CMS V, 1 B, no. 275, p. 270.

Epameinondas Kapranos

130 **Cylinder Seal**

Late Minoan IIIA2 (ca. 1375–1300 B.C.)
Faience
H. 0.019 m, diam. 0.009 m
Armenoi, Late Minoan cemetery, Chamber tomb 108
Rethymnon Archaeological Museum, Σ 94

This imported cylinder seal from Mesopotamia's Mitanni region depicts an antelope or a caprid and a bird, both left-facing and highly stylized. The combination of an antelope and a bird is unique. An antelope is depicted on another faience cylinder seal from the Armenoi cemetery, also imported from the Mitanni region.

The shape of the cylinder seal probably originates in southern Mesopotamia, where it first appeared about 3500 B.C. The presence of cylinder seals imported from the Mitanni region in Late Minoan III Crete demonstrates the existence of trade relations between the island and the East.

Selected Bibliography
CMS V, 1B, p. 251, no. 241.

Epameinondas Kapranos

Jewels, especially those made of gold and semiprecious stones, have traditionally been used as a means of displaying status and wealth, both during life and in death. Most examples of Minoan jewelry have been found in graves, placed on or around the body of the deceased.

The first gold and silver jewels appear in the middle of the third millennium B.C. (ca. 2600 B.C.) in the tombs of eastern Crete and of Mesara in central Crete. They take the form of leaves or flowers, with thin stems and finely crafted chains, and of gold bands and diadems that resemble similar types from Troia and the north Aegean.

Elaborate and sophisticated jewels, such as necklaces, rings, earrings, pendants, and amulets, were manufactured from the Protopalatial to the Final Palatial period (ca. 1900–1250 B.C.). Jewelry making involved several techniques: granulation, in which gold granules are soldered one by one onto a surface; filigree, in which fine gold wire is twisted delicately into intricate designs; hammering, to create embossed decoration; and cloisonné, or the application of enamel into raised cells, usually made of metal. Necklace beads, like seals, were made at specialized workshops of semiprecious stones, such as sard, agate, amethyst, and rock crystal, or of simpler veined rocks. Remains of these raw materials have been found mainly at Poros and Zakros. Necklace beads, earrings, and hairpins were also made in various shapes of vitreous materials, namely glass and faience, which were cast in molds and thus offered the opportunity for large-scale, cheap reproduction of precious originals.

Jewels in tombs are found alongside personal items of daily use for toilet and ornamentation, such as jewel boxes made of clay or ivory, ivory or bone combs, bronze mirrors, tweezers, ear picks, knives, and razors. These objects all reflect a belief in life after death for both wealthy urban citizens and ordinary people, who wished to carry both luxury and everyday objects on their final journey.

131A–B **Myrtle-Shape Leaves**

Early Minoan II period (ca. 2600–2300 B.C.)
Gold
131A (HM 325): L. 0.059 m
131B (HM 326): L. 0.052 m
Mochlos, Tomb III (131A); Tomb XIX (131B), 1908
Herakleion Archaeological Museum, HM 325 and 326

Two gold myrtle-shape leaves with punch-dotted outlines and
threadlike stems, bent at the end. They were probably attached
by the thin wire to holes on a diadem.

These leaves were made from hammered gold sheets cut into the
shape of a leaf and embellished with a simple punching technique to create a relief (repoussé). The precision and regularity
of the punched dots that shape the outline indicate an experienced and specialized craftsman.

Myrtle, a typical Cretan plant, was a popular decorative
motif in Minoan art. These gold leaves in the shape of myrtle,
which are some of the most interesting examples of naturalistic
art in the Prepalatial period, come from the cemetery of
Mochlos, where excavations produced one of the largest collections of Prepalatial gold jewelry on Crete.

Selected Bibliography
Branigan 1983, p. 16; Cameron 1968; Davaras 1975; Effinger 1996,
p. 256; Higgins 1961, p. 62; Seager 1912, p. 39; Televantou 1984,
pp. 27, 46.

Katerina Athanasaki

132A–B **Flower-Shape Pins**

Early Minoan II/III–Middle Minoan I period
(ca. 2500–1800 B.C.)
Gold
132A (HM 260): max. h. 0.053 m
132B (HM 261): max. h. 0.051 m
Mochlos, Tomb XIX, 1908
Herakleion Archaeological Museum, HM 260 and 261

Two identical, complete gold ornaments in a flower shape, with
long stems and eight petals each. On top of the pointed stem,
which is made of fine hammered wire, is a cutout sheet in the
shape of a flower. Flower-shape pins were probably used either
for securing gold diadems on the head or, on their own, for dec-
orating hair.

These two gold daisies were found in the larger chamber of
Tomb XIX at Mochlos, which despite the opulent grave gifts is
not one of the cemetery's most monumental graves. The daisies
were made using the simple, basic techniques of that period, but
the result is one of the most elegant and imaginative examples
of Prepalatial Minoan jewelry and was the work of an able
craftsman, possibly of a local workshop.

Selected Bibliography
Branigan 1974, pp. 38–39, pl. 19; Branigan 1991; Seager 1912,
pp. 70–72, figs. 41–42; Soles 1992, pp. 64–65.

Eirini Galli

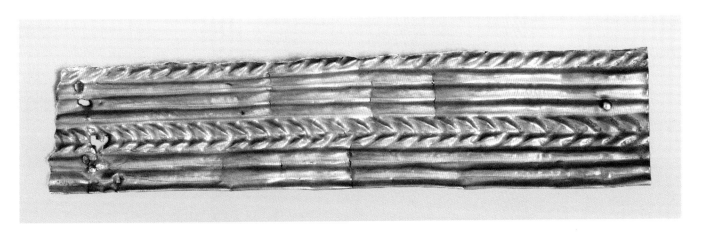

133A–B **Bands**

Early Minoan IIB–Early Minoan III (ca. 2600–2200 B.C.)
Gold
133A (HM 287): max. w. 0.022 m, max. l. 0.097 m
133B (HM 289): max. w. 0.021 m, max. l. 0.072 m
Mochlos, Tomb II, 1908
Herakleion Archaeological Museum, HM 287 and 289

Two joining bands of gold leaf have embossed decoration consisting of horizontal, parallel grooves alternating with herringbone motifs (a half-herringbone motif is preserved along the edge). One long edge is folded inward for securing the band on a perishable material, such as leather or textile. Holes along the short edges served the same purpose. Fragmentary joining.

These gold bands were found inside Tomb II at Mochlos, the richest and one of the most monumental of this cemetery's grave complexes. Jewelry in the form of gold-leaf bands are among the most important finds from the Mochlos cemetery. Depending on their size, the bands have been interpreted as diadems, appliqué ornaments for garments, or armbands. These two bands belonged originally to a larger piece of jewelry, probably an armband, as indicated by a complete example found in another grave, which was carefully cut into three or four pieces.

Mochlos's rich and well-built tombs are associated with the social elite that was able to acquire many luxury goods. Because the tombs were used over a long time period and contained several burials and mixed groups of grave gifts, it is difficult to define the social structure of this elite. In any case, the Mochlos finds illustrate an elaborately organized community that directly or indirectly supported the importation of raw materials for the manufacture and consumption of luxury goods through long-distance trade.

Selected Bibliography

Branigan 1974, pp. 43–44, pl. 22; Davaras 1975; Evely 1993–2000, 2 (2000), pp. 401–2, 404–11; Seager 1912, pp. 22–24, fig. 8.II.18a, c, fig. 38; Soles 1992, pp. 17–23.

Eirini Galli

134 Necklace with Beads and Pendants

Early Minoan III–Middle Minoan I period (ca. 2300–1800 B.C.)

Steatite

L. 0.088 m

Mesara, Marathokephalo, Tholos Tomb, 1917

Herakleion Archaeological Museum, HM 1229

Necklace grouping of seventy-three beads made of steatite. The beads have various forms: disc-shape, almond-shape, barrel-shape, biconical, pyramidal, and irregular four-sided; one bead is shaped like a drop. The arrangement of the necklace is modern.

These objects come from the tholos tomb at Marathokephalo, Mesara. The same funerary context yielded vases, daggers, seals, hundreds of small disc-shape steatite beads, dozens of larger beads of hard semiprecious stones, and pendants of stone and bone.

Jewelry does not necessarily indicate its owner's sex. Clay male figurines and male figures on frescoes usually wear jewelry, including necklaces, armbands, and bracelets.

Because the Marathokephalo grave was used for multiple burials over a long period of time, as was customary in Mesara, the beads' original arrangement is uncertain. The decorative effect of necklaces made of a single material, such as steatite, lies in the great variety of the stone's natural shades. One of the most common Cretan stones, steatite was widely used for vases and jewelry in the Prepalatial period. Its softness and lack of porosity allowed the creation of smooth surfaces without recourse to complex, specialized tools.

Selected Bibliography

Sakellarakis–Sapouna-Sakellaraki 1997, pp. 625–26; Warren 1969b, pp. 140–41; Xanthoudides 1918b, pp. 15–20, fig. 8.

Eirini Galli

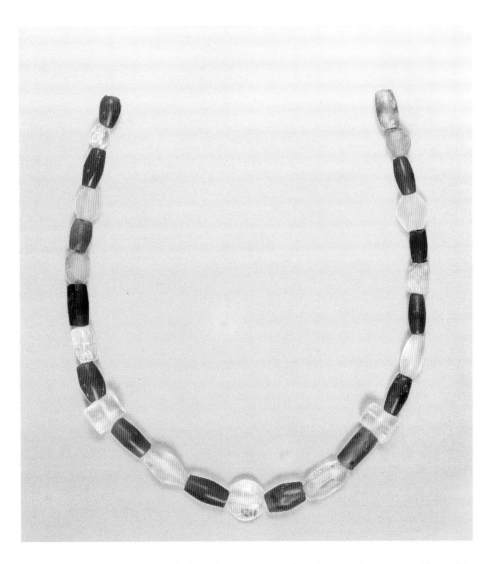

135 Necklace

Early Minoan III–Middle Minoan I period
(ca. 2300–1800 B.C.)
Rock crystal, sardonyx
L. 0.36 m
Mesara, Platanos, Tholos Tomb B, 1915
Herakleion Archaeological Museum, HM 1151

Necklace grouping of twenty-seven beads, of which thirteen are of rock crystal and fourteen of sardonyx. The beads have various shapes: cylindrical, lentoid, and barrel-shape; one is prismatic. They come from Tholos Tomb B at Platanos, one of the most impressive of the Mesara tombs. The three tombs at Platanos contained more than 2,000 beads, of which 1,800 are of steatite, the remaining beads being of sardonyx, rock crystal, and glass paste. The arrangement of this necklace is modern.

Beads found in their original position in the graves at Phourni in Archanes demonstrate that necklaces were often composed of beads of different materials and shapes arranged in various color combinations. Hard semiprecious stones, which require relatively advanced manufacturing techniques and specialized tools, were also used after the establishment of Crete's first palaces, along with the softer Cretan stones, such as steatite. The development of maritime communications from the end of the second millennium B.C. favored the importation of raw materials and the spread of ideas and new techniques. Sardonyx, amethyst, and lapis lazuli were imported from the East and Egypt. In combination with one another or with gold, the beads formed pieces of jewelry that accompanied their owners in death as in life.

Selected Bibliography

Krzyszkowska 2005a, p. 12; Sakellarakis–Sapouna-Sakellaraki 1997, p. 618, fig. 655; Warren 1969b, pp. 136–37; Xanthoudides 1924, pp. 90–92, 124, fig. LVIII.

Eirini Galli

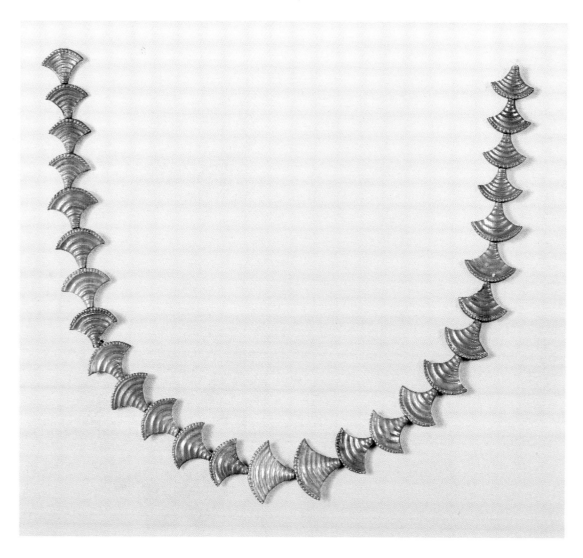

136 **Necklace**
  Late Minoan IIIA1 period (ca. 1400–1375 B.C.)
  Gold
  L. 0.384 m
  Sellopoulo, Tomb 4, 1968
  Herakleion Archaeological Museum, HM 1037

Necklace comprising twenty-seven golden beads of different sizes in the shape of papyrus, manufactured in three different molds. The beads are made up of two halves of the same shape joined together with a single piercing along the axis. Each piece has seven relief lines parallel to the arched dots of the edge.

The papyrus, a plant characteristic of Egypt and, according to some scholars, a native Minoan plant, was a motif very much loved by Minoan artists. Papyrus-shape beads occur in different guises and were often sewn onto cloth as ornaments. As for their manufacture, different materials were used, such as faience, glass, and lapis lazuli. Gold pieces of this type come for the most part from tombs of the Late Minoan IIIA1 period.

Selected Bibliography
Effinger 1996, pp. 34–35, 219; Popham–Catling–Catling 1974, pp. 202, 210–13, 223; Sakellarakis–Sapouna-Sakellaraki 1997, p. 616; Warren 1976.

Katerina Athanasaki

137 Diadem

Late Minoan IIIA1 period (ca. 1400–1375 B.C.)
Gold
L. 0.158 m
Knossos, Zapher Papoura cemetery, Chieftain's Grave
Herakleion Archaeological Museum, HM 206

Diadem of eighteen beads bearing relief (repoussé) decoration of schematic double nautilus/argonaut motifs, made by hammering into a mold. Good preservation.

The diadem was found in a pit grave at the Zapher Papoura cemetery, Knossos, known as the Chieftain's Grave. Two swords and two spears, among other grave gifts, indicate that this must have been one of the dozens of "warrior" graves in the Knossos region. Each bead of the diadem is made of two joint golden sheets with three suspension holes in their short axis.

Beads of this type, more than four hundred of which have been uncovered so far, usually have two or three parallel suspension holes and eyes in relief or depressed for the inlay of a different material, probably glass.

The nautilus/argonaut motif, attested already in Minoan iconography since the Middle Minoan period, became popular during the subsequent Neopalatial period, when the Marine Style was introduced into Minoan art. During the Late Minoan II and IIIA1 periods, the motif appears in the shape of double nautilus/argonaut. In addition to its decorative use, it might have had symbolic connotations as well, relating either to travel in general or to the navigating skills of the nautilus or "pontilus" creature as it travels in the sea, as vigorously described by Aristotle in his *Historia Animalium*. Furthermore, the motif is thought to symbolize perfection.

Selected Bibliography

Evans 1906, pp. 129–31, fig. 119, Effinger 1996, pp. 30–31, 75, 224, Alberti 2004, pp. 83–90.

Katerina Athanasaki

138 Necklace

Late Minoan II–IIIA2 period (ca. 1450–1350/1300 B.C.)
Gold
L. 0.417 m
Knossos, Zapher Papoura cemetery, Tomb 66, 1904
Herakleion Archaeological Museum, HM 204

Necklace comprising forty-six hollow relief gold beads in the shape of rosettes, with two parallel string holes. The beads are made of two separate leaves of gold joined at their edges. The bottom leaf is flat, and the top leaf forms an embossed schematic eight-petaled rosette with a rounded outline. The beads were made by hammering the gold on a mold.

The necklace comes from the cemetery of Zapher Papoura, northeast of the palace at Knossos. Golden beads made in various shapes inspired by imagery drawn from the natural world, such as rosettes, were frequently used as ornaments sewn onto clothing. The relief rosette is one of the most popular types of Late Minoan III jewelry making.

Selected Bibliography
Alberti 2004, pp. 83–90; Effinger 1996, pp. 37, 225; Evans 1906, pp. 129–30, fig. 119.

Katerina Athanasaki

139A–C Necklace

Middle of Late Minoan IIIB period (ca. 1250 B.C.)
139A (M 497 α-ι): gold
139B (Γ 189 α-λ), 139C (Γ 190 α-η): glass paste
Diam. 0.020–0.024 m.
City of Khania, Haghios Ioannis, Tomb I, 1984
Khania Archaeological Museum, M 497 α-ι, Γ 189 α-λ, Γ 190 α-η

The necklace arrangements are modern.

139A: Ten gold embossed rosettes, each with eight rounded double petals in relief around a central eye, also in relief. The glass-paste rosettes are rendered in the same manner. Each gold rosette consists of two thin gold sheets; the motif is rendered in low relief on the first, whereas the second forms the flat back. The two gold sheets are poorly joined. Both the gold and the glass-paste rosettes have double horizontal piercings, either for assembly into a necklace or for sewing onto a textile.

139B. Twelve well-preserved glass-paste rosettes. Six are chipped and one is fragmentary.

139C. Eight glass-paste rosettes. Flat reverse. Two are fairly worn. Six were made in the same mold. The other two are smaller, like those of 139B.

The rosette was a popular decorative motif, and rosette-shape beads in gold, ivory, glass, and faience were used in jewelry making or sewn onto luxury garments. These beads were found in a small pile next to and under a bronze "horned" sword in the chamber tomb where they came from.

Selected Bibliography
Im Labirynth des Minos, p. 332 (Preve); Karantzali 1986; Karetsou–Andreadaki-Vlazaki–Papadakis 2000, pp. 93–96, 111–12 (Andreadaki-Vlazaki); Xenaki-Sakellariou 1985, pp. 303–4, type 85b.

Sophia Preve

139A

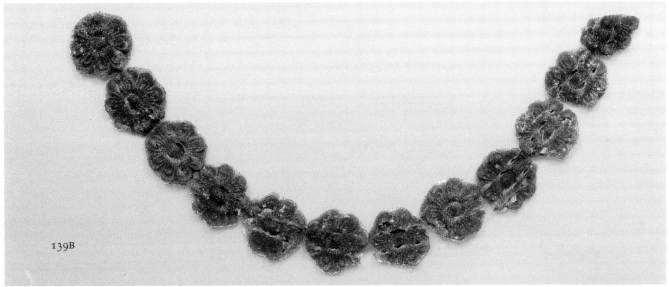

139B

139C

140 **Necklace**

Late Minoan II–Late Minoan IIIA1 period
(ca. 1450–1375 B.C.)
Amethyst (and carnelian?)
L. 0.17 m
Knossos, Mavrospelio cemetery
Herakleion Archaeological Museum, HM 1335

Necklace of twenty-one spherical beads in three different sizes; made of amethyst in a variety of colors with a central string hole.

This necklace comes from the Mavrospelio cemetery, northeast of the palace at Knossos, which was used almost without interruption from Middle Minoan IIB until the Late Minoan III period.

Amethyst, a semiprecious stone that the ancient Greeks believed to have shamanic, therapeutic properties, came mainly from a source in Egypt. Semiprecious stones of every kind began to reach Crete from the Middle Minoan II period onward, although they had been used sporadically as early as the Prepalatial period. It remains an open question, however, as to whether the amethyst beads found in Crete, more than 200 of them, were made in local workshops. Of particular relevance here are the unworked or semiworked pieces of amethyst found at the workshops of Poros, the harbor town of Knossos, which indicate that amethyst was worked on Crete as early as the Late Minoan I period.

Selected Bibliography
Dimopoulou-Rethemiotaki 1997, p. 436; Forsdyke 1926–27, pp. 278–79; Krzyskowska 2005b.

Katerina Athanasaki

141 **Necklace**

Late Minoan III period (ca. 1400–1200 B.C.)
Amethyst
Bead diam. 0.006–0.01 m
Rethymnon area
Rethymnon Archaeological Museum, Λ 731

Necklace made up of twenty-one spherical and squat-spherical amethyst beads. Spherical and squat-spherical beads are the most common bead shapes used in Minoan jewelry making. The amethyst was probably imported from Egypt; amethyst sources have been identified at Abu Simbel, near Aswan.

Pictorial sources show that Cretan women, men, and children adorned themselves with beads. Beads of various shapes and materials were arranged into necklaces, bracelets, and armbands, but beads were also used on head ornaments or sewn onto fabric. Most pieces of jewelry from this period were found inside graves, where they had been placed as grave offerings.

Selected Bibliography

Effinger 1996; Krzyszkowska 2005b; Löwe 1996; Sakellarakis–
Sapouna-Sakellaraki 1997.

Panagiota Karamaliki

142 **Necklace**
    Late Minoan IIIA period (ca. 1400–1350/1300 B.C.)
    Carnelian
    L. 0.572m
    Kalyvia cemetery of Phaistos, Tomb 4, 1901
    Herakleion Archaeological Museum, HM 239

Necklace of forty-one carnelian beads in the shape of lightly depressed spheres, with pairs of grooves parallel to their central string hole.

Beads of this shape are a variation on the simple spherical type and are made of different materials, such as gold, rock crystal, glass, faience, and steatite.

Carnelian, the material of which these beads are made, came mainly from Egypt, where, as on Crete, it was only sporadically used for jewelry making.

In addition to this necklace, the Postpalatial cemetery of Kalyvia-Phaistos was particularly rich in finds, which is why the tombs were dubbed the Tombs of the Nobles (*Tombe dei Nobili*).

Selected Bibliography
Effinger 1996, pp. 25, 277; Löwe 1996, pp. 243–46; Savignoni 1904, pp. 532, 605, no. 35, fig. 74.

Katerina Athanasaki

143 **Necklace**
    Late Minoan IIIA–B period (ca. 1400–1200 B.C.)
    Sardonyx
    Max. diam. of spherical beads 0.013 m; max. l. of biconical
    bead 0.02 m
    Armenoi, Late Minoan cemetery
    Rethymnon Archaeological Museum, Λ 735

Necklace made up of twenty-three beads from Graves 17, 23, 47, 98, 103, 108, 115, and 125 of the Late Minoan III cemetery at Armenoi, near Rethymnon. Various shapes are present, including cylindrical, amygdaloid (almond-shape), spherical, and barrel-shape. Similarly shaped beads are quite common in Late Minoan III Crete. Sardonyx, a semiprecious stone imported from the East, was often used in Minoan jewelry making during this period. The necklace's arrangement is modern.

Selected Bibliography
Effinger 1996; Löwe 1996; Sakellarakis–Sapouna-Sakellaraki 1997.

Panagiota Karamaliki

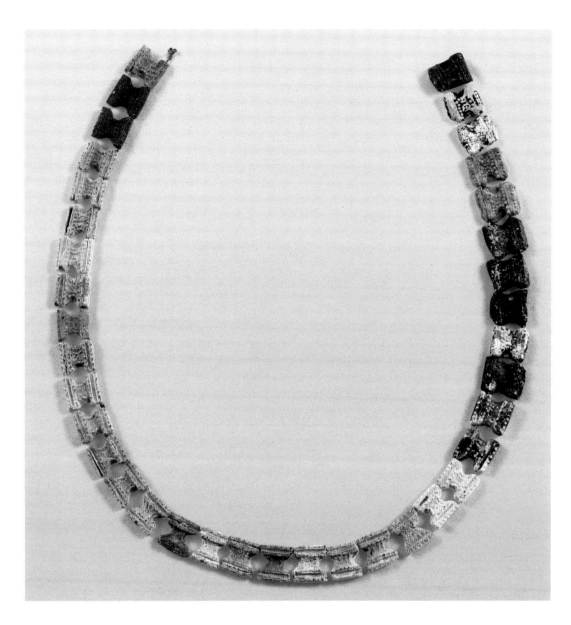

144 Necklace

Late Minoan IIIA period (ca. 1400–1300 B.C.)
Glass paste
H. and w. 0.012 m, th. 0.0035–0.005 m
City of Khania, Rovithakis plot, Tomb 2, 1996
Khania Archaeological Museum, Γ 293

Thirty-seven concave altar-shape beads. Each bead consists of two horizontal bands joined by a broad vertical stem with incurved sides. The horizontal bands have dotted decoration along the edge on the obverse only, and the upper band is pierced through. The necklace's arrangement is modern.

Although looted, the chamber tomb where this necklace was found preserved remarkable remains of rich grave goods, including jewelry of faience and rock crystal, gold-leaf discs, and necklace beads. Indicative of connections that wealthy families of the area likely had with the eastern Mediterranean is the presence of a Canaanite jar fragment in the tomb's entrance passage. These beads were found both scattered about and placed with others inside a vase.

Selected Bibliography
Im Labyrinth des Minos, p. 121, no. 100 (Preve); Xenaki-Sakellariou 1985, p. 302, type 81.

Sophia Preve

145 **Ring**

Late Minoan IIIC period (ca. 1200–1100 B.C.)
Gold
Bezel: l. 0.031 m, w. 0.02 m, hoop diam. 0.019 m
Praesos, "Photoula"
Herakleion Archaeological Museum, HM 765

Gold ring with elliptical bezel made of thick gold sheet. The hoop, which has three grooves along its outer side, is attached in two places to the rear surface of the bezel. The decoration of the visible surface of the bezel consists of a combination of gold granulation and wiring that creates a symmetrical scheme on both axes. There are two pairs of S-shape and opposing spirals of gold wire surrounded by granulation, each granule being attached to the surface one by one. Around the edge of the bezel, a double line of gold granules surrounds gold wire. There are larger granules of gold in the eyes of the spirals and in the middle of the bezel's ellipse.

This gold ring, which is outstanding in terms of its size, its composition, and the quality of its decoration, was used as a grave gift in a distinguished sarcophagus burial found in a rectangular, built tomb with corbelled walls, at the site of Photoula, Praesos, in eastern Crete. In addition to the ring, this burial yielded an ivory, gold-riveted scepter handle and pieces of thin gold foil found near the mouth of the deceased and bearing designs of nautili executed by a combination of incision and punched decoration. There was also a wooden basketlike vessel covered with bronze sheet, a spearhead, and clay pots. This was certainly one of the richest set of grave gifts found in a burial of the Mycenaean period in Crete, a period that generally saw few items of value in burials.

The ring is the earliest and most richly decorated example of a type made from gold sheet with a bulge in the place of a shield boss in the middle of the elliptical bezel. Later Submycenaean and Protogeometric examples with simple punched decoration come from the Kerameikos and Lefkandi. This type is quite rare in Crete, with a few examples from the Geometric cemeteries of Knossos.

This is a fine example of decorative gold work from the end of the Mycenaean period in Crete. Along with another example of the same date, from Mouliana, Siteia, which is decorated in a similar manner but with different motifs, this ring shows that local goldsmiths continued many years after the destruction of the palaces to produce works of high-quality craftsmanship, using specialized skills known from the earlier periods when jewelry-making was at its height.

Selected Bibliography
Effinger 1996, pp. 14, 291–92; Kraiker–Kübler 1939, p. 86, fig. 5; Platon 1960a, pl. 244b, c; Schachermeyer 1979, pp. 266–67.

Giorgos Rethemiotakis

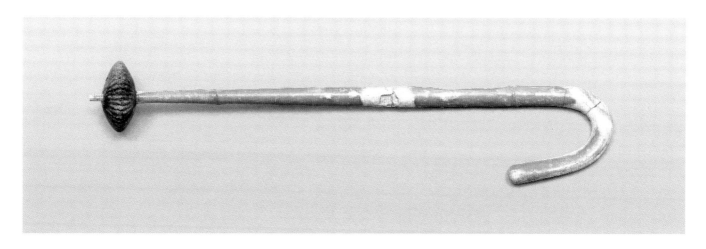

146 **Pin**

Late Minoan IIIB period (ca. 1300–1200 B.C.)
Glass
L. of stem 0.14 m, bead diam. 0.018 m
Cemetery of Metochi Kalou, Tomb B, inside Pyxis 13, 1976
Herakleion Archaeological Museum, HM 2643

This mended hooklike pin, probably a hairpin, was found inside a cylindrical pyxis, among the grave gifts of a rock-cut chamber tomb.

The pin was cast in a stone mold. It has a stem of blue glass, circular in section with a biconical bead-button wedged on the end, essential for securing the pin, since its smooth surface would make attachment difficult. The bead, with vitreous remains of a cobalt-blue glass on the exterior, has densely packed grooves parallel to the perforation.

Hooklike pins were probably a Minoan type, since there are few Helladic examples. They were usually made of bronze, although there are also examples in gold, silver, and glass, like this pin.

Glass, like faience, was first used as an imitation and replacement for precious stones and later as a luxury material in its own right. In Crete the craft of glass working was probably first introduced from Egypt or the Near East in the Neopalatial period, when relations between Crete and the broad Mediterranean region were particularly intense.

Glass was used in Minoan Crete to make beads, seals, and relief plaques, as well as vessels. A probable workshop for the production of vitreous materials has been located at Knossos. The raw material was probably imported from Egypt or the Near East, as can be deduced from the ingots found in the Ulu Burum shipwreck; this indicates a trade in unworked glass in the broad Mediterranean region.

Selected Bibliography

Cadogan 1976; Chatzi-Speliopoulou 2002; Dimopoulou-Rethemiotaki–Rethemiotakis 1978, pl. 21e; Effinger 1996, pp. 24, 248; Panagiotaki 1999a, pp. 621–22; Panagiotaki et al. 2004; Papadopoulos 2002; Papaefthymiou-Papanthimou 1979, 208–13.

Katerina Athanasaki

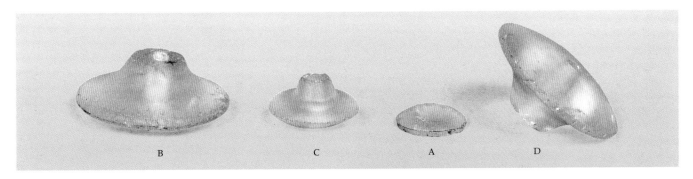

147A Discoid Rock Crystal Inlay

Late Minoan IB period (ca. 1450 B.C.)
Stone
Diam. 0.015 m, max. th. 0.004 m
Kato Zakros, Minoan palace, Banquet Hall of Shrine
Siteia Archaeological Museum, 13314

Complete.

This discoid rock crystal inlay was probably used as a decoration on a piece of furniture or other object.

147B Mushroomlike Pinhead

Late Minoan IB period (ca. 1450 B.C.)
Stone
Diam. 0.031 m, max. th. 0.014 m, diam. of perforation: top 0.004 m, bottom 0.005 m
Kato Zakros, Minoan palace, Workshop Sector of South Wing
Siteia Archaeological Museum, 13311

This pinhead was attached to a shaft. Complete.

147C Mushroomlike Pinhead

Late Minoan IB period (ca. 1450 B.C.)
Stone
Diam. 0.023 m, max. th. 0.009–0.010 m, diam. of perforation: top 0.004 m, bottom 0.005 m
Kato Zakros, Minoan palace, Workshop Sector of South Wing
Siteia Archaeological Museum, 13312

This pinhead was attached to a shaft. Complete.

147D Mushroomlike Pinhead

Late Minoan IB period (ca. 1450 B.C.)
Stone
Diam. 0.032 m, max. th. 0.013 m, diam. of perforation: top 0.004 m, bottom 0.005-0.006 m
Kato Zakros, Minoan palace, Workshop Sector of South Wing
Siteia Archaeological Museum, 13313

This pinhead was attached to a shaft. Complete.

E

147E Fragment of Rock Crystal (Quartz SiO_2)

Late Minoan IB period (ca. 1450 B.C.)
Stone
L. 0.071 m, w. 0.067 m, th. 0.059 m
Kato Zakros, Building G
Siteia Archaeological Museum, 13315

Partly worked fragment of rock crystal, with prismatic ends and one side polished.

Rock crystal, a hard semiprecious stone, is one of the materials used for making jewelry, necklace beads, amulets, and pinheads. The use of this material for making jewelry begins toward the end of the Prepalatial period, with examples of beads and amulets coming from tombs at Mochlos, the Mesara, and Archanes, and continued to be used for pinheads and inlaid decoration until the Postpalatial period. Pins with heads of rock crystal in different shapes have been found in tombs at Mycenae and in the final phase of the palace at Zakros. The pinheads in question were found in a room of the workshop sector of the palace, together with cores and semiworked fragments. These finds show that jewelry was a particular favorite in the Minoan and Mycenaean world for nearly a century. The mushroom-shape heads attached to pin shafts would have been used to adorn the hair along with other accoutrements.

Selected Bibliography

Marinatos 1931, pp. 158–59; Papaefthymiou-Papanthimou 1979; Platon 1965, p. 188; Platon 1966, p. 151; Platon 1969, p. 235; Televantou 1984, p. 47.

Evi Saliaka

148 **Mold for Casting Earrings**
Middle Minoan III–Late Minoan I period (ca. 1600 B.C.)
Schist
L. 0.04 m, w. 0.034 m
Mochlos, Cemetery, Burial Complex I/II/III (Tomb II of
Seager's excavation), 1908
Herakleion Archaeological Museum, HM 1305

One half of a complete two-piece mold with pouring funnel. On
its polished upper surface, a shallow channel has been carved
for casting earrings in the shape of an open circle, with narrowing and almost joining ends and a conical protuberance of nine
granules in the middle, resembling the form of a bunch of grapes
or mulberries. A hole pierced through the center of the surface
guided the carving of the circle as the mold was manufactured
and kept the two parts of the mold together during use. On the
edge of the narrow side, a small funnel-shape channel facilitated
the pouring of the molten metal.

Open-loop gold earrings with granules in the shape of a bunch
of grapes or mulberries are rare examples of a type of earring
commonly found in the Syro-Palestinian region and Cyprus during the seventeenth and sixteenth centuries B.C., with a few
examples also known from Crete.

The Mochlos mold, together with a similar example in the
Metaxas Collection (Herakleion Archaeological Museum) and a
third, now in the Ashmolean Museum, Oxford, with a probable
Cretan provenance, are of particular interest, since they point to
the local manufacture of this type of earring. In particular, the
material used for making the Mochlos mold, a kind of Cretan
schist, strengthens the argument for the local manufacture of
this type of earring, including all stages of production, from the
manufacture of the mold to the casting of the earring. Moreover,
its presence in the Mochlos cemetery is undoubtedly one of the
earliest indications of the manufacture of this particular type of
earring.

Selected Bibliography
AΔ 17 B (1961–62): 283, pl. 348 (Davaras–Platon); Boardman
1961, p. 127, no. 546, pl. XLVI; Effinger 1996, pp. 20–21; Evely
1993–2000, 2 (2000), p. 411; Higgins 1961, p. 73; Laffineur 1980,
p. 285; Lebessi 1967; Muhly 1992, pp. 121–23, pl. 26;
Sakellarakis–Sapouna-Sakellaraki 1997, p. 642; Stampolidis-
Karetsou 1998, p. 88, no. 60 (Dimopoulou-Rethemiotaki).

Katerina Athanasaki

149 Comb

Late Minoan IIIA2 period (ca. 1375–1300 B.C.)
Ivory
L. 0.132 m
Katsambas, near Herakleion, Tomb H
Herakleion Archaeological Museum, HM 341

Rectangular ivory comb with identical relief decoration on both sides, separated into two zones by three ridges. In the lower zone is depicted a pair of seated sphinxes facing one another, with open wings rendered in a linear manner, disproportionately strong facial features, and tall-crested diadem. The upper zone consists of a central eight-petal rosette and four spirals on each side. The vertical margins of both zones have triple-dotted bands separated by plain ridges, a motif recalling the granulation technique used in working gold. Groups of vertical incisions decorate the handle's flat top. Fragmentary, partly restored.

Essential for grooming hair, combs made of ivory and, more rarely, bone have been found in many Cretan sites, as well as on the Greek mainland and islands. The combs usually come from graves, where they were deposited as gifts. Most are rectangular in shape with a single row of teeth and often a long handle. The earliest known Cretan examples, from Archanes and Zakros, belong to the Protopalatial period. Its small size indicates that the Zakros comb may have been used for grooming eyebrows or a mustache. A semicircular comb with traces of gilding, so far a unique example, comes from Mycenae's Shaft Grave IV.

Ivory combs were precious objects made of raw material imported from Egypt and Syro-Palestine, and they were therefore often repaired rather than discarded. Wooden combs were probably also used, as in Egypt (and nowadays), but have not been preserved because of unfavorable environmental conditions. Comb handles could be decorated simply or lavishly, with elaborate relief scenes, usually divided into two zones. The various motifs—lizards, crocodiles, sphinxes, bulls, felines, argonauts, rosettes, and so on—creatively combine Egyptian and Eastern influences with Creto-Mycenaean artistic patterns. Combs decorated with sphinxes, a motif of Eastern or Egyptian origin that was particularly popular in the Mycenaean world, and eight-petal rosettes like the one on this comb were found at Spata, Prosymna, and Pylos.

Selected Bibliography
Alexiou 1967, pp. 57, 75, pls. 34, 35; Karetsou–Andreadaki-Vlazaki–Papadakis 2000, pp. 179–80 (Sapouna); Papaefthymiou-Papanthimou 1979, pp. 173, 197–201, pl. 57b; Poursat 1977b, p. 23, pl. X (5 and 6); Sakellarakis 1968; Sakellarakis–Sapouna-Sakellaraki 1997, pp. 730–31, fig. 851.

Christina Papadaki

150 Comb

Late Minoan IIIA2 period (ca. 1375–1300 B.C.)
Ivory
L. 0.082 m, h. 0.047 m
Maroulas cemetery, Chamber Tomb 5, 2001
Rethymnon Archaeological Museum, O 1489

Rectangular comb with simple, undecorated handle. Mended, some teeth missing.

The comb was deposited as a grave gift for a child about nine years old, possibly a girl, inside a clay sarcophagus. Combs were especially widespread throughout the eastern Mediterranean in the Late Bronze Age. Elephant or hippopotamus ivory combs were quite rare, however, being the luxury equivalent of bone or perishable wooden examples. In addition to those with a single row of teeth, combs with two rows of teeth are also known, particularly from Cyprus and Syria. The handles of some ivory examples are veritable works of art—richly decorated with a combination of various motifs. Some types of combs were not used for combing but as adornments for the hair.

Selected Bibliography

Papaefthemiou-Papanthimou 1979, p. 178, pl. 59c; Sakellarakis–Sapouna-Sakellaraki 1997, p. 729.

Eleni Papadopoulou

151 Spoon

Late Minoan IIIA2 period (ca. 1375–1300 B.C.)
Bone
L. 0.080 m, w. 0.020 m
Maroulas cemetery, Chamber Tomb 5, 2001
Rethymnon Archaeological Museum, O 1490

Complete miniature model of a human right arm, carefully carved into a vertically pierced fist with a hole through it on one side and a tiny spoon on the other. It was found with the ivory comb (see previous entry) accompanying a nine-year-old child in a sarcophagus.

Similar miniature spoons, usually in bronze or silver, are known from the Early Bronze Age onward, with a few examples dating from the Late Bronze Age. Although usually interpreted as ear cleaners, they were probably cosmetic implements used for scraping the remains of powdered pigments or ointments from the bottoms of pyxides or as ritual tools for spooning small quantities of such materials. Spoons shaped like human arms are particularly rare; a similar example comes from the Late Minoan IIIA2/B tholos tomb at Phylaki, Apokoronas, near Khania.

Selected Bibliography

Papaefthemiou-Papanthimou 1979, pp. 251–52; Sakellarakis–Sapouna-Sakellaraki 1997, p. 606, figs. 638–39.

Eleni Papadopoulou

152 Mirror

Late Minoan IIIA period (ca. 1400–1350/1300 B.C.)
Bronze
Diam. 0.183 m
Knossos, Zapher Papoura cemetery, probably Tomb 14
(Tomb of the Tripod Hearth)
Herakleion Archaeological Museum, HM 1524

Complete.

Mirrors in Bronze Age Crete were plain, solid bronze discs of medium size, whose surface was polished highly enough to permit reflection. The pair of small holes that is often found near the edge, as on this Knossian mirror, was used for inserting rivets to secure a handle. On luxury versions of this type, the handle would be made of ivory and decorated with relief or incised motifs, like the mirror from Tomb 49 of the same cemetery and a contemporary example from Tholos Tomb A at the Phourni cemetery of Archanes. Isolated ivory handles have also been found, their metal discs having been broken or perhaps even recycled in antiquity.

Clearly functional and closely linked to the refined habits of at least one sector of Minoan society, this implement, with the cast metal and the occasionally exotic material of its handle, acquired value and was deposited in tombs during the Mycenaean period as a grave gift of the dead.

Selected Bibliography

Evans 1906, p. 36; Papaefthymiou-Papanthimou 1979, pp. 137–38, nos. 30, 31; Sakellarakis–Sapouna-Sakellaraki 1997, pp. 602–3, 731–33.

Emmanouela Apostolaki

153 "Palette"

Late Minoan IB period (ca. 1450 B.C.)
Stone
H. 0.037 m, upper surface 0.139 x 0.235 m, underside
0.104 x 0.185 m
Kato Zakros, East Building, Room B, upper floor fill
Siteia Archaeological Museum, 3150

Rectangular upper surface, narrower underside with lightly curving ends. Incised line runs around the sides of the upper surface roughly 1 centimeter from the edges. Mended.

Palettes or stone-pigment tablets, a toiletry accessory, were used for rubbing pigments. Traces of wear are frequently preserved on the upper surface, as is the case with this palette from Zakros. Water was added to the crushed pigments to produce a paste that would be applied as makeup.

The Minoans' use of makeup is best confirmed by the wall paintings. Lips, cheeks, nails, and earlobes are usually painted a deep red. The eyes and eyelashes are heavily picked out with thick paint in a black outline that makes the eyes look particularly large and expressive. This palette was found with other toiletry objects, including pyxides, perfume and pigment containers, a mirror, tweezers, a spatula, bronze hairpins, combs, rubbing palettes, and elegantly decorated vases. The discovery of all these objects indicates the existence of a particularly well-equipped beauty parlor.

Selected Bibliography
Papaefthymiou-Papanthimou 1979, pp. 273, 280–81; Platon 1977, pp. 431–33.

Evi Saliaka

154 **Tweezers**

Late Minoan IIIA–B period (ca. 1400–1200 B.C.)

Bronze

L. 0.08 m, w. 0.006–0.01 m, th. 0.0012 m

Armenoi, Late Minoan cemetery, Tomb 100 (X. II), 1976

Rethymnon Archaeological Museum, M 558

Complete. Made from a bronze strip with an open eyelike loop at the top and ends that curve slightly inward. An incised line runs around the edge.

This is a cosmetic implement, although it may also have had other everyday uses. The shape remained unchanged from earliest Cretan examples of the Early Bronze Age and can be divided into two types: a strip of metal bent to form two arms, the ends of which are widened, and a strip bent to form two arms but with an eyelike loop at the top. This second type is considered later, since it normally dates to Late Helladic/Late Minoan times, although the eyelike loop is not a precise dating criterion. Tweezers are usually of bronze, although gold has also been used (e.g., Mochlos). The eye-loop type is known from the Cyclades, Euboea, and mainland Greece.

Selected Bibliography

Arnott 1999; Papaefthimiou-Papanthimou 1979, pp. 226–46; Sakellarakis–Sapouna-Sakellaraki 1997, p. 602; Tzedakis–Martlew 1999, p. 275: 285 (Arnott).

Irini Gavrilaki

155 **Pyxis with Lid**

Late Minoan IIIA1/2 period (ca. 1400–1300 B.C.)
Clay
Pyxis: h. 0.138 m, rim diam. 0.172 m, base diam. 0.21 m
Lid: h. 0.029 m, diam. 0.212 m
Mochlos, Late Minoan cemetery
Siteia Archaeological Museum, 11140

Cylindrical body with an inset rim to hold the lid; five pairs of small holes below the rim; discoid base projecting slightly to the side. A small hole in the center of the lid and decoration of concentric circles, zigzag lines, and bands that form a crosslike ornament. Mended.

Imported from Palaikastro, the vessel is covered over its whole body by painted decoration with a pictorial scene in five sections. The main motifs are a winged standing griffin, a wild goat, and a pair of birds, which are complemented by horns of consecration and framed by a multitude of filling ornaments, including vegetal and geometric forms, such as irises, crocuses, reeds, concentric circles, lozenges, zigzag bands, chevrons, and curves. All allude to a natural landscape with numerous flowers and some rocks.

The decoration of the pyxis, like other similarly painted vessels of the time, perfectly matches contemporary sarcophagus painting. It is related to the religious beliefs of the Creto-Mycenaean world with regard to the divinity, death, and the afterlife, as demonstrated by the presence of the griffin, birds, wild goat, and sacred horns. This type of vessel was often used as a jewel case.

Selected Bibliography
Banou 2005, fig. 24.

Chrysa Sophianou

156 Pyxis with Lid
   Late Minoan IIIA2–B period (ca. 1300 B.C.)
   Clay
   H. 0.205 m, rim diam. 0.228 m, base diam. 0.255 m
   Lid: h. 0.03 m, diam. 0.252 m
   Mochlos, Late Minoan cemetery
   Siteia Archaeological Museum, 9396

Cylindrical body with an inset rim to hold the lid; four small holes beneath the rim. The lid has a hole in the center and painted decoration of concentric circles, zigzag lines, and chevrons, which form a radiating ornament. Mended and restored with gypsum.

The pyxis itself has painted decoration all over its body that unfolds in a frieze consisting of horns of consecration with double axes and flowering plants of different sizes and of unidentifiable species. They are divided into two interesting scenes. In the first, a large bird and papyrus flower are depicted, reminiscent of a Nilotic landscape. In the second, three human figures are represented at different scales and on two levels. This unique scene possibly signifies the descent into Hades, with the deceased figure on the lower level being led by the escort of souls, Hermes, while on the upper level, the deceased is again depicted, this time larger and occupying the center of the scene. The Nilotic landscape in the other scene can also be given a theological meaning. With its probable religious character (horns of consecration), the decoration of the vessel possibly refers to beliefs involving the Netherworld.

The vase was imported from Palaikastro.

Selected Bibliography
Banou 2005.

Chrysa Sophianou

Minoan painters were the first to develop the art of large-scale wall painting in the Aegean region, including mainland Greece. Extensive decorative programs, of which only a few fragments survive owing to the perishable nature of the materials, covered the walls of palaces and opulent urban mansions, especially at Knossos, the largest and most powerful political center on the island.

Mural painters used the technique of fresco, applying earthy colors to wet surfaces to create compositions that even today retain their vivid quality. The artists drew inspiration from the natural world, especially the flora and fauna of Crete. Motifs include wild goats, wild cats, monkeys, and other exotic species, as well as birds (partridges and hoopoes), sea creatures (dolphins and octopus), and plants of the Cretan landscape, such as myrtle and olive trees, reeds, wild roses, and bushy shrubs. Other frescoes depict public life, featuring figures of palatial officials, Arthur Evans's "king-priest," attendants, and ladies of the court taking part in processions and public gatherings in urban courtyards or around the palaces, as well as athletic events, especially bull-leaping.

The Minoans were evidently eager to demonstrate the ostentatious life-style of their ruling class, the wealth and status of palatial and religious authorities, the power of the king, and the vigor and skill of their athletes. They were also deeply affected by the beauty of Crete's diverse and colorful environment, and their mural paintings of these terrestrial and marine worlds are exceptional in both quality and originality.

Detail of cat. no. 158

157 **Relief Wall Painting of Olive Tree**
Middle Minoan IIIA period (ca. 1700–1650 B.C.)
Painted plaster
H. 0.756 m, w. 0.705 m
Knossos, North Entrance, 1900
Herakleion Archaeological Museum, HM 36A

Incomplete. Mended, with painted restoration.

This relief wall painting depicting an olive tree is a typical example of Minoan landscape painting. It is part of a larger composition with a bull-hunting scene, of which few fragments have been preserved. The scene unfolded in a rocky landscape with olive trees and included at least two bulls, as well as two figures, one male and one female.

The surviving part of the wall painting depicts an olive-tree trunk with dense branches and dark green and red spearlike leaves on a blue-green ground, embellished with scattered white spots and dotted rosettes. The lack of convention in the rendering of the olive tree confirms the exceptional skill of the Minoan artists in the naturalistic style.

The technique of making painted relief plasters, which allowed the Minoans to attain the effect of light and shade and also to approach the three-dimensional prototype of the natural world, was especially used in the fresco decoration of the palace at Knossos, where most of the relief wall paintings were found.

The iconography of the olive tree in Minoan art, expressed in a variety of ways, was popular as early as the Early Minoan period, as seen on grave goods in the shape of olive leaves from the Mochlos cemetery. Later it is found on four of the well-known wall paintings from Knossos, on a fresco fragment from Tylissos, and on one side of the Haghia Triada sarcophagus.

Whether as a simple landscape reference or as an iconographic element with a symbolic dimension, the olive tree in wall paintings is one of the prominent examples of naturalistic art of the Neopalatial period and, at the same time, one of the many direct and indirect pieces of archaeological evidence that form an inextricable part of the Minoan landscape and culture.

Selected Bibliography
Boulotis 1996, pp. 46–51; Evans 1899–1900, pp. 51–52; Hood 2005, pp. 56–58; Immerwahr 1990, pp. 85–88, 162, 164; Kaiser 1976, pp. 271–73; Macdonald 2007, pp. 126–28; Sapouna-Sakellaraki 1969.

Katerina Athanasaki

158 The Partridge Fresco

Middle Minoan III–Late Minoan IA period
(ca. 1700–1525/1500 B.C.)
Dimensions of the restored piece: L. 1.94 m, w. 1.08 m,
w. of frieze 0.28 m
Knossos, Caravanserai
Herakleion Archaeological Museum, HM 13

Preserved in fragments. Artistic reconstruction. Cracks, bulges, and paint loss caused by decay.

Painted wall frieze with depiction of partridges and a hoopoe in a rocky landscape with vegetation. It is bordered by red, yellow, and black bands, with a wide dull yellow zone below. A vertical zone painted red with a rectangular end painted blue touches (on the underside) the horizontal zone painted dull yellow. The restoration is by E. Gilliéron fils.

This wall painting of partridges is part of the decoration of the upper section of the west wall in a raised, open, pillared propylaeum of the Loggia type in the so-called Caravanserai, a large building complex south of the palace at Knossos. According to the excavator, Arthur Evans, this building was a caravanserai for travelers on foot and was used for rest and residence before they entered the palace. Its wall paintings imitated architectural decoration. The vertical zones of red crowned with rectangles of blue, one of which was included in the Gilliéron's restoration, imitate pillars with capitals, and the broad zone of dull yellow paint, the color of wood, is a kind of architrave on top of which stood the "frieze" with the wall painting.

The section of the frieze that has been restored adorned the upper section of the Loggia's west wall, and the east wall seems to have had a similar scene. It is likely that the south wall had a wider zone with plant decoration, of which some pieces have been preserved.

There are seven partridges in the reconstructed section. Their plumage is depicted with fine strokes in ocher and reddish-brown, with oblique black lines beneath the wings and carefully painted red beaks, eyes, and legs. The hoopoe perched on a bush, the smallest and worst-preserved bird, is painted in yellow ocher and has a long beak and a tall fan-shape crest. Myrtle stalks and a bush or a small tree with small round green leaves, perhaps dittany, lie between the hoopoe and the partridges. The composition is bordered by wavy blue, yellow, and pink bands with thin lines and tufts at the edges, perhaps briars or, more likely, rocks or hillsides covered with greenery. Large and small polychrome pebbles lie on the ground at the right.

Other fragments exist of wall paintings from the same composition, but they have not been placed in the restoration. Some parts include another three partridges, one hoopoe, wavy bands, and myrtle stalks, as well as one bushy shrub with thin branches, perhaps spiny chicory, spiny burnet, or thyme.

The partridges, the most typical Cretan bird species, have been depicted with particular accuracy by the brush of a talented artist. The alternating white and black background of the scene (which according to Evans indicates the perpetual sequence of day and night, or the light of the open air and darkness of the cave where the partridges hid to sleep) and the polychrome landscape, which is rendered not faithfully but with obvious artistic license, contribute a unique decorative quality to the composition, making it one of the most successful and certainly the most attractive pictorial version of Cretan nature.

Selected Bibliography
PM II, pp. 109–16; Shaw 2005.

Giorgos Rethemiotakis

159 **Fragment of Wall Painting**
Late Minoan I period (ca. 1600–1450 B.C.)
Plaster
H. 0.535 m, w. 0.31 m
Epano Zakros, Minoan villa
Siteia Archaeological Museum, 13317

Painted on white ground is a net pattern of blue lozenges, with blue rosettes where the lozenges join and black lines at right angles on either side of them. The lozenges form a frame for red lily-papyruses. The central composition is framed by vertical bands with successive intersecting lilies.

The technique of fresco, which ranges in theme from geometric drawings to narrative scenes of a religious character taken from nature, is found on walls, floors, and the ceilings of important rooms, as well as on such objects as stone sarcophagi, hearths, and altars. This particular fragment probably comes from a geometric composition that covered a ceiling or floor. Geometric compositions also appear on the woven clothing of female and male figures in wall paintings. The quality of this fragment, which compares well with the finest examples from the palatial workshops of Knossos, reveals the presence of a Knossian artist in the region. Parallels for the blue rosettes at the junction of the lozenges can be found on the wall paintings of Akrotiri, Thera.

Selected Bibliography
Doumas 1992, p. 131, pls.136, 137; Platon 2002b, pp. 154–55, pls. XLIV–XLVIIIc; Shaw 2003, pp. 180, 184–85.
Evi Saliaka

In the Minoan religion, the figure of a female goddess, the protector of nature and fertility, occupies the predominant place in the hierarchy of deities. The goddess is represented for the first time in three-dimensional form in the clay figurines from Myrtos dating to about 2500 B.C. The idols with raised arms in a summoning gesture, an appeal for the sake of the votaries, constitute the first cult statuettes, which date to about 1300–1100 B.C. They were placed on benches in small communal sanctuaries, where they were worshiped and received offerings from believers.

Rituals in which the focus is the advent or presence of the female goddess are depicted on gold rings that show scenes of ecstatic worship, particularly of the *baetyl*, or venerated stone, and the tree cult, acts that appeal to the powers of nature personified by the great goddess. Ceremonial rituals were accompanied by music produced by such instruments as the lyre and the sistrum. Athletic events may also have taken place in some sanctuaries, similar to those of the later Olympic games, as suggested by a gold ring that bears the representation of a runner from the sanctuary of Symi, Viannos. Sacred symbols of Minoan religion include the horns of consecration and the double axe, which are depicted in religious scenes or attested on ritual vessels. Double axes made of bronze, silver, and gold were placed in areas of worship; oversize bronze versions were put on poles to protect sanctuary space.

In the Protopalatial period (ca.1900–1700 B.C.), public worship was practiced out of doors in peak sanctuaries and caves, where numerous votive figures of clay and occasionally bronze were deposited. Figurines depict worshipers, whereas replicas or human limbs were intended as requests for treatment on behalf of disabled votaries; animal figurines were symbolic offerings to protective deities. In the Neopalatial and the Final Palatial period of Knossos (ca. 1700–1300 B.C.), impressive public ceremonies were organized in the courts and halls of the palaces, where sumptuous vessels of metal and stone were used for libations and ceremonial feasts. Stone rhyta, conical or ovoid vases with a hole at the bottom for pouring liquids, were found primarily in the palaces at Knossos and Zakros, along with "communion cups," or chalices used during ritual feasts. Exceptional examples include a chalice known as the "Chieftain's Cup" from Haghia Triada and two bull's-head stone rhyta from the palaces at Knossos and Zakros.

A. DIVINE

160 **Ring**

Late Minoan IB period (ca. 1525/1500–1450 B.C.)
Gold
Bezel: l. 0.017 m, w. 0.013 m; hoop diam. 0.015 m
Phaistos, Kalyvia cemetery, Tomb 11
Herakleion Archaeological Museum, HM 45

Gold signet ring with elliptical bezel. Surface worn through use, resulting in a shallower engraving of the motifs in the representation, as well as of the engravings on the upper surface of the hoop, where the user held the ring while sealing. The wear pattern shows that, before it was used as a grave gift in the burial where it was found, the ring had been intensively used as a seal to produce clay sealings (seal impressions). Complete.

Hollow inside, the ring is made of two pieces of gold sheet or plate, one convex with the main scene and one concave for the back, which fits to the convex surface of the finger. The join made by the two pieces of sheet at the back and the soldering of the hoop onto the edge formed by the two pieces are not visible, since the pieces fit together perfectly and the soldering has been carefully rubbed to erase all traces. So the ring appears to be solid, not hollow, and this was the norm for the finest examples, technically speaking, of Minoan gold rings. The technique is actually revealed by a small hole on the rear plate, which confirms that the bezel is hollow. A similar hole exists on the well-known "Ring of Minos" just where the hoop merges into the back plate. These perforations at the back, which was not intended to be seen, were probably made to allow the escape of gases produced during assembly, so that they would not be trapped inside the bezel. The hoop has horizontal grooves on the outer surface.

The scene on the upper surface of the bezel has been engraved with fine tools, traces of which are visible under a microscope. At the left, a female figure with a voluminous backside and breasts is either naked or, more probably, wears a tight-fitting diaphanous veil, whose border can be made out just above the ankle. She is holding the trunk of a tree with both hands and turning her head back. The tree is supported by a

wooden structure that sits on a rock formation. A male is behind the female figure, touching or clutching an ovoid rock with both arms. A large flying bird and a column are behind them. The sky is defined by a dotted wavy line.

The ring was found in a chamber tomb (Tomb 11) belonging to the group of tombs in the Kalyvia cemetery of Phaistos, known as the Tombe dei Nobili. The tomb contained one burial on the floor, which was accompanied by a bronze mirror and knife in addition to the ring. A large number of similar necklace beads of gold and semiprecious stones came from other disturbed burials, along with four clay pots dating from the Final Palatial period (Late Minoan IIIA2–14th century B.C.).

The representation combines tree worship, a scene thought to represent a religious ritual that culminated in pulling on the branches of the "sacred tree," and *baetyl*-cult, a parallel and related scene of worship of the "sacred stone," thought to embody divine powers. It seems that these representations, also known from other signet rings, were iconographic renderings of a composite formal ritual with the epiphany of the deity at the core, the miraculous coming of the goddess in the form of a vision, from the transcendental dimension to the terrestrial and sensible world of the faithful. However, the goddess does not appear in her human form in the representation on this ring. Her imminent arrival is suggested by the flying bird, which is both a symbol and a companion of the goddess in her numinous appearances, just as it is impressed on two gold rings from Poros, Herakleion. The column at the right may be a shorthand indication of the sacred building in front of which the religious scene is unfolding.

The signet ring, as a prestigious symbolic object with strong social and religious connotations, accompanied the eminent owner in life and death.

Selected Bibliography

CMS II, 3: 114, pp. 113–14; Dimopoulou-Rethemiotaki–Rethemiotakis 2000; Effinger 1996, pp. 11–12, 280; Savignoni 1904, pp. 534, 577, fig. 50, pl. 40,6; Warren 1990.

Giorgos Rethemiotakis

Cat. no. 169

161 **Ring**

Late Minoan IA period (ca. 1600–1525/1500 B.C.)
Gold
Bezel: l. 0.018 m, w. 0.009 m, ring diam. 0.015 m
Symi
Herakleion Archaeological Museum, HM 1699

Misshapen hoop, left side of the bezel slightly deformed. Small hole in the skirt of the female figure caused by strong pressure from the engraving implement. Complete.

This gold signet ring, called the "Runner's Ring," has a long, elliptical bezel and is hollow inside. The bezel is made up of two pieces of gold sheet, the upper side with the representation being convex and the underside concave. The join between the two pieces around the edges is just visible at the back on the short side of the ellipse. The endings of the thin hoop penetrate the hollow interior of the bezel and are held in place by being soldered to the point of contact of the two pieces of gold sheet. The hoop has thin grooves across its breadth.

The representation on the bezel has been executed by engraving, impressing, beating, and carving with special tools, traces of which can be seen on the outlines and in the interior of the hollows.

A central figure dominates the scene, running with broad strides from right to left, with one arm held in front and the other behind as he races along. He turns his head up, and his long hair is blown back in the opposite direction of the movement. He is running toward a male figure dressed in a heavy gown with a curved hem at the knees and a pointed end behind, like a tail. An arched object is visible in front of his chest, probably the top of a scepter in the shape of the so-called snake frame. The third figure, a female, has a long skirt and sleeved bodice; her long hair is indicated by punched dots. She has her left hand on her breast, and her right hand is stretched out toward the runner. A wavy band above with a tufted end is shorthand for the sky, and a starry body may be the Milky Way, a comet, or a shooting star. The ground is indicated by a double band with pairs of small engraved vertical lines.

The ring was found at the sanctuary of Kato Symi in the area of the sacred enclosure, together with cult equipment, mainly large communion cups but also everyday vessels and animal bones.

The scene on the ring is unparalleled in Minoan iconography. An athlete is shown running on a flat surface, probably the running track. The figure in front has a priestly robe, recognizable from other scenes in which male priests are depicted, and a scepter with the snake frame device, a symbol of priestly rank. This may be a high-ranking overseer–priest, the official in charge of conducting this particular event. The female figure to the right is perhaps a priestess in a pose that underlines the religious importance of the event.

This unique depiction of the runner shows that Minoan athletes took part in running races, as well as in other competitions and sports, such as bull-leaping, boxing, wrestling, and acrobatics. Running was a highly competitive event that became popular in the later Olympic Games of antiquity, as well as in modern track events. From the representation on this ring, it would seem that this event took place under the supervision and in the presence of a high-ranking priest, whose position is indicated by the scepter.

The ring was almost certainly an important offering from an actual runner. The image is clearly one of value, showing that the person who left it really did run in a race at some time and won it; perhaps the event took place at the shrine where it was found. The valuable and undamaged material from which the ring is made demonstrates that the worshiper-dedicator intended to deposit at the shrine the depiction of his victory, unconquered by time.

Selected Bibliography
Lebessi–Muhly–Papasavvas 2004.

Giorgos Rethemiotakis

© CMS Archive, Marburg

162 **Seal Stone (Mistress of Animals)**
Late Minoan IIIA period (ca. 1400–1300 B.C.)
Steatite
Diam. 0.0175–0.018 m
Armenoi, Late Minoan cemetery, Chamber Tomb 24
Rethymnon Archaeological Museum, Σ 22

Complete lentoid seal with a little damage and a perpendicular string hole. It shows a seated female figure in a rocky place with flowers. She wears a flounced skirt and a necklace around her neck. Her head is turned to the left, and the head of a rampant lion near her left hand is turned toward her.

Naturalistic scenes and, more rarely, representations with more than one figure begin to occur on seals of the Neopalatial period at the same time as decorative and schematized motifs. The depiction of scenes of worship and ritual appears frequently. This particular scene depicts the well-known subject of the "Mistress of Animals" (Potnia Theron), here with only one animal, and has a religious content that is highlighted by the gesture of the arm of the female figure.

Selected Bibliography
CMS V, 1, p. 203, no. 253; Niemeier 1981, p. 211 (Tamvaki).

Epameinondas Kapranos

163 "Chieftain's Cup"
     Late Minoan IA–Late Minoan IB period
     (ca. 1550–1450 B.C.)
     Steatite
     H. 0.115 m; max. diam. 0.097 m
     Haghia Triada, Royal Villa
     Herakleion Archaeological Museum, HM 341

Footed conical goblet, with wheel-shape base decorated with incised relief bands and beadlike ornament; rim decorated with an incised relief band. The scene, beginning from a vertical relief and an incised band, includes five male figures, two facing each other and three in processional order. Mended and restored.

Of the two first figures, the one at the right is an adult male with long loose hair, a loincloth, and a codpiece, as well as boots on his feet. He wears a great deal of jewelry—three necklaces, the lowest with circular beads, as well as armbands and bracelets on both arms. He holds a staff or scepter in his outstretched right hand, a pose that has been interpreted as indicative of a high office or a projection of power. Muscular details are depicted with subtle relief and engraving on the calves, thighs, and lean chest. Facial features and the hair are rendered in detail, the latter in little curls with a hooked end on his forehead and long, wavy locks down his neck and chest.

The figure at the left is a young man with loincloth and codpiece who wears a simple necklace and bracelet. He has a sword in his right hand and in his left is an object with a curving, crescent-shape end. The object has been interpreted as a whip or a ritual sprinkler, although it may actually be a scabbard for the sword with decorative tassels at the end. His short haircut, with a fringe above his forehead, leaves visible his large ear, which is drawn in some anatomical detail. The face is realistically depicted with fullness of expression; whereas his musculature and body are rendered concisely with little attention to detail.

To the left, up to the vertical "ruler" that functions as a beginning and end of the scene, three male figures are depicted in procession carrying large bell-shape objects, probably large animal skins, most likely from oxen, since the peaked ends look like tails. One figure's head is preserved and shows long hair and a face rendered in detail and perfectly proportioned, which calls to mind standards of the Classical era.

This stone vase was found in the Royal Villa (Villa Reale) at Haghia Triada, together with other luxury vessels and equipment, including the famous "Harvester Vase" and the "Boxer Rhyton," which had been used in drinking rituals and liquid offerings by the occupants of the villa.

The main scene, which depicts the two male figures facing each other, has been interpreted as a scene in which a young male foot soldier presents arms to a commanding officer ("the Chieftain"). The young man stands at attention (a stance that gives the cup its name, which in Greek is "κύπελλο της ανα-φοράς" or "call to attention cup"). Or this could be the depiction of an incident of "sacred conversation" with a male deity. According to yet another interpretation, the scene on the cup and the vessel itself relate to initiation rites for young men, comparable to a ritual known from the aristocratic polity of Doric Crete. According to Classical and Hellenistic written sources, after completing their initiation, the young men, as aspiring citizens, took arms as a gift from the older men who had been in charge of the initiation procedure; in return they offered a cup and a bull, which was duly sacrificed. In this interpretation, the stone goblet is the object actually being offered, while the ox hides and the sword are the gifts being displayed and presented by the initiate and his companions to his mature tutor and patron, whose status is indicated by the scepter and large amount of jewelry, evidence of wealth and power.

Selected Bibliography
Koehl 1986; Paribeni 1903, p. 324.

Giorgos Rethemiotakis

164 Female Figurine with Male Figurine attached to the Chest

Late Minoan II–IIIA1 period (ca. 1450–1375 B.C.)
Clay
H. 0.103 m
Knossos, Mavrospelio cemetery
Herakleion Archaeological Museum, HM 8345

Mended, one arm and leg of the male figurine broken.

The female figurine has a cylindrical skirt, conical body, and hands brought to the chest. The sketchy face has been modeled by pinching the sides of the spherical head. The hairstyle comprises three solid locks that fall onto the shoulders. The male figurine is schematic with the hands on the chest and legs held apart. The male figurine is fixed to the chest of the female with a lump of clay and a nodule attached between the legs. The painted decoration emphasizes the outline of the female's face and hair. The eyes are painted on both figures; details of the female's dress are painted with dashes on the arms, continuous brushstrokes vertically arranged on the shoulder blades and skirt, rows of dots on the shoulders, and a wide band around the waist. Six iris and crocus flowers are painted on the armpit and in the abdominal area. The mouth of the female figure is indicated with red paint, as is the border of the shoulders, the inner curve of the arms of both figurines, and the back of the male.

This figurine was found in a cavelike tomb at Mavrospelio, Knossos, and was used as a dedication to one of the deceased, probably within the context of funeral rites.

Apart from the fact that the figurine is unusual and without parallel, its interpretation is made even more difficult by the rarity of Minoan figurines in tombs of the Neopalatial and Postpalatial periods. Although Mycenaean *kourotrophos* (child nurturer) figurines have a rather different form and are later in date, this figurine has been interpreted as a *kourotrophos*, that is, a divinity protecting children, because the small male figure sitting on her breast may represent a boy. The floral decoration on the dress also indicates a divine entity, and it is well known from other representations that the crocus played an important role in the worship of the great Minoan goddess.

Selected Bibliography
Forsdyke 1926–27, pp. 290–91, pl. XXI; Rethemiotakis 1998, pp. 62–63, 108, 150, pls. 14d–e, 15a, fig. 12.

Giorgos Rethemiotakis

165 Female Figurine

Late Minoan IIIA period (ca. 1400–1300 B.C.)
Clay
H. 0.366 m
Haghia Triada, Building-Room of the two pillars (100 m
NE of the mansion)
Herakleion Archaeological Museum, HM 3034

Mended and restored, this figurine was found in many fragments
on the upper level of a building that had been remodeled several
times before an area of the building was used as a cemetery.
Traces of white slip are preserved on both the skirt and torso.
The long and narrow cylindrical, slightly tapering skirt is wheel-
made, as indicated by the pronounced turning marks in the interior.
Dense, irregularly spaced conical bosses, or "nipples," cover the
skirt. These are the same size as the breasts of the solid torso,
whose base forms an angle with the skirt. The bent arms point
downward over the belly, in front of the skirt. This gesture is a
variation of the so-called gesture of two hands to the abdomen.

The skirt's conical bosses make this statue both extremely interesting and difficult to interpret for lack of sufficient parallels.
Although it is possible that the bosses were ornaments of the
garment, the similarity in shape and size between the bosses and
the breasts has led scholars to search for an early multibreasted
deity in Minoan Crete. In fact, the gesture, which is common in
many cult figurines, may indicate a desire to display the multibreasted garment. The analogy between this figurine and the
polymastos (multibreasted) Ephesian Artemis, who is depicted
wearing a complex skirt and having many breasts, was pointed
out early on. The Ephesian Artemis borrowed several features
from Eastern fertility cults and was worshiped as a fertility deity,
with a special priesthood composed of the *megabyzo*i or *mega-
lobyzoi* (large breasted). Despite the common cultural ties
between Crete and Asia Minor, it is difficult to see in this multibreasted Haghia Triada figurine a precursor of the Greek Artemis
of fertility.

Selected Bibliography
Paribeni 1904, p. 726, fig. 24; *PM* I, p. 567, fig. 413.

Dimitris Sfakianakis

166 Female Adorant
   Late Minoan IIIA period (ca. 1400–1350 B.C.)
   Clay
   H. 0.21 m, base diam. 0.11 m, max. diam. 0.09 m
   Myrsini, Siteia
   Haghios Nikolaos Archaeological Museum, 1860

Female figure with a cylindrical robe and arms clasped to the breast. The nose and ears are modeled, whereas the other facial features are painted. Mended at the neck.

The hair of the figure is pulled back in a hairstyle reminiscent of the later chignon. Interesting decoration in the upper part of the dress contrasts with the monochrome lower part. Painted wavy lines on the back of the figure may indicate priestly or stately robes.

This figure belongs to the class of Late Minoan III figures with cylindrical body and arms raised or clasped at the breast, known from Knossos (Shrine of the Double Axes), Gournia, Pangalochori, Gazi, and Karphi. Parallels are also found in Mycenaean figures that date to Late Helladic IIIA–B. The position of the hands, joined in front of the breast in a pose of supplication, may have its roots in Mesopotamia as an attribute of priests and votaries. The Myrsini figure, with a cylindrical body and arms in a particularly naturalistic pose, is considered an example of the transformation from the naturalistic to the schematic type in the advanced phase of the Creto-Mycenaean figure-making.

Selected Bibliography
Davaras n.d., p. 53; Sakellarakis–Sakellarakis 1973–74, Table XV.

Chrysa Sophianou

167 **Female Figurine**
Late Minoan IIIA2 period (ca. 1375–1300 B.C.)
Clay
H. 0.215 m
Knossos, Shrine of the Double Axes
Herakleion Archaeological Museum, HM 3861

Mended, slightly restored. The fingers of the right hand are missing.

Female figurine with a cylindrical skirt, hollow inside, solid cylindrical body, raised arms, and spherical head. The ears and nose are indicated in relief, and the buttonlike breasts, long lock of hair, and a bird figure stuck on top of the head are pieces of applied clay. The arms, with short upper arms and long forearms, are bent at right angles at the elbows. The oversize hands are twisted in different ways with the palm of the right held toward the viewer and the palm of the left toward the face.

Rich, painted decoration depicts the facial features—eyebrows, eyes, and mouth—as well as the nails, hair, details of the clothing, and various ornaments.

The figurine is wearing a kind of mantle made out of two pieces of cloth, which fall in a roughly triangular fashion on the chest and back and are held on by straps at the neck, shoulders, and elbows. The vertical border of the opening along the chest is indicated with paint, as is a second, leaf-shape opening on the back, which is filled with a net pattern. Hatched triangular zones and rows of dots represent jewelry, either woven in or sown onto the cloth. The belt and the ornamentation of the skirt or apron are indicated with paint, the latter with curving or S-shape strokes radiating out from the waist. The lower part is simply decorated with bands. Rows of necklaces and bracelets made of beads of several shapes and one seal on each hand are painted on the figurine.

Together with other objects of worship, this figurine was found in a small room-shrine with a bench on the southeast side of the palace at Knossos. The figurine was found on top of the bench, along with four other figurines—two female votaries, one male holding a bird, and one schematically made figure. There were also two plaster models of horns of consecration with sockets in the middle for the shafts of double axes. The floor of the room was strewn with pebbles. A large plaster table of offerings had been placed in front of the bench, and the rest of the space had been taken up by small and large pots, which probably contained liquid offerings.

The illustrated figurine is certainly the most important and prominent object of worship in this small shrine. It is the largest figurine and the only one with upraised arms. Evidence for its priestly nature is the richly embellished ritual mantle. Another indication of its preeminent position among the figures from the same shrine is the lavish amount of painted ornament, far more than the other figurines. There is no question but that the painted decoration depicts real jewelry of gold or semiprecious materials, bracelets, necklaces, and seals, all of them symbols of wealth, prestige, and high rank, as we know from the rich burials in tombs of the same date as the figurines.

The bird sitting on the figure's head reveals its divine nature, the bird being the symbol of the epiphany of the Minoan goddess, her companion, and the herald of her visionary revelations to the ecstatic worshipers. Therefore, this figurine, or in this instance idol, represents the Minoan goddess, who appears inside the shrine in a dramatized scene of worship involving other figurines of worshipers and miscellaneous religious symbols; the vases with liquid offerings from the faithful are evidence of ritual activity. At the same time, the emphasis placed on the gesture—the oversize forearms and hands compared with the rest of the anatomy—combined with an accentuation of the physiognomy, particularly the eyes, vividly brings to life the message and content of the prayer, the immediate visual and mental contact of the goddess with the praying faithful.

This particular idol is the oldest known example of a type of religious effigy of the goddess with upraised arms, a form that would become particularly popular in communal shrines of the Postpalatial period.

Selected Bibliography
Alexiou 1958, pp. 202–4, pl. Θ, fig. 1; *PM* II, pp. 335–44, fig.193a; Rethemiotakis 1998, pp. 66–68, 154–55, fig. 28.

Giorgos Rethemiotakis

168 Goddess with Upraised Arms
    Late Minoan IIIB–C period (ca. 1300–1100 B.C.)
    Clay
    H. 0.51 m
    Pangalochori, Rethymnon
    Rethymnon Archaeological Museum, Π 637

The upper body is solid, the lower bell-shape part hollow. This well-made figure represents a woman viewed frontally. She either has a conical chignon or wears a conical *polos* (hat); locks of hair, shown in relief, fall down her back. A painted band outlines her ears, which are unusually large compared to the rest of the head. The eyes and breasts are in relief. Painted bands denote the belt and necklace, and two fine vertical lines on the arms may denote the sleeves. The dress covers the entire body and is rendered in glossy paint, its lower part decorated with a checkered pattern. Forearms are missing.

This Late Minoan figure with upraised arms is a typical example of the way in which the female deity was represented at this time, perhaps in a gesture of benediction. Probably inspired by Eastern and Egyptian models, the type may have been imported to Crete in the Middle Minoan I–II periods. The detailed rendering of the garment and jewelry recalls a similar example from the Shrine of the Double Axes at Knossos (cat. no. 167).

The manufacture and decorative techniques, as well as the garment that covers the bosom (in earlier periods the breasts were exposed) and the checkered pattern, date this figure to the later years of the Late Minoan period. It is probably related to some ritual at a sanctuary in the area of Khamalevri-Pangalochori, where a large Minoan settlement developed.

Selected Bibliography
Alexiou 1958, pp. 187–88; Rethemiotakis 1998.

Epameinondas Kapranos

169 Figure

Late Minoan IIIC period (ca. 1200–1100 B.C.)
Clay
H. 0.579, max. w. 0.286 m
Gazi
Herakleion Archaeological Museum, HM 9308

Mended and restored in places.

Figure of the "goddess with upraised arms" type, with hollow interior, cylindrical skirt, conical torso, and open cup-shape head. The arms slant downward with the forearms vertical and the thumbs pointing back. Prominent relief and appliqué are used to depict the chest, nose, eyes, eyebrows, and ears. Three locks of hair in relief emerge from the border of the head and converge in a triangular shape down to the skirt. A bird figurine is attached to the border strip of the head's opening just above the forehead, and there are five other attachments: two tongue-shape and three forked strips. There are traces of white painted bands.

This figure was found in a room of the shrine complex in the region of Bairia near Gazi, where there was a large Minoan settlement. Found with this were four other figures, a table of offerings, and some clay vases, as well as a tubular piece of equipment. Such items are found in shrines of this category and were probably used for libations centered on the divine figures.

The example illustrated here is typical of the type of large-scale clay figures of the Postpalatial period. The gradual increase in size, from the earlier figures of the Shrine of the Double Axes at Knossos (cat. no. 167) and Kannia at Gortys to the goddesses from Karphi—that is, from a height of about 20 centimeters for the earliest example to 90 centimeters for the latest—is evidence of a comparative strengthening of the semantic content of the figure's form as an image of the goddess, which embodied and highlighted her attributes and essence, as well as its practical function as an object of worship. For this reason, the number and size of the symbols that define these attributes rise concomitantly.

There are five symbols on the Gazi figure that are particularly noticeable, because they are stuck onto the edge of the opening of the head, whose features are accentuated, probably because the head was considered far more important than the rest of the body. The bird figure, the symbol par excellence of the epiphany, is certainly the most important symbol and is placed on the central axis above the forehead. It is not certain what the other two symbols depict. However, attention has been called to the similarity between the forked strip symbol and the hieroglyphic sign for the "sprouting seed," and its shape resembles a plant stem with a leafy or flowery end. The likelihood of adding plant symbols that seem to be sprouting out of the head of the goddess could be interpreted as a direct, literal reference to her ability to summon the powers that regenerate nature.

Selected Bibliography

Alexiou 1958, pp. 188–92, pl. E, fig. 3; Marinatos 1937, figs. 1:5, 4, 10; Rethemiotakis 1998, pp. 80–81, pls. 44–45.

Giorgos Rethemiotakis

B. FIGURINES

170 Female Figurine

Early Minoan II period (ca. 2600–2300 B.C.)
Bone
H. 0.09 m
Haghios Charalampos, Lasithi Plain, burial cave
Haghios Nikolaos Archaeological Museum, 13067

Female figurine of animal bone. Rectangular face with abstract rendering of the eyes, nose, and mouth. Flattened body with carved folded arms and pubic triangle. Legs separated and fragmented below. Complete.

The figurine belongs to the so-called Siva type and has parallels from the Siva cemetery of the Mesara Plain. This particular type of figurine is thought to be a Cretan creation imitating Cycladic prototypes, particularly the marble figurines with folded arms. On the other hand, the rendering of the eyes and mouth, as well as the separated legs, are signs of divergence from the Cycladic iconography.

Cretan figure-making, at least until the Middle Minoan I period, did not have indigenous types, apart from some very abstract examples. Nearly all figurines manufactured in the Early Minoan period were imitations of or heavily influenced by Cycladic art, as this is most apparent in the folded arms and the abstract rendering of facial characteristics. The discovery of similar figurines in the Lasithi Plain and at Mesara indicates how very far Cycladic cultural influence had penetrated into the Cretan hinterland.

Selected Bibliography
Branigan 1971; Ferrence (in press); Papadatos 2003.

Yiannis Papadatos

171 **Cycladic-type Figurine**
Early Minoan II–III period (ca. 2600–2100 B.C.)
Marble
Max. h. 0.132 m
Teke, Herakleion, N. Nisioti field, 1933
Herakleion Archaeological Museum, HM 282

Marble Cycladic-type figurine depicting a standing female figure *en face*; complete. Incised straight lines denote the arms, which are folded over the belly with the left forearm under the right. An incision defines the pubic triangle, and two small protrusions mark the breasts. A rough incision separates the torso from the long neck, which ends in an almost lyre-shape head that tilts slightly back. The nose is shown in relief. The legs are joined down to the ankles but are separated by a deep groove. Two vertical incisions denote the toes on the raised feet.

This figurine was found at the area of Teke, near Knossos, together with other Cycladic-type figurines and two metal daggers. Cycladic-type figurines are a particular type of Prepalatial artifact, and they clearly demonstrate the prominent presence of a Cycladic element on Crete and the contacts between Crete and the Cyclades in the Early Bronze Age.

Of the rich repertory of Cycladic sculpture, the most popular type in Minoan Crete is the so-called canonical type in which female figures are rendered in *en face* with arms folded under the chest. In most cases, it is difficult to determine whether a figurine was imported from the Cyclades or manufactured locally.

This Teke figurine belongs to the Koumasa type, a variation of the canonical type, which as yet has occurred only in Crete and may have been a local creation. Koumasa-type figurines are smaller than their Cycladic equivalents, with a particularly thin and flat profile; wide, angular shoulders; and short legs.

In Crete, Cycladic-type figurines usually occur in the central and southern parts of the island; characteristic groups come from Archanes and the Mesara Plain. Most examples have been found in graves, which gives them a pronounced religious-symbolic character. The fragmentary state of many figurines may be caused not only by burial conditions, but also by the fact that they may have been smashed deliberately during funerary rituals.

Selected Bibliography
Branigan 1971; Doumas 2000, pp. 48, 52; Karantzali 1996, pp. 153–236; Marinatos 1933, figs. 9–14; Renfrew 1969, pp. 22–23; Sakellarakis–Sapouna-Sakellaraki 1997, vol. 1, pp. 338–49.

Eirini Galli

172 **Female Figurine**
   Middle Minoan I–II period (ca. 2000–1700 B.C.)
   Clay
   H. 0.098 m, max. w. 0.077 m, max. th. 0.065 m
   Prinias, peak sanctuary
   Haghios Nikolaos Archaeological Museum, 6028

Handmade figurine depicting a seated female figure and covered
with reddish-brown paint. The head is missing, as are the two
arms at shoulders. The figure wears a long skirt with an added
thick flounce. Part of the skirt has been restored with gypsum.
The torso is rather crudely molded without well-defined
anatomical details.

The important peak sanctuary of Prinias is located on the second highest (height a.s.l. 803 m.) peak that rises above the village of Zou, Siteia, and, like Piskokephalo, it is connected to the
Minoan town of Petras, Siteia. Because of its typical elliptical
shape and the fire that would have been lighted on it, the peak
sanctuary must have been visible from a great distance and from
most parts of the region. Even though the sanctuary was found
looted, a large quantity of anthropomorphic figurines of exceptional quality was collected during its excavation, along with
animal figurines, including clay models of small scarab beetles
of the subfamily *Oryctes rhinoceros* (coconut rhinoceros beetle),
which was considered sacred.

Selected Bibliography
AΔ 27 B2 (1972): 651 (Davaras); Davaras n.d., fig. 29; Rutkowski
1988, pp. 86–87, pls. XXI, XXII.

Vili Apostolakou

173 Female Figurine
Middle Minoan II–III period (ca. 1800–1600 B.C.)
Clay
H. 0.15 m, w. 0.075 m
Vrysinas, peak sanctuary, 1973
Rethymnon Archaeological Museum, Π 7618

The figurine represents a standing woman. Facial features are carelessly rendered, and the head is not differentiated from the neck. Slits mark the eyes, and triangular projections denote the nose and ears. The figure wears a cylindrical headdress and a garment that consists of a bell-shape skirt with double belt and tight bodice. The right arm is bent across the breasts, which are rendered in relief. Mended with lower part restored in plaster; left arm missing

Figurines in human or animal shapes are the most characteristic offerings found at the peak sanctuaries and were used in rituals performed in open-air places. By dedicating a figurine representing an adorant, the devotee fulfilled his need to communicate with the deity, perpetuated his presence at the sanctuary, and assured his permanent protection by the divinity.

The Vrysinas peak sanctuary, the largest and most important in western Crete, functioned during the Protopalatial and Neopalatial periods.

Selected Bibliography
Pilali-Papasteriou 1992, pp. 153–60; Rethemiotakis 1998, p. 107.

Eleni Papadopoulou

174 **Female Figurine**

Middle Minoan II–III period (ca. 1800–1600 B.C.)
Clay
H. 0.110 m, w. 0.052 m
Vrysinas, peak sanctuary, 1973
Rethymnon Archaeological Museum, Π 2060

The handmade figurine represents a standing woman in frontal position. The lower body, right arm, and left hand are missing. The facial features are rendered schematically. Impressed circles mark the eyes, and triangular projections denote the ears and nose. A Petsophas-type headdress, decorated with three applied clay roundels, covers the head. Similar roundels make up the necklace. The left arm is bent and rests under the schematically rendered breasts in a characteristic gesture of worship. Traces of black are visible on the surface throughout. Mended at the neck.

The Petsophas-type headdress is the most common headdress on female figurines, with examples known from most peak sanctuaries, indicating that this was a common fashion throughout Crete. Jewelry is rarely represented on Protopalatial figurines, and its presence is often interpreted as a possible sign of social differentiation through the individualization of the features of the offering.

Selected Bibliography
Papadopoulou–Tzachili (in press); Pilali-Papasteriou 1992, pp. 124–26, 131, nos. 41, 50.

Eleni Papadopoulou

175 **Head of Female Figurine**
Middle Minoan IIIB–Late Minoan IA period
(ca. 1650–1525/1500 B.C.)
Clay
H. 0.074 m
Piskokephalo
Herakleion Archaeological Museum, HM 9735

Slightly chipped head of female figurine with elaborate hairstyle. The nose, mouth, and eye sockets are executed in low relief. The face, neck, and hairband are covered with white paint, the hair itself with red-brown paint.

Many similar figurines with comparable characteristics come from the open-air sanctuary at Piskokephalo, Siteia. They were found with male figurines, house or shrine models, and figurines of the rhinoceros beetle. The modeling of the figural features, notably their hairstyles, places them among the best and most representative examples of clay sculpture in the Neopalatial period. The well-molded contours of the face and the realistic modeling indicate that the Piskokephalo figurines are products of a single specialist workshop that produced sculptural works, which were in high demand for the needs of a prominent group of votaries.

All the female figurines are distinguished by their impressive hairstyles. In this instance, the hairdo is shaped by a mass of fine, long locks, which are gathered up at the nape to create a complex plaited bun held in place by a broad ribbon, apparently a piece of cloth in the original. One of the plaits goes under the ribbon, falls free, and is cut or styled into a triangular shape on top of the forehead.

The composition and creation of such a striking hairstyle must have taken time and skill. The variety of styles with many variations, as seen on other figurines from the same sanctuary, demonstrates an emphasis on the aesthetics of the female haircut, as well as an apparent tendency toward display and prestige in a specific social context, a model of sophisticated behavior with recognizable values.

Selected Bibliography
Platon 1951b, pl. ΣΤ′, fig. 2.

Giorgos Rethemiotakis

176 Head of Female Figurine

Middle Minoan IIIB–Late Minoan IA period
(ca. 1650–1525/1500 B.C.)
Clay
H. 0.081 m
Piskokephalo
Herakleion Archaeological Museum, HM 9823

Head of female figurine with elaborate hairstyle. The nose, eyebrows, mouth, jawline, and ears are all executed in gentle relief with a naturalistic feel. There are traces of white paint on the face.

The sophisticated, impressive hairstyle doubles the height and mass of the head. It is made up of two groups of very long tresses with a part in the middle of the forehead. The locks, arranged in a thick, wavy manner, cover the temples above the ears and are supported with knots at the back of the head above the nape. From the point where the hair is held together at the bottom of the main hairdo, the tresses are divided into slim plaits and rise up vertically, forming loops at the end. The hair was probably all woven onto some kind of "skeleton" of pins and clips, although they do not show, since the impressive cylindrical shape of the hairdo is surrounded and held in place by a wide band, which would have been of real cloth.

The figurines of Piskokephalo—especially this example—illustrate the great depth of skill in styling women's hair. The particularly detailed way in which such a sophisticated and pretentious hairdo is treated in all the figurines from the sanctuary and the deliberate lack of detail in the face show that the hairstyle was the most important aspect of appearance, perhaps also evidence of prestige and social value in a defined group of female votaries.

Selected Bibliography
Platon 1951b, pl. H', fig. 1.

Giorgos Rethemiotakis

177 **Male Figurine**
Middle Minoan II period (ca. 1800–1700 B.C.)
Clay
H. 0.17 m, w. 0.085 m
Petsophas, peak sanctuary
Haghios Nikolaos Archaeological Museum, 9953

The figurine stands on a rectangular base; the head was manufactured separately and then fitted to the body. It probably held an offering, as perhaps indicated by an almost circular piece of clay between the palm and the body. Mended.

The figure is clothed in the simplest and most common Minoan male dress, including a codpiece, which is rendered sculpturally. The arms are folded on the chest, which is a gesture of worship, one of the most typical and common poses for male Minoan figurines. The head is inclined sharply backward as though looking up. This upward gaze is characteristic of the Petsophas figurines.

Most peak sanctuaries have been located at the eastern end of Crete, including Traostalos, Prinias, Piskokephalo, Modi, and Petsophas, where this figurine comes from. The last two peak sanctuaries are connected with the important town of Palaikastro. Through excavation at the peak sanctuary of Petsophas, it became clear that one of the ritual activities was lighting a pyre where the faithful would scatter their dedications.

Selected Bibliography
AΔ 27 B2 (1972): 652–54 (Davaras); *AΔ* 32 B2 (1977): 334, pl. 208a (Davaras); Davaras 1980, pp. 88–92; Davaras 1981; Dimopoulou-Rethemiotaki 2005, pp. 90 ff.; Marinatos 1993, pp. 115–23; Myres 1902–3; Platon 1951b, pp. 120–22; Rutkowski 1972, pp. 73–98; Rutkowski 1986; Rutkowski 1991; Sapouna-Sakellaraki 1971, pp. 8–9, 88–92.

Vasiliki Zographaki

178 Male Figurine

Middle Minoan II period (ca. 1800–1700 B.C.)
Clay
H. 0.235 m, max. w. 0.07
Petsophas, peak sanctuary
Haghios Nikolaos Archaeological Museum, 9955

Mended at the neck.

This male figurine is the most typical example from the peak sanctuary at Petsophas, as well as all contemporary sanctuaries. The care taken to achieve the relatively accurate proportions of the body, the significance given to the lower part of the body, and the formation of the slender waist are all characteristic of figurines made during this period.

The figurine wears a codpiece and the head is inclined lightly back, as though the artist wanted to show the eyes gazing upward. The arms are folded across the chest, a typical gesture for figurines and one that may reflect gestures used in real life, particularly in prayer or worship.

Selected Bibliography

ΑΔ 27 B2 (1972): 652–54 (Davaras); Myres 1902–3; Platon 1951b, pp. 120–22; Rutkowski 1991.

Vasiliki Zographaki

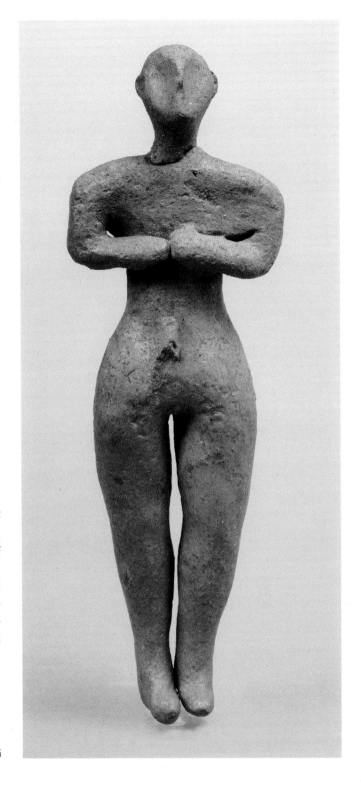

179 **Figurine**
Middle Minoan III–Late Minoan I period
(ca. 1700–1450 B.C.)
Bronze
H. 0.077 m
Skoteino cave
Herakleion Archaeological Museum, HM 2574

Bronze figurine of a male votary, missing feet and base. Torso heavily bent at the waist with the right hand raised to the forehead and the left at its side pointing down. Round elongated head, without facial features. The right ear and the hair, which consists of three locks reaching down to the waist and a mass of hair at neck level, are indicated in low relief. The figurine has a ring-shaped belt, hollow in section, perhaps with a metal frame, like most bronze figurines of this period. Two parts of the codpiece are fixed to the belt, the front elongated one with a leafy ending between the thighs and the back part shaped like a horseshoe to cover the buttocks.

This figurine was found in the excavation of the Skoteino cave in the Pediada, one of the largest and most spectacular sacred caves of Crete. Other bronze figurines were found in the same cave, as well as cult equipment, votive bronze strips, and pottery dating from the Middle Minoan period to the Roman period.

Although small in size, the figurine has all the general characteristics known from bronze figurines of the Neopalatial period: the organic articulation of the body, the realistic and proportional rendering of the limbs, and the backward bend of the torso. Also consistent with other such figurines is the generalized representation or complete absence of facial features, obviously because the face was not the principal element of the figure. Another standard feature of bronze figurines of the time is the devotional gesture with the right hand on the forehead, which expresses the act of praying, supplication, or the impulsive reaction of the votary at the climactic moment of spiritual communication with the deity. In addition, evidence for the priestly office or social status of the figure is the long front part of the codpiece and the long, loose hair, which may indicate a certain degree of maturity.

Selected Bibliography
Davaras 1969, pl. XI; Sapouna-Sakellaraki 1995; Verlinden 1984, pp. 112–14, 116, 192, pl. 22:44.

Giorgos Rethemiotakis

180 **Figurine**
   Middle Minoan III–Late Minoan I period
   (ca. 1700–1450 B.C.)
   Bronze
   H. 0.102 m
   Tylissos
   Herakleion Archaeological Museum, HM 1832

Bronze figurine of a male votary. Triangular torso curving sharply into the waist. The right hand is on the chest and the left is extended downward with a clenched fist. Spherical head with facial features (nose, eyes, ears) and button-shaped haircut in relief. Toes are indicated; the legs are bent slightly backward. The soles of the feet stand on a rectangular base, slanting forward in relation to the axis of the body. A double relief ring represents a belt with a phallus sheath shown below it. Complete.

A young man is shown in the pose of an adorant/votary. A feature common to most figurines of this period is the noticeable backward bend of the torso, as well as a corresponding but lesser bend of the legs at the knees and of the arms at the elbows. In the context of the singular semiotics of anthropomorphic Minoan sculpture, where all figural idioms express socioreligious perceptions and corresponding behaviors, this flexing has its own special meaning. It would appear that the worshiper's inner tension is externalized and given form in this way, as is the sense of awe that overcomes the faithful at the climactic moment of communing with the divinity. The "standing-to-attention" stance reveals respect, and the gesture indicates supplication or invocation of the deity being worshiped.

Selected Bibliohgraphy
Hazzidakis 1934, pp. 71–72, 95, pl. XXVIb; Sapouna-Sakellaraki 1995; Verlinden 1984, pp. 31, 130–31, 202, pl. 49:107.

Giorgos Rethemiotakis

181 **Model of a Female Body**
Middle Minoan I–II period (ca. 2000–1700 B.C.)
Clay
H. 0.105 m, max. w. 0.04 m
Petsophas, peak sanctuary
Haghios Nikolaos Archaeological Museum, 6079

Headless and handless. Particularly bold at flat chest with two perforations where the nipples should be; these could be used as suspension holes. Many incisions in the pubic region and belly. One deeper incision indicates the sex. Right knee mended, left foot restored in gypsum.

The presence of models in the form of individual human limbs or other parts of the body, often deformed, as well as some complete figurines with particularly bold characteristics, probably indicates an attempt by the faithful to gain the protection of the divinity, in order to heal the specific limb or, perhaps, give thanks for their cure. This particular female body with its special features may be indicative of a gynecological illness or infertility.

Selected Bibliography
AΔ 27 B2 (1972): 652–54 (Davaras); Davaras 1980, p. 91; *Im Labyrinth des Minos*, p. 252; Rutkowski 1986, pp. 87–89; Rutkowski 1991, pls. XLIII, 5–6.

Vasiliki Zographaki

182 **Model of Half a Human Figurine**
Middle Minoan IB–II period (ca. 1900–1700 B.C.)
Clay
Max. h. 0.123 m
Petsophas, peak sanctuary, 1903
Herakleion, Archaeological Museum, HM 3443

Terracotta male half figurine. The right half of the body is represented with the head thrown backward. It is standing with the right forearm held at right angles to the body. White painted decoration preserved on a brownish-black background denotes the eye, footwear, loincloth, and necklace. Mended from two pieces.

The figurine, which belongs to a particular category of votive offerings in the shape of human parts, was found at the Petsophas peak sanctuary. This figurine represents the entire right half of a male figure in the characteristic worship stance found on most complete worshiper figurines from peak sanctuaries. The brownish-black slip is a Minoan convention for representing the male gender. The great majority of the male figurines from Petsophas wear the characteristic Minoan loincloth. On this figurine, the loincloth is depicted with white paint as two curved pieces of fabric that cover the front and back of the pelvis down to the top of the thighs.

The careful application of the slip and paint on this section indicates that this is a complete figurine. Assuming that terracotta human parts were offered in exchange for healing, this half figurine may correspond to a case of hemiplegia, that is, paralysis of one side of the body.

Selected Bibliography
Myres 1902–3, p. 381, pl. XII.35; Peatfield 1990; Rutkowski 1991, pp. 32, 92, pls. XLII.13, XLII.12, fig. 8.2; Sapouna-Sakellaraki 1971, p. 16, fig. 2, pl. 10b.

Eirini Galli

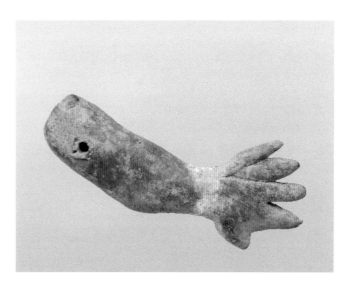

183A–B Two Models in the Shape of Legs
Middle Minoan I–II period (ca. 2000–1700 B.C.)
Clay
183A (5962): H. 0.14 m
183B (10586): H. 0.09 m
Petsophas, peak sanctuary
Haghios Nikolaos Archaeological Museum, 5962 and
10586

Two leg models with suspension holes. Catalogue number 183A is mended at the top of the ankle.

They belong to the same category as the naked female body (cat. no. 181): a group of dedications at peak sanctuaries consisting of models of individual limbs of the human body, sometimes deformed; half sections of the body; heads, or even complete figurines with emphasis given to some part of the body. Footwear is rendered in paint on some of the foot models.

These models were probably dedications—votives of ill people who sought a remedy for the corresponding affected limb or who gave thanks to the divinity for their cure. Votive limbs have also come to light at Minoan settlement sites, such as Tylissos and Malia.

Selected Bibliography
AΔ 27 B2 (1972): 652–54 (Davaras); Davaras 1976, p. 246, figs. 138–39; Davaras 1980, pp. 88–92; Myres 1902–3, p. 357, nos. 49–51, pl. 12; Nilsson 1950, pp. 174 ff.; Platon 1951b, pp. 110, 120–22, 147–60; *PM,* I, p. 152, figs. 111p–q; Rutkowski 1991, pls. XLV 9–12, 16–17, and XLVI.

Vasiliki Zographaki

184 Forearm
Middle Minoan IB–Middle Minoan II period
(ca. 1900–1700 B.C.)
Clay
L. 0.076 m
Petsophas, peak sanctuary, 1903
Herakleion Archaeological Museum, HM 3448

Complete clay model of an arm, from forearm to hand with straight fingers (thumb missing). A small lump on one side may represent the bent elbow. There is a suspension hole through the upper forearm. A shiny red slip covers the surface; a white painted band around the wrist may denote a bracelet.

Terracotta human limbs constitute a particular category of finds. Most of them come from peak sanctuaries—that is, Minoan centers of worship situated on the tops or slopes of hills—and were offered by the worshipers as an expression of religious beliefs during organized religious rituals. Terracotta limbs were probably offered to solicit divine help to heal an ailing limb, or to give thanks for the successful outcome of a request, or to request future protection. Characteristic examples of such votive offerings are a head with an overdeveloped thyroid gland and a seated woman with an obviously swollen foot. Paint is often used to depict the jewelry or garments, and many offerings have holes by which they were suspended in the sanctuary.

These votive offerings confirm the communal identity of peak sanctuaries. Although some were probably included in official palatial religious practices, all of them were deposited far from the developing proto-urban environments. Their offerings reflect the needs and concerns of the social groups that bolstered the agricultural economy.

Selected Bibliography
Marinatos 1993, pp. 115–23; Myres 1902–3, pl. XII.43; Platon 1951b, pp. 109, 120–22; Rutkowski 1986, pp. 73–98; Rutkowski 1991, pp. 32–34.

Eirini Galli

185 **Bull Figurine**

Middle Minoan II–III period (ca. 1800–1600 B.C.)
Clay
H. 0.12 m, l. 0.18 m
Vrysinas, peak sanctuary, 1973
Rethymnon Archaeological Museum, Π 24927

This handmade figurine has a solid cylindrical body and short legs. Deep hollows mark the eyes and nostrils, and an incision denotes the mouth. The modeled left ear is preserved under the horn. The tail is twisted to the right and rests on the bull's rump. Traces of brown paint are visible all over. Mended and restored.

The many bull figurines found at Minoan peak sanctuaries were an integral element of open-air rituals. By offering these, the faithful sought prosperity for their community and appealed for the fertility of their lands and herds. These figurines are often considered a substitute for the ritual sacrifice of real animals.

Selected Bibliography

ΑΔ 28 Β2 (1973): 583–84; Papadopoulou–Tzachili (in press).

Eleni Papadopoulou

186 **Bull Figurine**
   Middle Minoan II–III period (ca. 1800–1600 B.C.)
   Clay
   H. 0.095 m, l. 0.122 m
   Vrysinas, peak sanctuary, 1973
   Rethymnon Archaeological Museum, Π 7592

This extraordinary type of bull figurine has two heads on opposite sides. The horns and ears are modeled; a deep incision denotes the mouth. The eyes, represented by small discs, are preserved on one head only. Horns and legs are restored.

Although a rare type of offering at most Cretan peak sanctuaries, two-headed bull figurines abound at Vrysinas. By adding a second head, the donor was perhaps emphasizing the importance of the request he sent to the deity. A comparable offering is the double bull's-head rhyton from the Traostalos peak sanctuary near Zakros.

Selected Bibliography
Athanasopoulou-Tzedakis 2003, p. 172, no. 51; Papadopoulou–Tzachili (in press); Zeimbeki 2004, pp. 359–60.

Eleni Papadopoulou

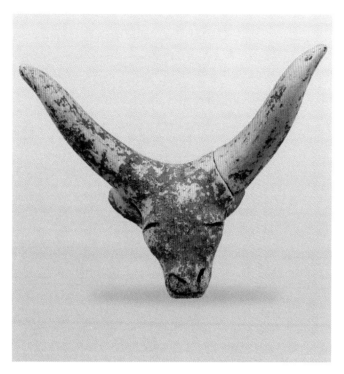

187 **Bull's Head**
Middle Minoan III period (ca. 1700–1600 B.C.)
Clay
H. 0.094 m
Vrysinas, peak sanctuary, 1973
Rethymnon Archaeological Museum, Π 7590

The bull's head is carefully rendered, with long curved horns and fully modeled ears. The powerful anatomical features, particularly the cheeks and muzzle, are represented realistically. Monochrome painted. Mended. Body entirely missing.

This fine example of a naturalistic trend in rendering figures is characteristic of Neopalatial art. The bull's-head rhyta from Knossos and Zakros are exquisite examples of this new style in Minoan art.

Selected Bibliography
Hatzaki 2005, pp. 184–85; Peatfield 1990, p. 127; Rethemiotakis 1998, p. 135.

Eleni Papadopoulou

188 **Bird Figurine**
Middle Minoan III period (ca. 1700–1600 B.C.)
Clay
H. 0.028 m, l. 0.070 m
Vrysinas, peak sanctuary, 1973
Rethymnon Archaeological Museum, Π 23672

This handmade figurine is solid, with long, well-formed wings and a slender body. The raised neck ends in a triangular head with an open beak and two grooves for the eyes. The naturalistic rendering is enhanced by the body's continuous curved outline. Almost complete, with a chip off the bottom.

Because of its size, this figurine probably stood alone on a short base, like similar examples from the Petsophas peak sanctuary. It was likely used together with other offerings for ritual purposes at the Vrysinas peak sanctuary. Birds were a very popular motif in Minoan iconography, particularly in religious and ritual pictorial cycles. They were associated with divine epiphany, either as the deity's heralds or as its zoomorphic incarnation.

Selected Bibliography
ΑΔ 28 B2 (1973): 583–84; Rutkowski 1991, pp. 110–11, pls. XLVII: 4, 5, 8; Tilmann–Pöhling 1990, p. 121, no. 124 (Papadopoulou).

Eleni Papadopoulou

189 **Beetle Figurine**
Middle Minoan III–Late Minoan I period
(ca. 1700–1525/1500 B.C.)
Clay
Max. l. 0.199 m
Piskokephalo, sanctuary, 1952
Herakleion Archaeological Museum, HM 9796

Terracotta figurine of a beetle, hollow, with a small hole at the rear. Two groups of deep parallel incisions denoting the wings cover the back; the head is flat, and no effort has been made to depict the legs. The beetle is covered with a red slip. Restored in places.

Terracotta figurines of beetles belong to the category of animal figurines of which large groups were found at peak and open-air sanctuaries, such as Piskokephalo. Although most animal figurines are smaller than life size, beetle figurines are very much larger than life size, with their main anatomical features emphasized in order for them to be recognizable. The beetle's symbolic role in the Minoan world is also suggested by the discovery at Palaikastro and at the Prinias peak sanctuary of pierced, hollow beetle figurines that may have served as ritual rhyta.

The beetles represented can be identified as dung beetles (*Copris hispanus*), a subspecies of the scarab (*Scarabaeidae*). Dung beetles feed off the feces of herd animals and pets, and their presence is therefore linked to them. The small terracotta nodules or balls found in the remains of ritual pyres are identified by some scholars as representing dung. Dung beetle figurines were offered at open-air sanctuaries and peak sanctuaries, which were associated with nature and rural life, probably to appeal for the successful outcome of agricultural and farming activities. Crete's involvement in maritime trade and its extensive contacts with Egypt probably fostered the belief that the beetle, like the Egyptian scarab, was a symbol of good fortune.

Selected Bibliography
Davaras 1988; Platon 1952, pp. 475–76; Rutkowski 1986, pp. 89–91.

Eirini Galli

C. MUSIC

190 **Sistrum**

Late Minoan IB period (ca. 1450 B.C.)

Bronze

H. from base to top 0.285 m, h. of frame 0.171 m, w. of frame 0.08–0.083 m, l. of horizontal pins 0.148–0.152 m, diam. of discs 0.021-0024 m, l. of handle 0.125 m, w. of U-shape support 0.055–0.064 m, diam. of handle 0.016–0.026–0.032 m, wt. 420 g.

Mochlos, Hoard from House of the Metal Merchant, House C3

Haghios Nikolaos Archaeological Museum, 14398

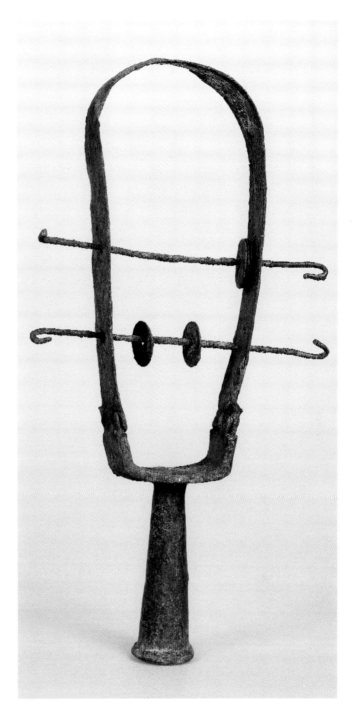

A closed ovoid shape with a curved frame made from a thin piece of metal joined to the interior of the U-shape support of the handle by two small rivets on each side. Two horizontal pins are inserted via pierced holes near the lower half of the frame, bent into a loop at each end. The upper horizontal pin has three discs and the lower pin has two. The handle is hollow with a turned base that tapers toward the U-shape support of the frame. This support is pierced where it joins the handle and tapers at each end where it joins the frame. It is stabilized on the lower part of the shoulders by two irregularly shaped pieces of metal. Mended and slightly restored.

The sistrum is of Egyptian origin and is connected to female deities. Two types of sistrum can be distinguished, the temple shape and the closed ovoid. The second type, to which this Mochlos sistrum belongs, was used widely in Egypt from the Middle Kingdom onward in religious processions, symposia, festive occasions, and as funerary offerings. The use of the sistrum outside Egypt was not only for music making but also for magical healing practices. Many seal stones are known from the cemetery at Phourni, Archanes, on which the hieroglyphic symbol of the sistrum is depicted. In Burial Building 9 of the same cemetery, a complete sistrum made of clay was found, but this may be an imitation of the real thing since clay is not a suitable material for producing sound. However, since it accompanied a child's burial and since its handle is hollow and its construction light, it may have been a child's toy.

When a sistrum is shaken, the discs clang against each other and the side of the frame, and the pins move backward and forward in the frame. A relief stone vase from Haghia Triada, the "Harvester Vase," reproduces the image of such a sistrum and points to its use in religious ceremonies, in this instance, at a harvest festival.

This sistrum was probably imported from Egypt, where no bronze example appears to have survived from a time as early as this, although a type with a loop-shape frame and similar handle is painted in the tomb of Menkheperrasonb, which dates to the reign of Tuthmosis III, and it also appears frequently in reliefs at Amarna. The construction details of the Mochlos sistrum are the same as those on the later Egyptian bronze sistra, and the findspot of the Mochlos instrument, next to the ingot in catalogue number no. 65, indicates that it could have been imported to the area in the same load.

Selected Bibliography

Andrikou et al. 2003, p. 111; Karetsou–Andreadaki-Vlazaki–Papadakis 2000, p. 267 (Sapouna); Mikrakis 2000, pp. 163–64; Sakellarakis–Sapouna-Sakellaraki 1997, pp. 351–57; Soles 2005.

Maria Kyriakaki

Detail of cat. no. 192

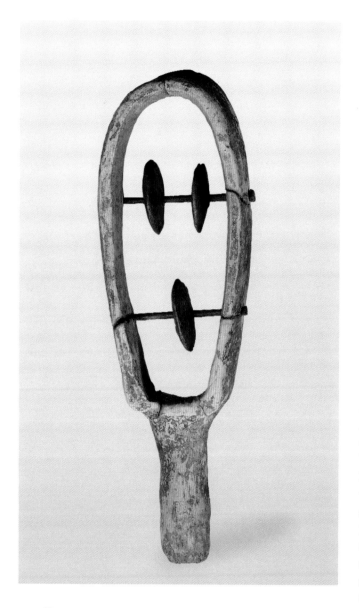

191 **Sistrum**

Middle Minoan I–II period (ca. 2100–1700 B.C.)
Clay
H. 0.18 m, handle diam. 0.018 m, max. w. 0.054 m
Burial cave of Haghios Charalampos, Lasithi Plain
Haghios Nikolaos Archaeological Museum, 13976

Clay sistrum with solid cylindrical handle and strap hoop with two pairs of holes. Mended and restored.

Three perforated clay discs were found next to the sistrum and were probably put on wooden shafts that were held in place by the two holes of the hoop. The hoop has painted decoration consisting of white bands on a dark background. Five similar sistra were found in the same cave, associated with burials.

The sistrum was a very common musical instrument in Egypt, where it was used to accompany singing and dancing, although it has also been found in tombs. Usually made of metal, the discs would hit each other and the loop when shaken vigorously, thus creating a rhythmic sound.

In Crete this instrument seems to have been well known and prolific. Apart from the Haghios Charalampos examples, another clay sistrum was found in the Phourni cemetery at Archanes. It is not known whether clay sistra were symbolic copies of metal prototypes destined for the grave, as opposed to being functional musical instruments in their own right. However, it is certain that metal sistra existed on Crete and were used as musical instruments, as demonstrated by the metal sistrum found recently in the Late Minoan I settlement at Mochlos (cat. no. 190), as well as by the scene on the stone rhyton from Haghia Triada, where harvesters are represented singing to the accompaniment of a sistrum. Lastly, the widespread acquaintance with and significance of sistra in Minoan Crete are also apparent from their depiction in scripts, both Hieroglyphic and Linear A.

The sistra constitute undeniable evidence for a strong relationship between Crete and Egypt and of the influences exerted by Egypt on Minoan civilization. The sistra from Haghios Charalampos are especially important, since they reveal that these contacts had begun at a very early stage, very probably before the construction of the first palaces. They also show that familiarity with that distant civilization was not confined to large and important seaside towns but that resonances of it reached even remote parts of the Cretan hinterland, such as the Lasithi mountain plain.

Selected Bibliography

Betancourt–Muhly 2006, dr. 2 right; Mikrakis 2000; Sakellaraki–Sapouna-Sakellaraki 1997, pp. 351–55; Soles 2005, p. 433.

Yiannis Papadatos

192 **Pyxis**

Late Minoan IIIB early period (ca. 1300–1250 B.C.)
Fine, yellowish clay
H. 0.15 m, max. diam. 0.167 m
Kalami cemetery (area of prehistoric Aptara), Chamber
Tomb I, 1969
Khania Archaeological Museum, P 2308

Cylindrical body and short, vertical rim. Four handles, immediately below the rim, alternating horizontal and vertical. Attachment holes for the missing lid flank the horizontal handles. Complete. Monochrome interior. Exterior covered with a large number of motifs divided up into panels and rendered according to the stylized trend of the period: horns of consecration, double axes, birds in flight, chains of shells, wavy and zigzag lines. The most important panel depicts a musical scene: a man with short hair dressed in a sleeveless robe, his head in profile and his body *en face*, is holding a branch in one hand; the other hand is touching a large, upright seven-stringed musical instrument, a lyre (κίθαρις in Homer) amid birds, horns of consecration and double axes. The musical instrument is shaped like a horseshoe and has vertical horns (Greek πήχεις, Latin *cornua*) with S-shape decoration, a straight bridge (Greek ζυγόν, Latin *transtillum*), and lunate sounding box. The two painted protuberances on the outside on the upper part of the sounding box probably depict the flutes (holes) that let the sound out of the hollow sounding box.

The musical scene, known from examples in the Creto-Mycenaean world (e.g., Haghia Triada sarcophagus, procession wall painting of Haghia Triada and wall painting of a musician at Pylos, a krater from Nauplion, and an amphora sherd from Tiryns), is interpreted as a religious ritual. The discovery of the vase in a tomb may link the scene to funeral rites. The direct relationship between the music of religious worship and funeral rites is well known in the prehistoric period. The musician can be interpreted as Apollo or Orpheus but also as a simple singer or priest. If the male figure depicts a divinity, this is a religious scene; if it is a singer, then an epic scene as described in Homer is more likely. If he is a priest honoring the deceased with music or calling the deceased to Hades, then it is a depiction of funeral rites.

The tomb was found by chance during the construction of the National Road from Khania to Rethymnon, on the side of the Aptera hill, a short distance before the river Koiliaris. The Kalami pyxis is the best-known representative example of the Kydonia ceramic workshop, which flourished in the Khania region during the fourteenth and thirteenth centuries B.C. (Late Minoan IIIA and IIB phases). Its products, which can be distinguished by their high quality, are characterized by a white or yellowish clay, yellowish-white slip, and orange-red paint. Examples from the Kydonia workshop have been found in Rethymnon, Knossos, eastern Crete, the Peloponnese, Thebes, Cyprus, and Sardinia, and they show the range and importance of the Khaniote export market (mainly in scented olive oils) during the period of the so-called Mycenaean *koine*.

Selected Bibliography
Andrikou 2003; Andrikou et al. 2003, pp. 122–23 (Andreadaki-Vlazaki) but also pp. 114–15 (Mandalaki), 120 (Chatzi–Speliopoulou), 124 (Papademetriou); Demakopoulou 1988, p. 153, no. 105 (Andreadaki-Vlazaki); Dragona-Latsoudi 1977, pp. 95, 98, pl. 22a; Tzedakis 1969b; Tzedakis 1970, figs. 1–2.

Maria Andreadaki-Vlazaki

D. RITUAL EQUIPMENT

193 Tripod Table Leg

Middle Minoan IIIB–Late Minoan IA period
(ca. 1625–1575 B.C.)
Plaster
H. 0.249 m
Palaikastro, Minoan town, Building 7
Siteia Archaeological Museum, 11365

One leg and a small part of the body from a tripod table of offerings. Painted decoration depicting narcissus flowers covers the exterior. The decoration is in white, blue, green, red, and yellow. Mended.

Tables of offering are part of the paraphernalia of worship in Minoan religion. They are usually made of stone, clay, or plaster held up by three legs. Offerings to the divinity such as fruit and grain would be placed on top of these tables.

This tripod table was a very fine and fragile vessel, thanks to the material of which it is made. It is a characteristic example of the artistic skill of the Minoans, who rendered their natural environment on wall paintings with great realism and particularly fine technique. The excavations at Palaikastro have brought to light notable quantities of plaster with polychrome decorative motifs belonging to wall paintings.

Selected Bibliography

MacGillivray et al. 1991, p.139, fig. 15.

Chrysa Sophianou

194 **Votive Axe**
  Middle Minoan IIIB period (ca. 1650–1600 B.C.)
  Gold
  L. of axe 0.0493 m, l. of haft 0.057 m
  Arkalochori cave, 1934
  Herakleion Archaeological Museum, HM 599

A gold votive double axe with engraved linear decoration on the wings of the axe and the edges of the haft. The haft is circular in section with slightly thicker ends. Two perforation holes are at the lower end, one of which has a thin gold wire running through it.

The axe comes from the Arkalochori cave, which produced a notable amount of bronze, silver, and gold double axes. Ritual or votive axes vary in size and come from sacred places and religious sites, such as that described above, and from settlement complexes, such as the huge axes from the Villa of Nirou, where they are found from the Early Minoan period to the Late Minoan period and beyond.

The double axe, a preeminent symbol of Minoan religion, occurs often in iconography either on its own or in combination with other motifs, such as the horns of consecration.

Selected Bibliography
Bucholz 1959; Dietrich 1998; Hazzidakis 1912–13; Marinatos 1935a; Marinatos 1962; Moss 2005, pp. 117–19, 197; Nillson 1950; Rutkowski–Nowicki 1996, pp. 24–25.

Katerina Athanasaki

195 Votive Double Axe

Middle Minoan III–Late Minoan I period
(ca. 1700–1450 B.C.)
Bronze
L. 0.50 m
Arkalochori cave
Herakleion Archaeological Museum, HM 2418

Blades widening toward the curved cutting edges. Decorated with double relief lines and oblique bands with consecutive crescent-shaped motifs. It was found together with other similar artifacts inside the Arkalochori cave. Complete, edges chipped.

Several small gold and silver double axes were found at the center of the cave. Hundreds of bronze axes of different sizes and uses (e.g., thin votive axes, utilitarian axes), as well as a large number of votive swords and daggers, remains of cylindrical wooden objects, small copper ingots, and copper slags, had been deposited at the cave's northernmost end. Most of the axes have engraved decoration, and three are inscribed with Cretan hiero-glyphic symbols.

At first Marinatos believed that during the Middle Minoan III–Late Minoan I period the cave was dedicated to some war deity, to whom the swords and double axes were offered. He later suggested that the cave served as a metallurgical workshop.

Worship in caves was widespread in Crete in the Neo-palatial period. Some caves have yielded examples of the double axe, the emblematic symbol of Minoan religion, and the Psychro cave even contained a steatite stepped base to hold the pole of a large double axe.

The Arkalochori cave, however, is unique, because of the great number of double axes and votive weapons and the ab-sence of any other type of ritual or votive object.

Selected Bibliography

Buchholz 1959, pp. 8–9, 33, pl. 1; Hazzidakis 1912–13; Marinatos 1935a; Marinatos 1935b; Moss 2005, pp. 115–19; Rethemiotakis 2002, pp. 64–65; Rutkowski–Nowicki 1996, pp. 24–26; Tyree 1975, pp. 28–30, 306–11; Tyree 2001, p. 41.

Deukalion Manidakis

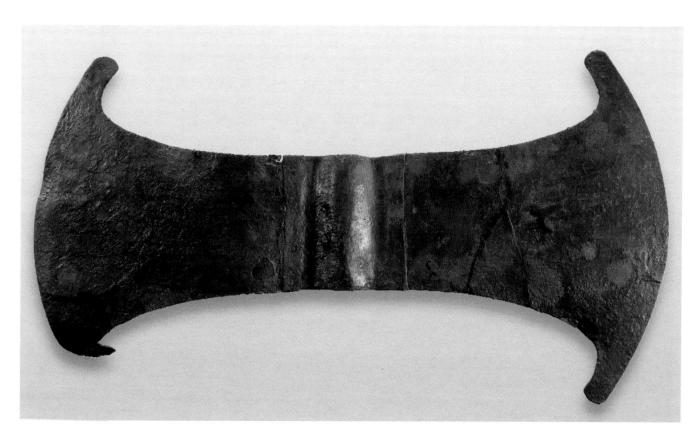

196 Double Axe

Late Minoan I period (ca. 1600–1450 B.C.)
Bronze
L. 1.118 m, max. h. 0.63 m
Nirou Chani, Room 7
Herakleion Archaeological Museum, HM 2049

This double axe is made up of four thin sheets of bronze. The two larger sheets form the blades, which widen toward the curved ends with tongue-shape tips. The two smaller, almost square sheets cover the middle of the blades and hold them together with rivets, at the same time forming the shaft hole. Almost complete, mended.

This is the largest of the four similar axes discovered in the Minoan villa in the coastal settlement at Nirou Chani. Covering an area of 1,000 square meters, the villa had about forty rooms and two paved courtyards, one of which contained a stepped construction and a pair of stone horns of consecration.

The double axe is the emblem of Minoan religion. Large ritual or votive axes have been found at many sites, including settlements, palaces, and sacred caves. The axes were probably fitted onto tall poles that were set into stepped stone bases, like those discovered in the Palace and the Little Palace at Knossos and in the Psychro cave, but also outside Crete, at Mycenae. A pair of large double axes with tall poles on similar stepped bases is pictured in the offering scene on the Haghia Triada sarcophagus, providing evidence for the rituals in which these objects were used.

The stepped construction and the stone horns of consecration found inside the east paved court of the Nirou villa suggest a ritual use of that space, possibly in relation with the large four axes.

Selected Bibliography

Buchholz 1959, p. 8; Hakulin 2004, pp. 12–13; Marinatos 1993, p. 5; Nilsson 1950, pp. 217–19; *PM* IV.2, pp. 437–47; Xanthoudides 1922, pp. 6, 12–13, fig. 10.

Deukalion Manidakis

197 Double Axe

Late Minoan IB period (ca. 1525/1500–1450 B.C.)
Bronze
L. 0.48 m, w. 0.30 m
Zakros, Palace, West Wing, Room XXV (Treasury of the Shrine)
Herakleion Archaeological Museum, HM 5829

Bronze double axe, with double blades on each side. It is made of two thick sheets, folded in the middle to form the shaft hole. Mended. The embossed decoration includes small, closely set circles on both sides of the blades and on either side of the shaft hole. Most of the decoration is engraved, comprising stems of papyrus and isolated flowers of the same plant with punched eyes arranged horizontally. Stems of papyrus are also found arranged vertically on the socket. The horizontal papyri on the sides are denticulate, embellished with engraved running spirals with punched eyes. Small engraved circles are found on both the front and the reverse sides.

Of all the religious symbols of the Minoan world, the double axe is the most important. Double axes make their appearance in the Early Minoan II period, both as working tools and as grave goods. However, in the same period, objects such as this were manufactured in such a manner that they would be considered useless on a practical level as tools.

The origin of such strong symbolism remains an enigma. A. Evans hypothesized that the double axe was an aniconic form of the Great Mother Goddess. Other scholars thought that the double axe was in fact the sacrificial implement par excellence in Minoan rituals, with the result that over time its presence acquired symbolic religious significance.

The earliest confirmed involvement of the double axe in Minoan religious ritual is its clearly deliberate deposition inside the defined open-air spaces of Prepalatial and Protopalatial circular tombs, where it is thought that communal burial rites took place. Examples of double axes come from the surrounding areas of circular tombs in the Mesara, particularly the sites of Kamilari, Apesokari, Platanos, and Sopata Kouse. At the same time, double axes began to be dedicated in sacred caves. Typical of this kind of deposition in the Neopalatial period that followed are the great bronze axes and the miniature gold and silver axes from the Arkalochori cave, most of which have beautifully engraved ornamentation. Nonetheless, the largest examples come from the building at Nirou Chani, with all its religious connotations. Hypothetically, these enormous double axes, held up by very tall wooden shafts, stood in front of the façade of the building performing the function of a religious emblem. As far as the shape is concerned, the closest parallels to the large bronze axe from Zakros are the miniature double axes of ivory, also with double blades, found in a room near the treasury.

The singular, in some instances emblematic, character of this object is confirmed by the role it occupied in Minoan religious iconography. On a seal stone from Knossos and a signet ring sealing from Zakros, a female deity is represented carrying a large axe with a haft; and, in the case of the Zakros sealing, the axe is depicted with double blades exactly like the bronze example in question from the palatial treasury. On a matrix from Palaikastro, a female figure, identified as a deity, holds double axes in her two upraised arms. However, the most important evidence for the use of the double axe is provided by the libation scene on the Haghia Triada sarcophagus. In front of a structure that has been identified as a burial monument, a large double axe of the double-bladed type represented by the bronze Zakros example is depicted on a tall haft. Priestesses are making libations around the base of the axe, and a bird sits on top of it.

The double axe frequently appears as symbol in its own right, lending sanctity to a vessel or an object that is to be used in some kind of religious ritual. Thus it is found in relief, engraved, or painted on tables of offering, ritual vessels, and clay sarcophagi. The image developed as a fairly common decorative motif on clay vases and vessels, particularly from the Neopalatial period onward. At any rate, the axe definitely seems to be connected with the involvement of the objects it adorns in sacred ritual.

Iconography also confirms that double axes equipped with tall hafts were set up in stepped stone or clay bases. Many examples of such bases have been found at Minoan sites, including the palaces at Knossos, Malia, and Zakros.

Selected Bibliography

Long 1974, p. 36, pl. 15; Nillson 1950, pp. 194–235; Platon 1974, pp. 127, 130; *PM.*

Lefteris Platon

198 **Lid**

Late Minoan IB period (ca. 1450 B.C.)
Clay (Knossian)
H. with handle 0.029 m, diam. 0.213 m
Pseira, Minoan settlement
Siteia Archaeological Museum, 7141

Flat, with a raised lip and strap handle in the middle. Four double-bladed, double axes decorate the surface around the handle. Mended and restored.

As a decorative motif, the double axe is found on vases, pithoi (storage jars), and sarcophagi. It is without doubt one of the sacred symbols of Minoan religion and is connected with ceremonies. The lid was found together with two bull-shape rhyta and a basket vase also decorated with double axes in a room of Building BQ. Both decoration and shape of these vessels lead to the conclusion that they were equipment used in religious ceremonies that probably took place in that room.

Selected Bibliography
Betancourt–Davaras 1999, p. 136, no. BQ4, pl. 21A, fig. 15; Seager 1910, p. 31.

Chrysa Sophianou

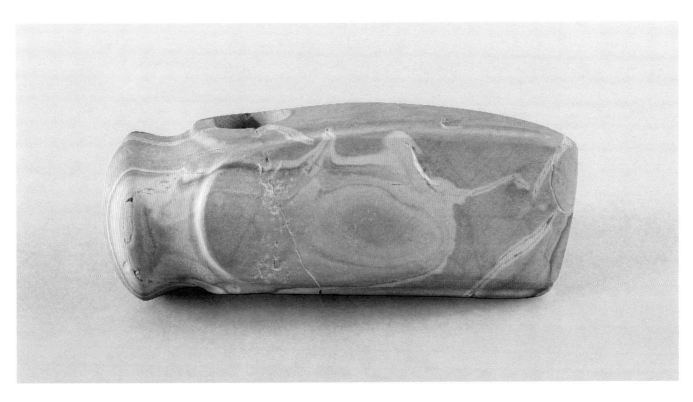

199 **Hammer-Axe**

> Late Minoan I period (ca. 1600–1450 B.C.)
> Conglomerate veined limestone
> L. 0.108 m, W. 0.41 m, diam. of striking surface 0.038 m,
> diam. of shaft hole 0.016–0.018 m
> Poros, tomb at Vlastos Plot, 1967
> Herakleion Archaeological Museum, HM 3174

Mended, slightly restored.

As indicated by the name, hammer-axes resemble both hammers (*sphyra*), for their rounded striking surface, and axes (*pelekis*), for their sharpened edge. Hence they are assumed to have been used for hammering and cutting or chopping and as tools and weapons at the same time. They were attached haft handles through pierced holes like common utilitarian axes.

The hammer-axe from Poros is very well made, with a smooth surface and a shallow groove running along both sides of the blade. The stone veining, which is rarely attested on tools, the care in which it was treated, and the lack of traces of use at any point on its surface have led to the hypothesis that this object must have served as a ceremonial axe. Its prototypes are foreign to Crete, but its emblematic function parallels that represented on some Minoan seals, where similar tools are depicted together with individual figures.

Hammers and axes that were never used as tools, judging from their find contexts, sizes, materials, and the absence of use marks on their surfaces, have been found at various sites in Crete, mainly of the Neopalatial period (Knossos, Archanes, Zakros, etc.). A unique and revealing feature of all these objects is a single-edged stone axe from the palace at Malia, broadly contemporary with the Poros find, whose blade bears a normal edge at one end and an animal figure with engraved embellishment at the other.

Selected Bibliography

Lebessi 1967, 208–9; Manti-Platonos 1981, p. 79; Marinatos 1993, p. 7; Muhly 1992, pp. 134–40, 285.

Emmanouela Apostolaki

200 **Ritual Hammer**

Late Minoan IB period (ca. 1525/1500–1450 B.C.)

Marble

L. 0.103 m, diam. of shaft hole 0.022 m, max. diam. 0.07 m, diam. of percussion head 0.06 m

Zakros, Palace, West Wing, Room XXV (Treasury of the Shrine)

Herakleion Archaeological Museum, HM 2698

Complete ritual hammer of white marble, with a little dark veining in places. Slender, spindlelike shape, with curved percussion surfaces at either end, clearly differentiated from the rest of the body. Shaft hole, circular in section in the middle of the hammer. Two shallow grooves around the body, nearly touching the edge of the shaft hole, probably for securing twine.

This is one of three complete stone hammers found in the southwest corner of the so-called Treasury of the Shrine in the palace at Zakros. The superb carving of the material places it among the finest examples of this particular category, which comprises about twenty objects (without counting hammers of similar shape, but made of bronze, from Haghia Triada).

The religious symbolism and ritual use of objects in this category is, in most cases, suggested by their excavation context. In the case of Zakros, the ritual use of the corpus of equipment from the Treasury of the Shrine, which included the three hammers, is very clear because of its character. The remaining examples in this category come from other shrine treasuries, peak sanctuaries, burial caves, and the tombs of priests or other eminent individuals.

One hammer, from the Metaxas Collection in Herakleion Museum, has a hole in one of the percussion surfaces, which indicates that the object served as a rhyton.

However, the main use of these hammers as cult symbols is confirmed by the way they are portrayed in ritual scenes in contemporary iconography. On two Minoan amygdaloid seal stones from House Delta at Malia and the Vapheio tholos tomb in Laconia, figures with long robes, probably priests, walk in a ritual procession, each holding a hammer with a long haft supported on one shoulder. On two seal stones, from Kastelli, Khania, and Haghia Triada, priestly figures brandish similar objects before them or above their heads. These representations bolster the idea that the hammer in Minoan Crete, along with the double axe, was used mainly as a religious emblem. However, the enigmatic question of the symbol's origin appears to be a more difficult matter, along with the likely initial use of the objects in religious ritual. It has been suggested that hammers, like double axes, were first used for ritual animal sacrifice. Another hypothesis suggests that the symbolic character of the object originated in the ritual of knocking on the shrine's door so that it would be opened for the appearance of the goddess (a ritual that is also found in other ancient religions related to Minoan). In addition, it is well known that hammers similar to the Minoan examples, both in Pharaonic Egypt and the Syro-Palestinian region, were used as scepters or religious symbols.

Selected Bibliography

Platon 1974, p. 127; Platonos 1981; *PM*; Schiering 1972.

Lefteris Platon

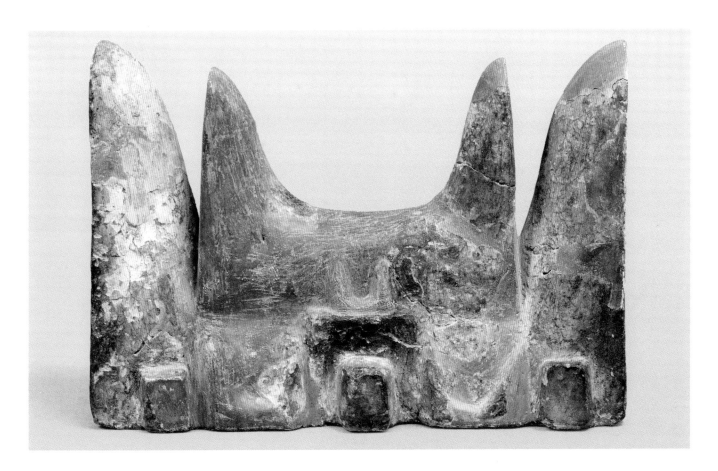

201 Composite Horns of Consecration

Middle Minoan IB–II period (ca. 1900–1700 B.C.)
Plaster
L. 0.14 m, w. 0.044 m, h. 0.098 m
Petsophas, peak sanctuary
Haghios Nikolaos Archaeological Museum, 6805

One pair of horns is flanked by another, larger pair. There are three additional miniature pairs of horns on the front and three square protruding altars in a composition reminiscent of the tripartite arrangement of Minoan shrines. Mended and restored with gypsum. The model has been thought to depict the actual shrine building or the two peaks of hills adjacent to Petsophas, as they appear from the site of the shrine.

The double sacred horns, or "horns of consecration," as Arthur Evans called them, made of clay, stone, or plaster—as in this example—constitute the symbol par excellence of Minoan religion and symbolize the animal force and potency of the bull, the most sacred animal of the Mediterranean region and the Near and Middle East, as well as of southern Asia. Excavated finds attest the central role of the bull in ceremonial ritual as early as the Middle Minoan period, and the double horns occur as a typical part of worship and are indicative of shrines and altars. Painted and plastic depictions of sacred horns, common in Minoan and Mycenaean iconography, turn up on sarcophagi, religious equipment, pithoi (large storage jars), and seal stones.

The peak sanctuary of Petsophas (height a.s.l. 255 m.), the most important in eastern Crete, is linked to the Minoan town of Palaikastro. The *temenos* encloses an area of 500 to 700 square meters and probably extends onto the neighboring peak. The sanctuary comprised a complex of five rooms, some of which were roofed. It had a particularly long life, beginning in Early Minoan III and lasting to Late Minoan I (ca. 2300–1500 B.C.). It yielded a large number of offerings, more than a thousand human and animal figurines, clay cups, and miniature vessels. Among the finds there are two important stone tables of offerings with inscriptions in the Linear A script, probably of a religious character.

Selected Bibliography

AΔ 27 B2 (1972): 652–54 (Davaras); *AΔ* 31 (1976): 380 ff. (Davaras); Davaras n.d., p. 22, fig. 31; Davaras 1976, pp. 273–74; Myres 1902–3, pp. 356–87; Platon 1951b, pp. 120–22; Rutkowski 1991.

Vili Apostolakou

202 **Stand**

Late Minoan IIIA2 period (ca. 1350 B.C.)
Clay
H. 0.245 m, diam. 0.22–0.24 m
Gra Lygia, Hierapetra, rock-cut chamber tomb 1
Haghios Nikolaos Archaeological Museum, 12684

An exceptionally well-preserved vessel with a cylindrical body open at the top and bottom. Three raised, broad ribs at the base, the middle, and the top encircle the body and define two main decorative zones. Each of these consists of vertical metopes—decorated with successive zigzag lines, a simple net pattern, alternating V's, and a net pattern with solid-painted lozenges—which alternate with openings, each of roughly the same size, in the shape of double windows separated by columns. A row of alternating monochrome and unpainted plastic double sacred horns, divided from one another by a vertical inscribed line, crowns the vessel. These features may be based on actual architectural constructions of a sacred nature. Mended ring top with the double horns.

The stand was found in a rock-cut chamber tomb that also contained three sarcophagi; forty vases in a very good state of preservation and dating to the Late Minoan IIIA2 and Late Minoan IIIB periods; a bronze knife and two bronze tools; fragments of ivory combs, plaques, and pins; 1,401 beads of a faience necklace; and one amulet of rock crystal. A cover for an incense burner, found in a nearby tomb, is surmounted by double sacred horns, alternately monochrome and unpainted, just like the stand.

This shape of stand first appears in the Late Minoan IIIA period, although it is not represented by many examples. It was meant to support vases that had small or unstable bases; since it was decorated with religious symbols, its use was probably related to a cult.

The well-known piece from Gournia, Hierapetra (Herakleion Archaeological Museum), is very similar in shape and general decorative concept to the Gra Lygia stand. The small stand from Elounda, Mirabello, which is a more simply made stand, is also surmounted by double sacred horns. A clay stand with fenestrated walls in the shape of horns of consecration comes from the Late Minoan IIIC–Subminoan settlement of Karphi.

Selected Bibliography
Apostolakou 1998; Hägg 1989.

Vili Apostolakou

203 House Model

Late Minoan IIIC period (ca. 1200 1100 B.C.)
Clay
H. 0.111 m, base diam. 0.105 m
City of Khania, Kastelli Hill, Vakalounakis plot,
10 Katre Street, 1973
Khania Archaeological Museum, Π 3717

Cylindrical house model with a flat base for the floor and a low domed roof, now largely restored. Two vertical handles on either side of the well-carved rectangular opening serve as hinges for the missing door. A slight bulge on the floor may have served to position a portable object inside the house. Mended and restored with plaster.

Similar house models date from Late Minoan IIIA2 (ca. 1375–1300 B.C.) until the late Geometric period (ca. 800–700 B.C.), with most of them, so far, from the Late Minoan IIIC to the sub-Mycenaean periods (ca. 1200–1000 B.C.). Almost all of the Cretan examples come from settlements. The excavations at Kastelli hill, Khania, yielded another clay model and the door of a third example. The most widely accepted interpretation for these objects is that they represent houses and were dedicated at small house shrines, which often contained figurines of Minoan deities.

Selected Bibliography

Hägg 1990; *Im Labyrinth des Minos*, p. 261 (Andreadaki-Vlazaki).

Sophia Preve

204 Quadruple Kernos

Early Minoan II–III period (ca. 2900–2100 B.C.)
Chlorite
H. 0.053 m, w. 0.095 m.
Koumasa, Tomb B
Herakleion Archaeological Museum, 677

Quadruple, square kernos, mended and restored. The four deep hollows have obvious tool-mark traces from the carving, such as pronounced rings on the inside and a knob at the center. Between the hollows is a shaft that widens into an ovoid socket at the base. Four more shallow circular sockets at the corners of the base may have served for securing the object onto a base. The engraved decoration on the top and sides consists of geometric motifs filled with hatching. The top is decorated with two antithetical triangles and a motif that follows the outline of the two pairs of circular hollows and ends in a lozenge at the center. A horizontal ladderlike band divides the sides into two zones. The zones alternately present hatched pendent semicircles and vertical ladderlike bands.

The kernos form probably comes from the need to separate and display small quantities of goods or materials. They are usually associated with ritual funerary practices. When used as grave gifts, they probably contained offerings for the deceased.

Selected Bibliography

Warren 1969b, pp. 12–13, P 46; Xanthoudides 1905–6; Xanthoudides 1924, pp. 17–18.

Nektaria Mavroudi

205 Bull's-Head Rhyton

Late Minoan IB period (ca. 1450 B.C.)
Chlorite
H. 0.15 m, h. with horns 0.215 m
Zakros palace, West Wing, light well of Room XXVIII
Herakleion Archaeological Museum, HM 2713

Chlorite rhyton in the shape of a bull's head. Mended and restored, particularly the snout and most of the left side. The nape, crown, forehead, eyes, snout, and two folds of the skin at the neck are rendered sculpturally. The hide is rendered both in relief and with incisions: small, wavy curls begin at the crown and spread toward the forehead, swirling between the eyes and diverging from one another under the eyes to cover the snout. Wavy incisions denote the skin's folds around the eyes and on the snout, neck, and nape. Incised zigzags outline the eyes, and groups of curved incisions decorate the cheeks. Vertical ridges ending in wavy incisions decorate the interior of the ears (only one is preserved), which were secured to the head with square pegs. A plaque, carefully smoothed and with incised lines on its edges, closes the opening of the neck. This plaque was shaped to fit the sculpturally rendered part of the artifact, but some kind of binding agent must also have been used.

This libation vase from Zakros is one of the most elaborate and important creations of the Creto-Mycenaean world. Together with the famous stone bull's head from the Little Palace at Knossos, it is the best-preserved example of a particular type of religious vessel, of which fewer than twenty-five examples are known. The Knossian bull's head preserves one of the inlaid eyes, which is made of precious stones. The eyes of the Zakros vessel would have been inlaid in a similar manner. The hypothetical reconstruction of the animal's gilded wooden horns was inspired by a silver bull's-head rhyton from Mycenae's Grave Circle A.

Stone bull's-head rhyta are the acme of the Minoan artistic expression of a theme that appears to have had a long history and particular religious significance for the inhabitants of prehistoric Crete. Clay bull's-head rhyta appear during the period of the first palaces, and clay bull figurines, occasionally with figures of bull leapers on their horns, were used for ritual libations as early as the Prepalatial period, as indicated by examples from tholos tombs in the Mesara.

All of the known stone bull's-head rhyta date to the Neopalatial period. Fifteen examples, most of them partially preserved, come from Crete (eleven from Knossos, three from Zakros, and one from Palaikastro). Another eight fragmentary rhyta come from the Greek mainland: six from Mycenae and two from Pylos. Their presence in mainland Greece should not be considered fortuitous, as both sites had strong political ties with Minoan Crete. The exchange of gifts by rulers for diplomatic purposes was a common practice in the eastern Mediterranean during the Bronze Age. Bull's-head rhyta are included among the gifts presented to the pharaohs by figures identified as Cretans (Keftiu) on the wall paintings that decorate the tombs of Egyptian officials of the 18th Dynasty and date to the first half of the fifteenth century B.C.

Apart from their great artistic value, which made them first-class gifts, bull's-head rhyta also had symbolic and religious significance. Their fragmentary state of preservation is noteworthy. In fact, what usually remains is the front part of the snout. Even in the case of the two reconstructed bull's heads from Knossos and Zakros, the excavators remarked that, despite their efforts, they were unable to recover any other fragments. The archaeological contexts that produced these artifacts are also interesting. Objects of similar artistic value are usually found inside sacred areas or stored within the "treasuries" of palace sanctuaries. If such objects were a sign of their owner's status, they would have accompanied the deceased to his or her grave, yet none of the surviving fragments comes from a funerary context. The fragments from the Little Palace at Knossos were found inside a kind of depression in a stairwell, whereas those from Zakros come from the light well of the palace's West Wing. This has led to the assumption that the bull's heads were broken during a ritual of particular religious and possibly political significance. The symbolic dismembering and scattering of the vessel's fragments would substitute for the actual sacrifice of a bull, as it appears on the Haghia Triada sarcophagus and was probably performed in Tholos Tomb A at Archanes.

Either way, the symbolism of the bull appears to be all-powerful, especially during the Neopalatial period. The animal is often depicted alone or in bull-leaping scenes both on wall paintings and clay sealings made by gold, possibly Knossian, signet rings and found in various Neopalatial sites. Because Knossos appears to be at the center of this iconography, several scholars have assumed they involved a kind of political propaganda exercised by Knossos toward the periphery and expressed through the image of the bull—the symbol of Knossian power. This may explain why one of the finest examples of bull's-head vessels comes from the last palace at Zakros, which was probably subject to strong Knossian influence during the Neopalatial period.

Selected Bibliography

Hallager–Hallager 1995, pp. 547–54; Koehl 2006; Platon 1974, pp. 150–52; Rehak 1995; Wachsmann 1987, pp. 56–57, pls. XXVII, XXXVIII; Warren 1969b, pp. 89–90.

Lefteris Platon

206 Bull-Shape Rhyton

Middle Minoan IB period (ca. 1900–1800 B.C.)
Clay
H. 0.13 m, l. 0.22 m
Mochlos, Tomb XI
Siteia Archaeological Museum, 6206

The animal's body is plastically rendered, the belly and neck muscles all indicated. There is a hole at the back of the neck, and the nose and eyes are pierced. The vase is decorated with solid-painted brown discs linked by lines that cover the entire body, head, and legs. Mended at the left hind leg and two forelegs, and one horn restored in gypsum.

Initially it was thought that the decoration on the rhyton represented a kind of harness, but more recent scholars believe it represents the net with which the bull is captured before it takes part in a religious ceremony. The bull-shape rhyton is connected with the libations of devotional and funerary rites that were carried out at Tomb XI.

The bull, like the snake, was considered a sacred animal in Minoan religion as early as the Prepalatial period, although its worship cannot be proved. Bulls were dedicated to the divinity as a luxury good and were sacrificed in her honor. Bull figurines are some of the most common offerings found on peak sanctuaries. The horns of the bull became a sacred symbol of Minoan religion and, as elements of religious architecture, identified places as sacred. Sacred horns, or "horns of consecration," as well as bucrania (bulls' heads), decorated a variety of ritual vessels, pithoi (storage jars), and sarcophagi.

Selected Bibliography

Seager 1912, p. 31; Soles 1992, pp. 94–97.

Chrysa Sophianou

207 Bull-Shape Rhyton

Late Minoan IB period (ca. 1525/1500–1450 B.C.)
Clay
H. 0.17 m, l. 0.26 m
Pseira, House A (Seager), Building AA (Betancourt–
Davaras)
Herakleion Archaeological Museum, HM 5413

Hollow bovine figurine, partly restored. The body, particularly the musculature, is rendered in a naturalistic manner. The horns appear to have been cut off near the middle before firing. A ring at the base of each horn binds the horn and ear tighly together. At the nape, behind the horns, is a circular filling hole; a small pouring hole is located on the muzzle. A lustrous whitish slip covers the bull's body. A highly naturalistic orange net covers the body, closely following the relief of the musculature. The net, which has double stitching along the edges and triple stitching on the knots, leaves the head and the lower part of the belly uncovered. The legs are joined as if tied together, indicating the animal's immobility.

Scholars originally believed that the motif of the orange net on the whitish slip was a ceramic technique unknown at the time this vase was manufactured, a remarkable "archaicism" in the production of these ritual vessels. The white bull was perhaps the most important animal victim of ritual sacrifices. The iconographic features of this figurine—the net covering the fat body, the tied and possibly cut horns, the tied legs, and so on—suggest that the animal was intended for sacrifice. Of course, the fine, featherweight net is not the same as the heavy, resistant net known from bull-hunting scenes but was a ritual cover, symbolic of the animal's capture and designation. It is possible that the blood of the sacrificial animal was gathered in this kind of vessel, but this example was found inside a private house, where it may have served in private daily rituals. This libation vase is called a rhyton, although both its function and its form recall an animal-hide askos more than a rhyton. Bull-shape rhyta are considered to be Eastern in origin and have a long history in the Cretan civilization of the second millennium B.C.

Selected Bibliography

Koehl 2006, pp. 16–17, pl. 3:22; *PM* IV, pp. 259–60, fig. 154b; Seager 1910, pp. 22–23, fig. 7, pl. IX.

Dimitris Sfakianakis

208 Model of Triton Shell

Middle Minoan IIIB–Late Minoan I period
(ca. 1650–1450 B.C.)
Alabaster
Max. h. 0.317 m, max. w. 0.137 m
Knossos, Palace, Central Palace Sanctuary
Herakleion Archaeological Museum, HM 45

Life-size stone model of a triton shell, a common Mediterranean gastropod mollusk of the *Charonia* family. In imitation of the real shell, the diameter gradually increases as the form spirals, creating a conical vessel. The spiral begins at the apex and ends at the opening. In natural shells, the rings join at the stitch lines, which are denoted by deep grooves on the replica. Half of the rim is decorated with dense, parallel, wavy incisions, which imitate the folds and dents of the rim of natural triton shells. The other half has four small holes, possibly for attaching ornaments. The siphon canal is circular in section and separate from the rim. Mended and restored.

This imitation triton shell is made of alabaster, an off-white, semitranslucent mineral stone, usually imported from Egypt for the manufacture of precious vases. It was found in the West Wing of the palace at Knossos, in the so-called Central Palace Sanctuary, a group of rooms containing an impressive number of objects related to religious practices. The replica belongs to the palace's famous group of ritual stone vases that are thought to have fallen from a room in the upper story, which may functioned as a shrine or a storeroom for ritual objects until the palace's final destruction.

Natural triton shells are found in settlements starting in the Prepalatial period. They may be food remains, but their reworked ends suggest they were used as vessels for drawing water or as sound-producing instruments, a use attested in Crete as recently as the beginning of the twentieth century A.D. After the foundation of the palaces and particularly during the Neopalatial period, triton shells appear to have played an important role in organized Minoan rituals. Imitations of triton shells in stone, clay, and faience have been found in shrines, settlements, and graves (Knossos, Malia, Zakros, Kalyvia, and Haghia Triada). Stone triton shells are among the great achievements of Minoan stone carvers. They were probably standard religious symbols and not just utilitarian or decorative objects.

The shape and context of the shells suggest that they were used in the ritual consumption or offering of liquids, even though most of them are not pierced at the base like rhyta, the libation vessels par excellence. A characteristic example is the famous stone triton shell from Malia, which depicts in relief Minoan lion-shape daemons performing libation in a rocky landscape or perhaps a seascape. The role of triton shells in religious practices, even after the final destruction of the Minoan palaces, is revealed in a scene depicted on a stone seal from the Idaean cave, which shows a human figure standing before an altar holding a triton shell at shoulder level. Although it is uncertain whether the figure performs a libation on the altar, offers the triton shell itself, or blows into the shell to summon a deity, the gesture clearly refers to worship and emphasizes the significance of the sea in Minoan art, economy, and religion.

Selected Bibliography

Äström–Reese 1990, pp. 5–14; Baurain–Darcque 1983, pp. 5–58; Darcque 1983, pp. 59–73; Marinatos 1993, pp. 193–200, fig. 209; Panagiotaki 1999b, pp. 274–75; *PM* IV, pp. 211, 820–23, figs. 288, 537, 539; Warren 1969b, pp. 91, 125–26, pl. 498.

Eirini Galli

209 Conical Rhyton

Late Minoan I period (ca. 1600–1450 B.C.)
Veined limestone
H. with restored handle 0.405 m, rim diam. 0.117 m
Haghia Triada, NW Royal Apartments, Portico
Herakleion Archaeological Museum, HM 336

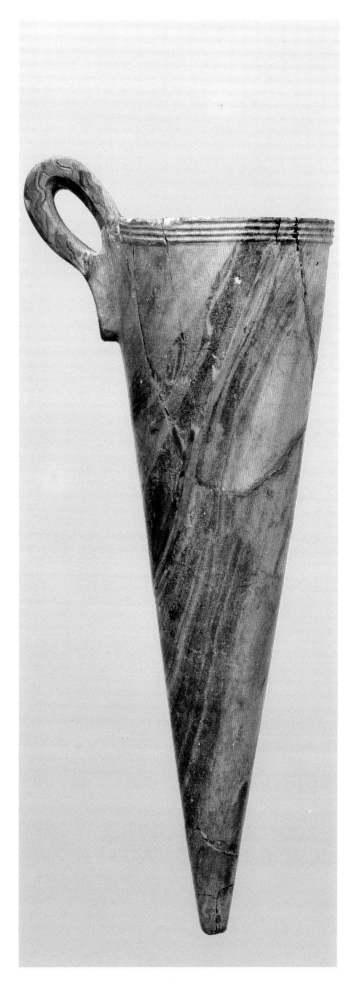

Tall rhyton, with symmetrical conical walls, a rim embellished with a relief band of four very narrow horizontal rings, and a markedly pointed bottom, where the discharge hole is. The raised strap handle has been restored on the basis of preserved examples, where the handle is usually manufactured of a separate piece of stone.

The manner in which the stone carver has taken advantage of the natural veins of the rock to make the greatest aesthetic impression, the fine carving of the relief band on the rim, and the even polish of its surface reveal the care with which this rhyton was made.

Conical rhyta are very common, also known from many examples in clay and from depictions on seal stones and wall paintings. Like the ovoid ones, conical rhyta were used as ritual libation vessels, as grave gifts for the dead, and on occasion as a kind of funnel to transfer liquids into another vessel. The luxury versions of this type were offered as formal gifts, as the parallels from wall paintings show: the famous figure of the "Cup [rhyton] Bearer," a fragment of a larger composition from the palace at Knossos depicting a priestly procession, carries a large conical rhyton to offer to a female figure—a goddess. Similarly, the Minoans/Keftiu on the wall paintings of the tomb of Rekh-mi-re at Egyptian Thebes (18th Dynasty) bring conical rhyta as gifts, among other luxury items and valuable raw materials, to the pharaoh on the occasion of some special event.

The Haghia Triada rhyton was found in the portico at the entrance to the Royal Apartments in the northwest part of the wealthy villa, together with a notable number of Linear A tablets.

Selected Bibliography

Halbherr–Stefani–Banti 1977, p. 84; Koehl 2000, pp. 97–99; Koehl 2006, pp. 330–32, 342–45; Warren 1969b.

Emmanouela Apostolaki

210 Ovoid Rhyton
  Late Minoan I period (ca. 1600–1450 B.C.)
  Breccia
  H. 0.325 m, max. diam. 0.173 m
  Pseira, House D5 Room 1/ Area CB
  Herakleion Archaeological Museum, HM 1126

Mended and restored.

A large version of the ovoid type of stone rhyton, this example is noticeable for its relief ring, which is carved directly around its mouth, thus omitting the neck. Two pairs of holes on the upper wall of the vessel were used for attaching the now-missing handles. It was manufactured from a conglomerate stone with dark-colored inclusions in a reddish matrix and was polished sufficiently at the surface to achieve a shiny, glassy look. The unusual choice of shape for this particular stone and the quality of the work on the vessel demonstrate, as with most stone vessels, the high degree of specialization of the craftsmen who worked stone during this period.

The shape and material used are similar to another ovoid rhyton from Knossos.

Selected Bibliography
Koehl 2006, p. 106 (224); Seager 1910, p. 37; Warren 1969b, p. 88 (P488a).

Emmanouela Apostolaki

211 **Ovoid Rhyton**
Late Minoan I period (ca. 1600–1450 B.C.)
Egyptian alabaster
H. 0.39 m
Archanes, Phourni, Burial Building 3
Herakleion Archaeological Museum, HM 3041

Mended.

This is a common type of ritual vessel of the Neopalatial period, with a narrow mouth, ovoid body, and rounded bottom with a discharge hole for liquids. Rhyta of this type frequently have separate attached necks and/or separate relief rings, where the neck is attached to the body, although in this example from Archanes, the vessel was made from one piece of alabaster, thereby demonstrating indirectly the skill and experience of the stone craftsman who made it. It has no handles but it does have decorative chasing on the lip and on the relief ring at the junction between the neck and body.

The rhyton was found underneath a clay burial sarcophagus, together with one silver cup and three bronze weapons in an excavation context later than the likely period of its manufacture. This indicates that the vase was preserved for a long time until it was used in a ritual or as a grave gift in the Burial Building at Archanes.

Selected Bibliography
Koehl 2006, p. 104 (212); Sakellarakis–Sapouna-Sakellaraki 1997, pp. 198, 579; Warren 1969b, p. 87.

Emmanouela Apostolaki

of the rim. Tritons are below and around the starfish, as well as on the neck of the vessel, where they are smaller. The modeled ring is decorated with groups of three vertical S-shape lines that alternate with thicker S-shape strokes. Small vertical dashes on the edge of the lip.

This shape of ovoid rhyton was as popular in stone as it was in clay and appears only in the last phase of the Neopalatial period on Crete, i.e., the Late Minoan IB period. Most examples are decorated in the Marine Style and are certainly products of palatial ceramic workshops. The outstanding, sometimes almost finicky, rendering of the details of sea organisms—and of the undersea world generally—combined with the scarcity of works in this style, have tempted some to identify the "hands" of individual painters. Scholars such as Betancourt and Müller have suggested that vessels of this type were made in pairs. Indeed, House A on the NW hill at Zakros yielded part of a similar vase, probably a twin ovoid rhyton. This hypothesis is supported by finds from other Neopalatial sites such as Knossos, Palaikastro, and Pseira, even if the practice may not have been exclusive to Marine Style rhyta but included other outstanding ritual vessels.

Ovoid rhyta, particularly the variant with a small vertical handle beneath the rim, could have served practical purposes, such as transferring liquid from a large vessel to a smaller one. If a rhyton is plunged into a larger wide-mouthed vessel containing liquid, it then fills up through the hole in its base, owing to the system of communicating vessels. By temporarily sealing the vessel's mouth with the palm of the hand, one can prevent the liquid from flowing (due to air pressure) until the mouth is unblocked.

However, there is no doubt that rhyta were mainly intended for use in libation rituals and other religious activities. Not only are they usually found in treasuries for shrines and other places of religious significance, but precious primary materials were used to manufacture stone examples of this type and they were decorated almost exclusively in the Marine Style and related styles. These decorative styles are found on a relatively limited number of examples and only on specific vase types, a fact that leads one to surmise that they are specially produced by palatial workshops, with a clearly ritualistic purpose.

From an iconographic standpoint, the well-known "Cup-bearer" (or rhyton bearer) from the "Procession Fresco" in the palace at Knossos is certainly taking part in a ritual by offering libations to a deity, probably female. Lastly, on the famous gold "Ring of Minos," a lamenting male figure is depicted shaking the sacred tree with one hand, as he holds an object in the other. This object is very like a rhyton of the type represented by the example from House A at Zakros.

212 Ovoid Rhyton with Marine Style Decoration

Late Minoan IB period (ca. 1525/1500–1450 B.C.)
Clay
H. 0.341 m
Zakros, NW hill, House A
Herakleion Archaeological Museum, HM 2085

Ovoid body, gradually narrowing to an almost conical bottom equipped with a discharge hole. Modeled ring at the transition from shoulder to neck. Reel-like neck. Flat, everted rim. Small, vertical handle under the rim ending in the middle of the neck. Mended and restored.

The vessel is decorated in the so-called Marine Style. Starfish are the central motif in the middle of the body, with concentric-circle eyes in the middle of each and simple circles between their arms. Marine rocks with coral appear on the lower part of the body and on the shoulder, neck, and upper side

Selected Bibliography
Betancourt 1985, pp. 135, 144–45; Hogarth 1902, pl. XII; Koehl 2006, pp. 31–32, 108, 264 (fig. 11); Müller 1997, pp. 25–26, 265–69, 362–63.

Lefteris Platon

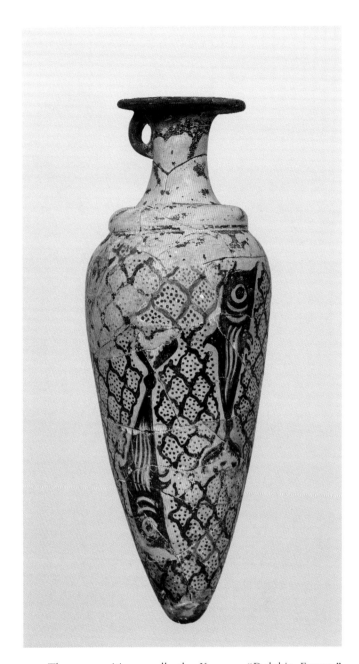

213 Dolphin Rhyton

Late Minoan IB period (ca. 1525/1500–1450 B.C.)
Clay
H. 0.285 m, rim diam. 0.07 m, max. diam. 0.099 m
Pseira
Herakleion Archaeological Museum, HM 5408

Ovoid rhyton with a broad, flat rim and a small handle with a circular section. Mended and restored. The relief collar ring marking the joint between the neck and body reflects a metal prototype.

The rhyton's shape is particularly characteristic of the Late Minoan IB period. Alternating dolphins arranged vertically cover the rhyton's body conforming to the shape of the vase. The rest of the surface is decorated with a grid of wavy lozenges filled with dots. Seaweed and coral-like motifs adorn the neck and upper lip surfaces.

The composition recalls the Knossos "Dolphin Fresco." The grid, which represents the reflection of sunlight on a calm liquid surface, and the rendering of the dolphins, with their fins pointing downward and their tails turned toward the viewer, are common to both representations.

The Dolphin rhyton is thought to form a pair with a similar Marine Style rhyton also from Pseira. Both were found together in a stepped street that leads directly from the coast to the settlement's main square. They were probably used during ritual processions that followed this route.

Selected Bibliography

Betancourt 1985, pp. 196–203; Koehl 2006, pp. 29–31, 330–32; Marinatos–Hirmer 1960, p. 94; Mountjoy 1976; *PM* II.1, pp. 223–26, II.2, pp. 507–11, IV.1, p. 269; Seager 1910, pp. 29–30.

Nektaria Mavroudi

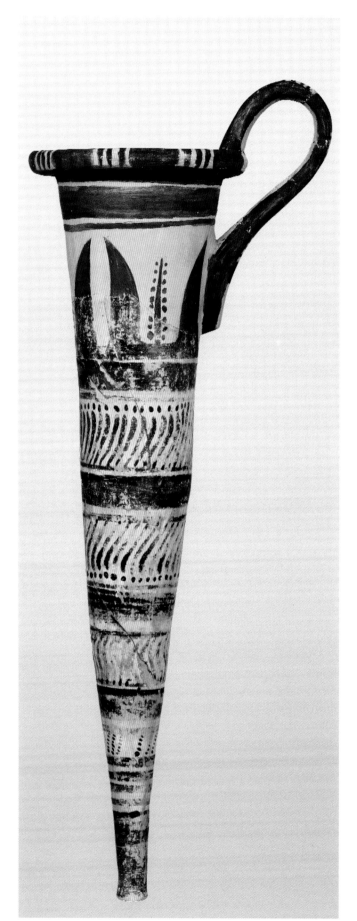

214 **Conical Rhyton**
Late Minoan IIIA2 period (ca. 1375–1300 B.C.)
Clay
H. 0.435 m
Knossos, Gypsades, House A
Herakleion Archaeological Museum, HM 2493

Elongated conical vase with pierced, pointed bottom (rhyton). Mended and restored. Parallel bands define four zones that are decorated with vertical, assymetrically parallel, linear motifs: (from bottom to top), groups of three dotted lines, sinuous lines, curved lines over dots, and curved lines below dots. Three pairs of horns of consecration, each with a leafy branch in the middle, fill the incomplete uppermost and tallest zone. The decoration was restored on the basis of similar compositions.

This vase was found on the floor of the Late Minoan IIIA2 phase of a much earlier building. The few other finds do not allow for a secure interpretation of the building's use during the Mycenaean period. The rhyton, or libation vase, is one of the most characteristic ritual vases in second millennium B.C. Crete. This particular type of rhyton was most popular during this period and until the end of the Bronze Age. Its representational decoration includes major cult symbols, which may refer to the religious ritual in which the rhyton was used. The depiction of horns of concecration on rhytons is not considered coincidental, and, indeed, such rhytons are thought to reflect the real bovine horns used for libations. Horns of consecration were usually placed on altars, with other symbols, such as double axes or even libation vases, such as jugs, at their center. On this rhyton, the horns of consecration are associated with leafy branches, which refer to the cult of the vegetal cycle. This association is particularly common in cult representations and on similar conical rhyta.

Selected Bibliography
Hogarth 1899–1900, p. 73, fig. 16; Koehl 2006, pp. 45–53; *PM* II, pp. 547–48.

Dimitris Sfakianakis

215　**Goblet of the "Communion Cup" Type**

Late Minoan IB period (ca. 1525/1500–1450 B.C.)

Gabbro

H. 0.075 m, rim diam. 0.095 m, base diam. 0.08 m

Zakros, Palace, West Wing. Room XXV (Treasury of the Shrine)

Herakleion Archaeological Museum, HM 2711

Conical main body, gradually widening upward. Straight rim. Separate spindle-shape base with the main body fitted on top. Complete.

This elegant goblet of the "communion cup" type is one of four discovered in the Treasury of the Shrine in the palace at Zakros. Of particular interest is part of another cup of the same type with bronze plating, again from Zakros. The first cups of this group, certainly products of Minoan Neopalatial workshops, were found outside Crete, in the shaft graves at Mycenae. Other examples from outside Crete have been found on Kea and Thera, two islands where Minoan cultural presence was strong.

In all, this type of ritual vase includes more than twenty examples so far. Of interest is the variety of material used in their manufacture, among which are included many stones imported to Crete from other regions, namely obsidian, a white-spotted variety from Giali on Nisyros; Spartan basalt, or *Lapis lacedaemonius*, from the Peloponnese; different polychrome marbles and veined limestone from the Aegean islands; and Egyptian alabaster. These precious, exotic primary materials, combined with the high technical proficiency of the Minoan craftsmen, enable the cups to be ranked among the finest creations of the prehistoric Aegean.

The ritual use of vessels in this particular category is not demonstrated only by the excavation context in which they occurred. On the basis of the Knossian "Campstool Fresco," which seems to have decorated the Sanctuary Hall in the West Wing of the palace at Knossos, first A. Evans and then N. Platon described a ritual act, which they called "Holy Communion." Apart from kylikes, the seated figures in the wall painting (the famous "La Parisienne" among them) are holding stemmed goblets of the type discussed here and receiving libation from ritual jugs held by standing figures. A marvelous example of a cup of comparable form is depicted on the Tiryns signet ring. A procession of daemons (*Tawaret*) is depicted offering libations to a seated goddess who is lifting a goblet of the "communion cup" type in front of her.

The iconographic evidence makes a strong case for such rituals taking place in open-air areas of the palace. Groups of priests and priestesses, each playing the part of different deities of the Minoan pantheon, would receive libations, which were probably offered by the participants in the ritual procession, in stone goblets perfectly represented by the present example from Zakros.

Selected Bibliography

Platon 1974, pp. 123–26; Platon 1959; *PM*; Warren 1969b, pp. 36–37.

Lefteris Platon

216 **Chalice**

Late Minoan I period (ca. 1600–1450 B.C.)
Veined limestone
H. 0.225 m, rim diam. 0.098 m, base diam. 0,059 m
Haghia Triada, NW Royal Apartment, Portico
Herakleion Archaeological Museum, HM 338

Mended and restored.

This kind of high conical cup without handles, conventionally called a "chalice" or "communion cup," had a long tradition in the ceramic production of Crete during the Bronze Age and appears to have been very popular in stone during the Neopalatial period. The Haghia Triada cup is made of grayish-white limestone with veining, chosen with great care by the craftsman to follow the direction of the body as it narrows toward the base, thus emphasizing the conical shape.

Luxury versions of chalices, like this example, have been interpreted as a kind of formal vessel that was used in contexts usually related to the consumption of wine and on special occasions (celebrations, festivities, ritual symposia). From this point of view, chalices reflect a perception of social behavior defined by specific rules and modes of expression. In addition to their practical use, they functioned symbolically to mark or display the formal character of a certain occasion within the palatial society.

Chalices have been found at various sites in Crete, the most impressive being a collection of such cups in a variety of stones from the palace at Zakros. A second vessel similar to the example described here was found in the same place at Haghia Triada.

Selected Bibliography
Halbherr–Stefani–Banti 1977, p. 85; Platon 2002a; Warren 1969b; Wright 2004.

Emmanouela Apostolaki

217 One-Handled Stemmed Cup-Rhyton
Late Minoan IB period (ca. 1525/1500–1450 B.C.)
Clay
H. 0.196 m, diam. rim 0.147 m, diam. base 0.066 m
Knossos, Tomb east of Hogarth's House B
Herakleion Archaeological Museum, HM 2484

Narrow-stemmed cup-rhyton with a flat, pierced off-center circular base; low foot; hemispherical body; broad, slanted rim;
and raised handle. Bands with dentate motifs, known as adder-
marks, alternating with dots, decorate the foot, body, and rim's
outer surface. Mended and restored.

Minoan rhyta (a term first used for animal-shape classical Greek
vases) are ritual vessels for liquid offerings. Their shape and
material vary; they may be conical, ovoid, spherical, or zoomorphic and made of select stones (serpentinite, chlorite, steatite,
rock crystal, strikingly veined stones) or clay. Numerous clay

rhyta are decorated with either sacred symbols (horns of consecration, double axe, sacral knot) or according to the refined
styles of the palatial workshops, like this example. A most interesting group of clay Neopalatial rhyta of various types was
found in the room C58 of the Gournia settlement.

Vases of the so-called Special Palatial Tradition, such as this
one, are characterized by refined and precise shapes influenced
by metal prototypes and by elaborate decoration, which became
increasingly schematized over the course of time.

Selected Bibliography

Betancourt 1985, pp. 185, 191 pls. 102, 196; Dimopoulou-
Rethemiotaki 2005, pp. 151–66, 223, 287; Evely 1999, p. 192;
Hogarth 1899–1900; Karetsou–Andreadaki-Vlazaki–Papadakis
2000, pp. 91–92 (Betancourt); Koehl 2006, p. 227, fig. 44: 1247.

Christina Papadaki

218 Ritual Vessel

Late Minoan IB period (ca. 1525/1500–1450 B.C.)
Clay
H. 0.406 m, max. w. 0.282 m
Zakros, Palace, east of the NE entrance, Room LXVII
Herakleion Archaeological Museum, HM 19820

Unique clay vessel made up of four hollow rings in a cruciform arrangement with a greater vertical axis. The tubular rings are joined together in such a manner as to form a continuous cavity. The system of four clay rings is crossed from top to bottom by two vertical, compact, rodlike supports. At the top, between the ends of the two supports, is a small, conical cup with upper walls curving sharply inward. The inside of the cup communicates with the cavity of the upper ring through a small hole in its bottom. Based on parallels, the entirely restored conical base has been connected to the lower ring through a hole in its upper part.

The vessel is decorated in two ways: with the attachment of small sculpted figures on selective parts and with painted decoration of different motifs all over its surface. The sculptural decoration includes two small birds with spread wings, probably doves, sitting on the two side rings; a fish diving downward on one vertical support; and a four legged animal, perhaps a wild goat or bull, although only the legs are preserved, on the base of the upper ring. Lastly, another applied figure, difficult to identify, is preserved beneath the rim of the small vessel at the top. The painted decoration includes a double axe on the cup on top with sharply curved blades and a shaft ending in a solid semicircle and rows of slanting leaves for the front surface of the rings. The upper part of the rod-shape supports is decorated with a checkerboard motif and closely spaced horizontal lines; on the right hand rod, below the checkerboard is a deformed papyrus-like plant.

The shape of this object is unique and its derivation problematic. No similar vessel is known from the Creto-Mycenaean region, and nothing comparable has been found in Cyprus, Anatolia, Syria, or Egypt. Despite this, even if the vessel is an isolated example, the upper ring with the vase growing out of it is similar to a type that was relatively popular during the Late Bronze Age in the eastern Mediterranean. In many instances, more than one miniature vessel are attached to these ring-shape objects so that they form a composite vessel—often called a *kernos*. The vertical positioning of the rings on the Zakros vessel, however, is paralleled only by a fragmentarily preserved object from the Late Minoan III cemetery at Myrsini, Siteia. It is a clay tubular ring with a small cup attached on top. Two breaks in the lower part of the ring introduce the possibility that the object was composite, in that it was connected to other hollow rings, just like the Zakros vessel.

The fact that the rings are hollow and communicate internally with each other, in combination with the vertical orientation, indicates that the maker wanted the Zakros object to be able to have a continuous flow of some kind of liquid from its upper section to the lower section. It therefore follows that there must have been an exit hole in the lower part of the lowest ring. If this is so, the hypothetical restoration of the solid conical base appears to be wrong. The object had probably been designed as a rhyton, or libation vessel, with a hole in the bottom. Of course, one cannot exclude the evacuation of liquid through a sculpted form such as a bull's head, an idea that finds support from some rather later examples of ring vases from Cyprus.

Thus, there can be no doubt as to the ritual character of the composite vessel from Zakros. Its similarity to other composite vessels—*kernoi*—supports its religious function. This hypothesis is strengthened still further by the presence of small applied sculptural figures. The birds in particular are a very common decorative theme on Minoan vessels and equipment, as early as the Prepalatial period. The worship of the so-called Dove Goddess caught A. Evans's imagination as it has other scholars of Minoan religion over the years. Today it is generally accepted that doves and birds in general are indicative of the epiphany of the Dove Goddess in her heavenly manifestation. It seems that her two other manifestations, the earthly and the chthonic, are represented on the Zakros vessel by the quadruped and the fish.

The three manifestations of the Divine (heavenly, earthly, and chthonic) appear to be common ground in different religions both ancient and modern. However, the shape—four joined circles—despite perhaps having particular local significance for the inhabitants of Zakros, is not found elsewhere. Thus, every attempt to discuss its religious or other symbolism could be considered risky, based on existing archaeological evidence.

Selected Bibliography

Karayianni 1984; *Κρητ. Χρονικά ΙΓ'* (1959): 373 (Platon); Nillson 1950, pp. 331–40; Platon 1990.

Lefteris Platon

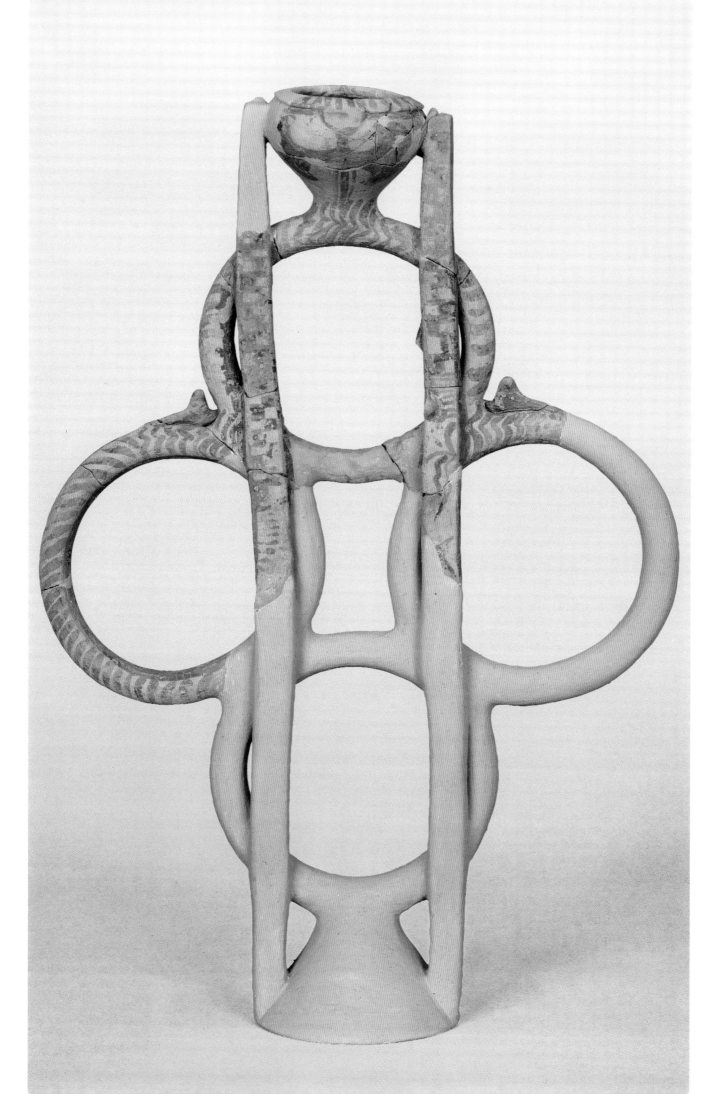

219A–B Ritual Vessels with Figure-of-Eight Handles
Late Minoan IB period (ca. 1525/1500–1450 B.C.)
Clay
219A (HM 13927): H. 0.309 m, w. 0.323 m
219B (HM 14006): H. 0.314 m, w. (at point of contact
of handles) 0.33 m, base diam. 0.107 m, rim diam.
0.246 m
Zakros, Palace, West Wing, Room XI
Herakleion Archaeological Museum, HM 13927,
14006

Ledged disc base, mended and restored. Almost cylindrical body below, opening like a funnel toward the top. Flat, everted rim. On opposite sides of the mouth, two figure-of-eight handles coiled and raised above the rim. A perforated division on the interior below the rim, with a series of small perforations around the edge and a larger hole in the center. Sporadic traces of brown to red-brown paint.

These are two of four restored examples of this type from Zakros. They were found together in the West Wing of the palace, in the same excavation context with a large number of piriform jars decorated with successive zones of plant and geometric motifs. The excavator thought that this important group had fallen to the ground floor from the upper-story apartment when the building was destroyed.

The peculiar treatment of the interior of the vessels, with a perforated division, is found in comparable vases from the West House in the Late Cycladic I settlement of Akrotiri, Thera. The two Theran vases are frustum-shape and decorated on the exterior with white lilies painted on a brown ground. S. Marinatos called them "flowerpots" and suggested that the central cavity was used for bunches of flowers, while the smaller ones around it were for individual flowers.

Works of art that depict flowerpots of a comparable type filled with lilies were found carefully painted on the window frames of the same house. These vases were rendered with multicolored spots, suggesting that they were made from some veined stone. Both the position of the wall paintings and the depiction of marbled dadoes beneath the flowerpots unquestionably confirm the custom of placing real flowerpots and potted plants on the windowsills of houses in the prehistoric Aegean.

Also termed "flower-pots" are cylindrical vases with everted rims and perforated interior partitions. They too are decorated with lilies and come from the palatial building at Archanes. Vases of comparable shape and decoration, but without the perforated interior partition, have been found both at Akroteri, Thera, and at Knossos, and their use as vases for flowers seems perfectly plausible.

A vase from the Isopata Royal Tomb at Knossos is very similar to the Zakros vases, even though it has no perforated partition within the vase. It is decorated outside with helmets and interlocking spirals. A depiction of a similar vessel, proffered to a deity, occurs on a clay matrix of a signet ring found at Knossos, as well as on a sealing from Zakros. And, last of all, frustum-shape vessels with raised handles at the rim are depicted in the libation offering scene on the Haghia Triada sarcophagus. These vases are carried by priestesses, who empty their contents (probably a liquid, perhaps even the blood of the sacrificed bull) into a large krater depicted at the far left of the scene.

Even if their ritual character seems indisputable, the parallels from Akroteri and Archanes support the hypothesis that, on a practical level at least, these peculiar Zakros vessels were used as flowerpots. Furthermore, the general shape of flowerpots represented in Aegean wall paintings, in and outside Crete, is similar to the vases in question. The decoration of Minoan palaces and villas with beautiful and different varieties of plants and flowers, whether planted in gardens or placed in pots, seems to serve both aesthetic and religious standards. There are many examples in Minoan art of ceremonial scenes of a religious nature directly linked to the ideological circle of the death and rebirth of vegetation and, by extension, of nature itself.

Selected Bibliography
Έργον 1989 (Αρχάνες), p. 145, fig. 136; Long 1974, p. 36, pl. 15; Marinatos 1971, p. 37, pls. 83?84; Marinatos 1977, pls. 49–51; Platonos 1987; *PM*.

Lefteris Platon

220 Squat Alabastron

Late Minoan II–IIIA2 period (ca. 1450–1350/1300 B.C.)
Limestone
H. 0.117 m, max. diam. 0.463 m, rim diam. 0.225 m
Knossos, Palace, Throne Room
Herakleion Archaeological Museum, HM 884

Very squat hemispherical body with three horizontal handles, a very short cylindrical neck, and a broad rim decorated with a relief running spiral. Mended and restored.

This is one of at least seven similar vases (some with a lid) found by Arthur Evans on the floor of the Throne Room, together with fragments of a large storage jar. Although the shape is peculiar, the craftsmanship on these vases recalls a palatial lapidary workshop.

Squat alabastra appear in Crete from the Late Minoan II period onward, possibly reflecting Mycenaean influence. Other than the group from the Throne Room, only few other stone examples are known, from graves at Sellopoulo near Knossos and from Mycenae and Asine. Similar vessels made of clay are more common, but these too occur primarily in funerary contexts and bear fine, elaborate decoration.

The shape and the heavy weight of the stone alabastra from the Throne Room, combined with the limited relevant excavation evidence, prevent us from drawing firm conclusions about their use. Arthur Evans assumed that olive oil was transferred into the alabastra from the storage jar found nearby by means of a scoop, like the one found together with a similar vase in a grave at Vapheio, Lakonia. Their presence in the Throne Room—which, together with the adjacent lustral basin, the anteroom, and the auxiliary rooms on the north and west, constitute one of the most official and sacred areas in the palace—demonstrates the distinctiveness of these vessels and confirms their use in some ritual of particular importance.

Selected Bibliography

Magrill 1987; Marinatos 1993, pp. 106–9; *PM*, IV.2, pp. 936–40, fig. 910; Von Arbin 1984; Warren 1969b, pp. 4–6, 71, pls. 11, 12; Warren 1989; Waterhouse 1988.

Deukalion Manidakis

221 Twenty Conical Cups

Early in Late Minoan IA period (ca. 1600 B.C.)
Clay
H. 0.039–0.034 m, rim diam. 0.076–0.067 m, base diam.
0.039–3.332 m
Nopighia, Kissamos, ritual deposit
Kissamos Archaeological Museum, P 765–784

Complete or almost complete cups without handles carelessly made, with white concretions of the surface in places The cups have a conical body; a narrow, usually flat base; and a rounded rim. They are but a few of the thousands of cups that constitute—together with a few bell-shape cups, cooking pots, braziers, and other domestic vessels and animal bones—the deposit excavated in the Drapanias-Nopighia region at Kissamos. The find consists of a long, narrow cutting that was filled with consecutive ritual deposits over a short period of time. It is dated to a troubled period, when the southeast Aegean was plagued by continuous seismic tremors that culminated in the eruption of the Theran volcano.

Selected Bibliography

Andreadaki-Vlazaki 1994–96; Andreadaki-Vlazaki (in press).

Eftychia Protopapadaki

222 **Jug with Painted and Relief Decoration**

Late Minoan IIIA1 period (ca. 1400–1375 B.C.)
Clay
H. 0.452 m, max. body diam. 0.265 m, base diam. 0.182 m
Knossos, Little Palace, Rooms 28, 29
Herakleion Archaeological Museum, HM 5749

Jug with a spherical body, low foot, ring base, tall neck, beak-shaped spout, and raised strap handle. Rows of conical projections decorate the shoulder, rim, and spout. A relief ivy-leaf adorns the neck. Relief bands form four four-sided panels with thickly painted wavy lines in between. On three panels painted heart-shaped motifs surround a relief ornament that represents a highly stylized sacral knot with a trilobed top. In the fourth panel, below the handle, a relief bilobed ornament and painted scale patterns possibly represent a seascape. Mended and restored.

This jug was found in the Little Palace at Knossos, along with such finds as a bull's-head rhyton, clay alabastra, and a stepped steatite stand. Both its shape and its decoration are singular. The tall neck, strap handle, conical projections, and relief bands on the body indicate metal prototypes, on which rows of rivets were used to hold different parts of the vase together. Both the shape and relief decoration closely resemble those of a jug from Tomb B at Katsambas. The schematic rendering of the sacred knot with trilobed top derive from earlier representations of this motif in combination with a double axe.

The vase's excavation context and characteristics, as well as the presence of religious symbols, such as the sacral knot and ivy leaf, suggest a symbolic ritual use. Jugs often appear in Minoan religious representations, primarily on seals. They are usually placed in the hands of daemonic figures in association with horns of consecration, ivy leaves, and other plant motifs. A similar jug is depicted on the famous Haghia Triada sarcophagus, in a scene showing offerings at an altar before a double axe and a sanctuary.

Most scholars agree that the use of such vases in rituals is related to the cycle of vegetation and the regeneration of nature.

Selected Bibliography
Alexiou 1952, pp. 25–41; Alexiou 1967, pp. 44, 59–61, pls. 5, 6; Dimopoulou-Rethemiotaki 1999a, pp. 218–20; Evans 1914, pp. 75–78, fig. 86; Hatzaki 2005, pp. 109–10, 119, 174, fig. 4.32, pl. 20b–d; Niemeier 1985, pp. 117–18, abb. 57; Platonos-Yiota 1995, pp. 777–78; Warren 2005, pp. 225–26.

Deukalion Manidakis

223 Ritual Double Jug

Late Minoan IIIA2 period (ca. 1350–1300 B.C.)
Ultra-white fine clay
H. with handle 0.208 m, max. base diam. 0.047 m
Khania, Karabinakis-Sinanis plot, 1987
Khania Archaeological Museum, Π 6339

This complete vase consists of two pear-shape jugs connected by a horizontal tripartite tube and a basket handle. The top of the closed jug is shaped like an animal head with pellet eyes, a short muzzle, and long ears that rest upon the high-swung handle. The open jug has a tall neck, a strainer, and an outwardly curved rim with a slight spout. The strainer consists of several small holes and one larger hole. A small bird figurine sits near the handle.

Closely arranged painted decoration covers the vase. Dots adorn the animal's face and neck, and circles denote its eyes and mouth. Fine bands and a wavy line outline the ears, and stylized flowers decorate the body of the closed jug. A wide band and vertical strokes adorn the open jug's rim. Circles surround the strainer holes. A band and repeated semicircles decorate the jug's neck, and a bird with a fine beak, large wings, and an open tail, among stylized flowers, occupies the body.

A ritual vessel of Cretan type known since Prepalatial times, the double jug is a popular offering in Minoan graves of the Mycenaean period. It occurs at various funerary sites in Crete, particularly at Khania. The double jug is most common, but quite a few examples of double baskets are also known. A popular product of the local Kydonia workshop, this vase displays the animal head with painted and relief decoration that appears on another four similar examples. It comes from a pit cave, part of a group of seventeen graves (chamber tombs, pit caves, and pit graves) situated in the west section of the Kydonia cemetery.

Selected Bibliography
Hallager–McGeorge 1992, p. 19; Karayianni 1984.

Sophia Preve

224 Composite Vase

Late Minoan IIIA2 period (ca. 1375–1300 B.C.)
Clay
H. with handle 0.22 m, max. diam. 0.20 m
Myrsini, site of Asprospelia, Tomb IB
Haghios Nikolaos Archaeological Museum, 1973

A complete triple vase for ritual use, made up of a wide-mouthed jug and two closed jugs; a high, arched double handle. The three vases, arranged in a triangle, are joined to each other at the belly by three cylindrical tubular stems. There is both relief and painted decoration. Applied to the mouth of the closed jugs are a bucranium (bull head) and a bird; there are two small birds on the lip of the open jug. Three of the birds are restored in gypsum.

The relief decoration on the composite vase in the form of sacred symbols shows that it had a cult function. The double horns, a well-known sacred symbol in Minoan religion, just like bucrania, refer to the bull, the sacred animal of the Minoans. The birds were the symbol of the epiphany of the divinity.

Selected Bibliography

Davaras n.d., p. 26, fig. 55; Karayianni 1984, p. 97; Κρητ. Χρονικά ΙΓ΄ (1959), pp. 372–73 (Platon).

Chrysa Sophianou

Human destiny—or the fate of humans after death—greatly preoccupied the Minoans, as it did many other prehistoric peoples. Representations on clay sarcophagi, particularly the sarcophagus from Haghia Triada, indicate that the Minoans believed in the continuation of life in another world, a concept similar to that of the Christian paradise. This peaceful land, like the Homeric description of the Elysian Fields as an evergreen garden where the blessed dead would live forever in joy, is evoked in the images on many Postpalatial clay sarcophagi (ca. 1300–1100 B.C.). Depictions of plants, trees, mammals, birds, and marine creatures inhabit the metaphysical land that was believed to be the final destination for human beings.

Clay sarcophagi served as coffins for the dead and were placed in graves. The dead were positioned in a seated position, curled up like embryos in utero, perhaps expressing a return to the beginning of life and serving as a symbolic harbinger of new life to come.

Beginning about 1200 B.C., cremation of the dead began to occur occasionally and eventually became standard practice in the early Hellenic years. The ashes were put into burial pithoi, or storage vessels, and placed inside communal tombs, together with grave gifts.

Detail of cat. no. 227

225 **Sarcophagus**
Late Minoan IIIA2 period (ca. 1375–1300 B.C.)
Clay
H. 0.75 m, l. 1.29 m, w. 0.48 m
Armenoi, Late Minoan cemetery, Tomb 10
Rethymnon Archaeological Museum, Π 1710

Mended, feet restored. The body of this rectangular clay sarcophagus is supported on four feet, and a molded frame, wider over the feet, surrounds each side. Two holes at the top of each side were used for securing the lid, now lost. Twelve holes in the bottom allowed the purification liquids to flow out. Pairs of monochrome painted bulls facing to the right are arrayed along the long sides. The body of one bull is decorated with rosettes and semicircles. Horns of consecration fill the empty spaces on the panels and on the frame's vertical section. One of the short sides has a striding deer with a papyrus flower over its back and horns of consecration with a double axe in the middle. A large papyrus-like flower occupies the other short side.

This is a typical example of the large group of sarcophagi from the Armenoi cemetery decorated with representational art. The use of clay sarcophagi was particularly widespread in the Armenoi cemetery, as in the rest of Crete, except for the Khania area, where wooden biers were used, in accordance with Mycenaean customs. Sarcophagi were decorated with animal and plant motifs, as well as with ritual symbols, and a combination of these motifs is evident on this example. Bulls, a deer, and a flower are associated with horns of consecration and a double axe—the most common sacred symbols of Minoan iconography. The frequent presence of bulls and sacred symbols on sarcophagi is believed to reflect the religious and burial practices of that period.

Selected Bibliography
Löwe 1996; Rutkowski 1968; Sakellarakis–Sapouna-Sakellaraki 1997; Tzedakis 1971; Watrous 1991.

Panagiota Karamaliki

226 **Sarcophagus**
Late Minoan IIIA2–B period (ca. 1350–1200 B.C.)
Clay
H. (with lid) 0.75 m, l. 0.95 m, w. 0.40 m
Armenoi, Late Minoan cemetery
Rethymnon Archaeological Museum, Π 1703

Clay, box-shape sarcophagus with gabled lid. Black painted decoration. The shape, essentially cuboid, is supported on four protruding feet. The lid has a curved back that juts out at each end and is surrounded by a ledged border that is deeper at the ends. A series of eight holes in the upper part of the box and ten in the lid were used to hold a rope for tying the parts together and holding them fast. The sarcophagus is complete, but the lid is slightly restored.

Three schematic octopuses in a row are represented in the main decorative zone of one long side. The other long side has an array of three horns of consecration; a double axe with a handle is fixed at the center of the horns. The upper part of the field is decorated with the zone of isolated spirals. On one short side, there is a somewhat abstract representation of a plant with acanthus-like excrescences in the upper part. Three rhomboid elements filled with chevrons appear as fill ornaments above the plant. On the other short side, a papyrus-like flower with a triple vertical stem and a radiating tuft is depicted inclining toward the right. The lid has similar decoration with groups of concentric arcs arranged antithetically on both sides.

In the Final Palatial period, the use of clay sarcophagi in tombs for depositing the dead in a contracted position is quite common. The cemetery at Armenoi has yielded by far the largest known group of sarcophagi of the period. The sarcophagus frequently highlights its origin as a wooden form and displays a relationship with contemporary vase painting. It is generally thought that the subject matter on sarcophagi reflects the religious perceptions of the period, since sacred symbols are very often present. It has also been claimed that the representations are echoes of religious rituals, and that by using religious symbols, they express a close connection to religious ceremonies. It is common to see animal and plant motifs, such as the octopus, in the iconography of sarcophagi. Similarly, the flowers on the narrow sides—particularly the papyrus—often make an appearance as decoration on sarcophagi of the Late Minoan III period, probably to give a suggestion of scenery.

Selected Bibliography
Long 1974; Löwe 1996; Rutkowski 1968; Sakellarakis–Sapouna-Sakellaraki 1997; Tzedakis 1971; Watrous 1991.

Panagiota Karamaliki

227 Bathtub-Shape Larnax

Late Minoan IIIC period (ca. 1200–1100 B.C.)
Clay
H. 0.47 m, l. 1.00 m, w. 0.60 m
Siteia, Petras, chamber tomb
Haghios Nikolaos Archaeological Museum, 262

Flat ledged base, elliptical body, and four horizontal cylindrical handles, one on each side. The lip is squared in section and inverted, with a ridge underneath. There is a hole in the bottom. Complete.

This larnax (clay coffin) has painted decoration all over the body, both inside and out. In the middle of the two long external sides, two octopuses are depicted with wavy tentacles embracing the whole exterior surface of the vessel. In the interior, two fish are depicted along with pendant semicircles, perhaps imitating rocks. In the bottom, dense wavy bands represent sea waves.

Marine subjects, and octopuses in particular, were favorite decorative motifs on Minoan larnakes throughout the Late Minoan period. Doubtless there was some symbolic connection of significance between the sea and Minoan perceptions concerning death.

Based on its typological features (shape, manufacturing details, decorative motifs and their execution), this particular larnax was made by a workshop or a craftsman whose products have been found at other sites in the broader Siteia region (Haghios Georgios–Tourtouloi and Piskokephalo) within a ten-kilometer radius of Petras.

Selected Bibliography
Laffineur 1991; Marinatos 1993, pp. 231–32; Tsipopoulou–Vagnetti 1997, figs. CLXXXI, CLXXXIIIa; Watrous 1991.

Yiannis Papadatos

228 Pyxis/Cinerary Urn

Late Minoan IIIC period (ca. 1200–1100 B.C.)
Clay
H. 0.34 m, body diam. 0.36 m, rim diam. 0.16 m
Kritsa–Katharo
Haghios Nikolaos Archaeological Museum, 173

Complete. The decorative motifs on this vessel are arranged in panels. Dominating the two central panels on the main side are highly stylized horns of consecration and a schematic double axe with fringed and dotted outlines and fill decoration.

Both the horns and the axe are among the most sacred Minoan religious symbols and are linked to the cult function of this vessel, which was to contain a cremation and take the place of the sarcophagus. This is demonstrated by the decorative motifs, which clearly relate to Minoan eschatological sentiments. The double axe is one of the most sacred symbols of Minoan religion, which is why it is found in all shapes and sizes among dedicatory offerings.

The shape of vase is known from tombs and settlements alike (Karphi, Phaistos, Palaikastro, Kastri, Praisos, Vrokastro, and Mouliana), and even the decorative motifs are relatively common on pyxides of this period. Pyxides with similar decoration from settlements would have also have had a ritual use.

The two funerary urns that came from the same tomb, which was excavated on the road from Kritsa to the Katharo plateau, are two of the earliest cremations of the Late Minoan IIIC period, during which time the practice of cremation was adopted, a burial custom linked with the arrival of new groups of people.

The discovery of a ceramic wheel may indicate that one of the deceased was a potter.

Selected Bibliography

Alexiou 1954, pp. 404–12; Borda 1946, pl. XXXVI; Davaras 1973b, pp. 162–63; Kanta 1980, pp. 138, 282–83, figs. 54.4, 5; Platon 1951a; Popham 1967, 349–50, figs. b–c. 90; Seiradaki 1960, fig. 24 a2; Tsipopoulou–Little 2001; Tsipopoulou–Vagnetti 2006, fig. 2e.

Vasiliki Zographaki

GENERAL BIBLIOGRAPHY

Akrivaki 2003
Akrivaki, N. "Τοιχογραφία με παράσταση οδοντόφρακτου κράνους από την Ξεστή 4 του Ακρωτηρίου Θήρας." In Vlachopoulos and Birtacha, eds. Αργοναύτης (2003), pp. 527–41.

Alberti 2004
Alberti, L. "Οι νεκροπόλεις της Κνωσού κατά την υστερομινωική ΙΙ–ΙΙΙΑ1 περίοδο." Ph.D. diss. Athens, 2004.

Alexiou 1951
Alexiou, S. "Πρωτομινωικαί ταφαί παρά το Κανλί Καστέλλι Ηρακλείου." Κρητ. Χρονικά Ε′ (1951): 275–94.

Alexiou 1952
Alexiou, S. "Νέα στοιχεία δια την υστέραν αιγαιακήν χρονολογίαν και ιστορίαν." Κρητ. Χρονικά ΣΤ′ (1952): 9–41.

Alexiou 1954
Alexiou, S. "Υστερομινωικός τάφος Παχυάμμου." Κρητ. Χρονικά Η′ (1954): 399–412.

Alexiou 1958
Alexiou, S. "Η μινωική θεά μεθ′ υψωμένων χειρών." Κρητ. Χρονικά ΙΒ′ (1958): 179–299.

Alexiou 1967
Alexiou, S. Υστερομινωικοί τάφοι λιμένος Κνωσού (Κατσαμπά). Βιβλιοθήκη της εν Αθήναις Αρχαιολογικής Εταιρείας 56. Athens, 1967.

Alexiou–Warren 2004
Alexiou, S., and P. Warren. The Early Minoan Tombs of Lebena, Southern Crete. SIMA 30. Savedalen, 2004.

Andreadaki-Vlazaki (in press)
Andreadaki-Vlazaki, M. "Τελετουργικές αποθέσεις των νεοανα-κτορικών χρόνων στη Δυτική Κρήτη." In Πεπραγμένα του Ι′ Διεθνούς Κρητολογικού Συνεδρίου, Khania, 1–8 October 2006 (in press).

Andreadaki-Vlazaki 1994–96
Andreadaki-Vlazaki, M. "Προϊστορικός οικισμός στα Νοπήγεια Κισάμου." Κρητική Εστία, Περίοδος Δ′-Τόμος 5. Khania, 1994–96, pp. 11–45.

Andreadaki-Vlazaki 1997
Andreadaki-Vlazaki, M. "La nécropole du Minoen Récent III de la ville de la Canée." In Driessen and Farnoux, eds. La Crète Mycénienne, 1997, pp. 487–509.

Andreadaki-Vlazaki–Hallager 2007
Andreadaki-Vlazaki, M., and E. Hallager. "New and Unpublished Linear A and Linear B Inscriptions from Khania." In Proceedings of the Danish Institute at Athens V. Athens, 2007, pp. 7–22.

Andreadaki-Vlazaki–Papadopoulou 2005
Andreadaki-Vlazaki, M., and E. Papadopoulou. "The Habitation at Khamalevri, Rethymnon during the 12th Century B.C." In D'Agata and Moody, eds. Ariadne's Threads (2005), pp. 353–97.

Andrikou 2003
Andrikou, E. "La musique dans le monde grec préhistorique." In Andrikou et al., eds. Dons des Muses (2003), pp. 20–25.

Andrikou et al. 2003
Andrikou, E., et al., eds. Dons des Muses. Musique et danse dans la Grèce ancienne. Exh. cat. Athens, 2003.

Apostolakou 1998
Apostolakou, V. "Υστερομινωικοί τάφοι στη Γρα Λυγιά Ιεράπετρας." ΑΔ 53 (1998): 25–88.

Arnott 1999
Arnott, R. "War Wounds and other Treatment in the Aegean Bronze Age." In Laffineur, ed. Polemos (1999), pp. 499–504.

Åström–Reese 1990
Åström, P., and D. S. Reese. "Triton Shells in East Mediterranean Cults." JPR 3–4 (1990): 5–14.

Athanasopoulou-Tzedakis 2003
Athanasopoulou, S., and Y. Tzedakis, eds. Ο ταύρος στο μεσογειακό κόσμο. Μύθοι και λατρείες. Exh. cat. Πολιτιστική Ολυμπιάδα 2001–4. Barcelona–Athens, 2003.

Avila 1983
Avila, A. J. Bronzene Lanzen–und Pfeilspitzen der griechischen Spätbronzezeit. Prähistorische Bronzefunde 5, 1. Munich, 1983.

Banou 1990
Banou, E. "Οδοντόφρακτο κράνος από τους Αρμένους Ρεθύμνης." In Πεπραγμένα του Στ′ Διεθνούς Κρητολογικού Συνεδρίου (Χανιά 24–30 Αυγ. 1986). Α2. Khania, 1990, pp. 39–47.

Banou 2005
Banou, E. "LM III Mokhlos (East Crete) Versus LM III Viannos (Central Eastern Crete): Differences and Similiarities." In D'Agata and Moody, eds. Ariadne's Threads (2005), pp. 145–73.

Banti 1930–31
Banti, L. "La grande tomba a tholos di Haghia Triada." ASAtene 13–14 (1930–31): 155–251.

Banti 1939–40
Banti, L. "Chronologia e ceramica del palazzo minoico di Festos." ASAtene 1–2 (1939–40): 9–39.

Barnard–Brogan 2003
Barnard, K. A., and Th. Brogan. Mochlos IB, Period III. Neopalatial Settlement on the Coast, the Artisans' Quarter and the Farmhouse at Chalinomouri. The Neopalatial Pottery. Prehistory Monographs 8. Philadelphia, 2003.

Bass 1986
Bass, G. F. "A Bronze Age Shipwreck at Ulu Burun (Kas): 1984 Campaign." AJA 90 (1986): 269–96.

Baurain–Darcque 1983
Baurain, C., and P. Darcque. "Un triton en pierre à Malia." BCH 107 (1983): 3–58.

Bennett 1985
Bennet, J. "The Structure of the Linear B Administration at Knossos." AJA 89 (1985): 231–49.

Betancourt 1980
Betancourt, P. P. Cooking Vessels from Minoan Kommos. A Preliminary Report. Los Angeles, 1980.

Betancourt 1985
Betancourt, P. P. The History of Minoan Pottery. Princeton, 1985.

Betancourt 1998
Betancourt, P. P. "The Legged Flask from Pseira." In
V. Karageorghis and N. Stampolidis, eds. *Eastern Mediterranean.
Cyprus–Dodecanese–Crete 16th–6th cent. B.C. Proceedings of the
International Symposium held at Rethymnon, Crete, in May 1997.*
Athens, 1998, pp. 49–52.

Betancourt 1999
Betancourt, P. P. "What is Minoan? FN/EM I in the Gulf of
Mirabello Region." In Betancourt et al., eds. *Meletemata 1999*,
pp. 33–39.

Betancourt et al. 1979
Betancourt, P. P., T. K. Gaisser, E. Koss, R. F. Lyon, F. R. Matson,
S. Montgomery, G. H. Myer, and C. P. Swann. *Vasilike Ware. An
Early Bronze Age Pottery Style in Crete: Results of the Philadelphia
Vasilike Ware Project.* SIMA 56. Gothenburg, 1979.

Betancourt et al. 1999
Betancourt, P. P., V. Karageorghis, R. Laffineur, and W.-D.
Niemeier, eds. *Meletemata: Studies in Aegean Archaeology
Presented to Malcolm H. Wiener as He Enters His 65th Year.*
Aegaeum 20. Liege and Austin, 1999.

Betancourt–Davaras 1999
Betancourt, P. P., and C. Davaras. *Pseira IV. Minoan Buildings in
Areas B, C, D and F.* University Museum Monograph 105.
Philadelphia, 1999.

Betancourt–Muhly 2006
Betancourt, P. P., and J. D. Muhly. "The sistra from the Minoan
Burial Cave at Hagios Charalambos." In E. Czerny, I. Hein,
H. Hunger, D. Melman, and A. Schwab, eds. *Timelines. Studies
in Honour of Manfred Bietak.* Vol. 2. Orientalia Lovaniensia
Analecta 149. Leuven–Paris–Dudley, 2006, pp. 429–36.

Boardman 1961
Boardman, J. *The Cretan Collection in Oxford. The Dictaen Cave
and Iron Age Crete.* Oxford, 1961.

Borchhardt 1972
Borchhardt, J. *Homerische Helme. Helmformen der Ägäis in ihren
Beziehungen zu orientalischen und europäischen Helmen in der
Bronze- und frühen Eisenzeit.* Mainz, 1972.

Borda 1946
Borda, M. *Arte cretese micenea nel Museo Pigorini di Roma.*
Rome, 1946.

Bosanquet 1901–2
Bosanquet, R. C. "Excavations at Palaikastro." *BSA* 8 (1901–2):
286–316.

Bosanquet–Dawkins 1923
Bosanquet, R. C., and R. M. Dawkins. *The Unpublished Objects
from the Palaikastro Excavations, 1902–1906.* BSA Suppl. Paper 1.
London, 1923.

Boulotis 1989
Boulotis, Chr. "La déesse minoenne à la rame gouvernail."
In *TROPIS I. Proceedings of the 1st International Symposium on
Ship Construction in Antiquity. Piraeus 1985.* Athens, 1989,
pp. 55–73.

Boulotis 1996
Boulotis, Chr. "Η ελιά και το λάδι στις ανακτορικές κοινωνίες
της Κρήτης και της μυκηναϊκής Ελλάδας: ό ψεις και απόψεις."
In *Ελιά και λάδι. Τριήμερο Εργασίας, Καλαμάτα 7-9 Μαϊου 1993.*
Athens, 1996, pp. 19–58.

Bradfer-Burdet–Detournay–Laffineur 2005
Bradfer-Burdet, Is., B. Detournay, and R. Laffineur, eds. *Κρης
Τεχνίτης. L'Artisan Crétois. Recueil d' articles en l' honneur de
Jean-Claude Poursat, publié à l'occasion des 40 ans de la découverte
du Quartier Mu.* Aegaeum 26. Liège and Austin, 2005.

Branigan 1968
Branigan, K. *Copper and Bronze Working in Early Bronze Age
Crete.* SIMA 19. Lund, 1968.

Branigan 1971
Branigan, K. "Cycladic Figurines and Their Derivatives in Crete."
BSA 66 (1971): 57–78.

Branigan 1974
Branigan, K. *Aegean Metalwork of the Early and Middle Bronze
Age.* Oxford, 1974.

Branigan 1983
Branigan, K. "Gold and Goldworking in the Early Bronze Age
Crete." *TUAS* 8 (1983): 15–20.

Branigan 1987
Branigan, K. "Ritual Interference with Human Bones in the
Mesara Tholoi." In R. Laffineur, ed. *Thanatos. Les coutumes
funéraires en Egée à l'Age du Bronze. Actes colloque de Liege,
21–23 avril 1986.* Aegaeum 1. Liège, 1987, pp. 43–51.

Branigan 1991
Branigan, K. "Mochlos—An Early Aegean 'Gateway Community'?"
In R. Laffineur and L. Basch, eds. *Thalassa: L'Égée préhistorique
et la mer. Actes de la troisième Rencontre égéenne internationale
de l'Université de Liège, Station de recherches sous-marines et
océanographiques (StaReSO), Calvi, Corse (23–25 avril 1990).*
Aegaeum 7. Liège, 1991, pp. 97–105.

Branigan 1993
Branigan, K. *Dancing with Death: Life and Death in Southern
Crete, c. 3000–2000 BC.* Amsterdam, 1993.

Brice 1961
Brice, W. C., ed. *Inscriptions in the Minoan Linear Script of Class A.*
Oxford, 1961.

Brogan 2006
Brogan, Th. "Tipping the Scales: Evidence for Weight Measure-
ment from the Wider Neopalatial Community at Mochlos."
In M. E. Alberti, E. Ascalone, and L. Peyronel, eds. *Weights in
Context. Bronze Age Weighing Systems of Eastern Mediterranean.
Chronology, Typology, Material and Archaeological Context.
Proceedings of the International Colloquium, Rome, 22–24
November 2004.* Rome, 2006, pp. 265–92.

Buchholz 1959
Buchholz, H. G. *Zur Herkunft der kretischen Doppelaxt.
Geschichte und auswärtige Beziehungen eines minoischen
Kultsymbols.* Munich, 1959.

Cadogan 1976
Cadogan, G. "Some Faience, Blue Frit and Glass from Fifteenth Century Knossos." In P. P. Betancourt, ed. *TUAS* 1 (1976): 18–19.

Cadogan–Hatzaki–Vasilakis 2004
Cadogan, G., E. Hatzaki, and A. Vasilakis, eds. *Knossos: Palace, City, State. Proceedings of the Conference in Herakleion organized by the British School at Athens and the 23rd Ephoreia of Prehistoric and Classical Antiquities of Herakleion, in November 2000, for the Centenary of Sir Arthur Evan's Excavations at Knossos.* BSA Studies 12. London, 2004.

Cameron 1968
Cameron, M. A. S. "A Graffito Related to a Myrtle Composition on a Minoan Fresco from Knossos." *Kadmos* 7 (1968): 97–99.

Carinci 1997
Carinci, F. M. "Pottery Workshops at Phaistos and Haghia Triada in the Protopalatial Period." In Laffineur and Betancourt, eds. *Τέχνη* (1997), pp. 317–22.

Carter 1994
Carter, T. "Southern Aegean Fashion Victims: An Overlooked Aspect of Early Bronze Age Burial Practices." In N. Ashton and A. David, eds. *Stories in Stone.* Lithic Studies Society Occasional Paper 4. London, 1994, pp. 127–44.

Carter 1998
Carter, T. "Reverberations of the International Spirit: Thoughts upon 'Cycladica' in the Mesara." In K. Branigan, ed. *Cemetery and Society in the Aegean Bronze Age.* Sheffield, 1998, pp. 59–77.

Catling 1979–80
Catling, H. W. "Archaeology in Greece, 1979–1980." *AR* 26 (1979–80): 3–53.

Catling–Catling 1984
Catling, H. W., and E. Catling. "The Bronzes and Metalworking Equipment." In Popham, ed. *The Minoan Unexplored Mansion* (1984), pp. 203–22.

Chadwick et al. 1986
Chadwick, J., L. Godart, J. T. Killen, J. P. Olivier, A. Sacconi, and I. A. Sakellarakis. *Corpus of Mycenaean Inscriptions from Knossos.* Vol. 1. Incunabula Graeca 88. Cambridge, New York, and Rome, 1986.

Chatzi-Speliopoulou 2002
Chatze-Speliopoulou, G. "Μυκηναϊκό γυαλί." In G. Kordas and A. Antonaras, eds. *Ιστορία και τεχνολογία αρχαίου γυαλιού.* Athens, 2002, pp. 63–87.

Chatzoudi 2002
Chatzoudi, A. "Νεολιθικός οικισμός Σταυρούπολης Θεσσαλονίκης. Προκαταρκτική μελέτη των οστέινων αντικειμένων." In D. B. Grammenos and S. Kotsos, eds. *Σωστικές ανασκαφές στο νεολιθικό οικισμό Σταυρούπολης Θεσσαλονίκης. Δημοσιεύματα του Αρχαιολογικού Ινστιτούτου Βόρειας Ελλάδας 2.* Thessaloniki, 2002, pp. 609–26.

Chouliara-Raios 1989
Chouliara-Raios, H. *L'abeille et le miel en Egypte d' après les papyrus grecs.* Δωδώνη Suppl. 30. Ioannina, 1989.

Christakis 2005
Christakis, K. *Cretan Bronze Age Pithoi. Traditions and Trends in the Production and Consumption of Storage Containers in Bronze Age Crete.* Prehistory Monographs 18. Philadelphia, 2005.

D'Agata–Moody 2005
D'Agata, A.-L., and J. Moody, eds. *Ariadne's Threads: Connections between Crete and the Greek Mainland in the Post Palatial Period (Late Minoan III A2 to LM IIIC). Proceedings of the International Workshop held at Athens, Scuola Archeologica Italiana, 5–6 April 2003.* Tripodes 3. Athens, 2005.

Darcque 1983
Darcque, P. "Les coquillages en pierre, en terre cuite et en faience dans le monde égéen (Annexe)." *BCH* 107 (1983): 59–73.

Davaras 1969
Davaras, C. "Trois bronzes minoens de Skoteino." *BCH* 93 (1969): 620–50.

Davaras 1971
Davaras, C. "Πρωτομινωικόν νεκροταφείον Αγίας Φωτιάς Σητείας." *AAA* 4 (1971): 392–96.

Davaras 1973–74
Davaras, C. "Cremations in Minoan and Subminoan Crete." In *Antichità Cretesi. Studi in onore di Doro Levi, I.* Cronache di Archeologia 12. Catania, 1973–74, pp. 158–67.

Davaras 1975
Davaras, C. "Early Minoan Jewellery from Mochlos." *BSA* 70 (1975): 101–14.

Davaras 1976
Davaras, C. *Guide to Cretan Antiquities.* Park Ridge, N.J., 1976.

Davaras 1980
Davaras, C. "A Minoan Graffito from Traostalos." *Kadmos* 19 (1980): 87–92.

Davaras 1981
Davaras, C. "Three New Linear A Libation Vessel Fragments from Petsophas." *Kadmos* 20 (1981): 1–6.

Davaras 1988
Davaras, C. "A Minoan Beetle-rhyton from Prinias Siteias." *BSA* 83 (1988): 45–54.

Davaras 1989
Davaras, C. "Μινωικά μελισσουργικά σκεύη." In *Φίλια Έπη εις Γεώργιον Ε. Μυλωνάν: δια τα 60 έτη του ανασκαφικού του έργου.* Vol. C'. Athens, 1989, pp. 1–7.

Davaras 1992
Davaras, C. "Χάλκινοι διπλοί πελέκεις" and "Χρυσοί διπλοί πελέκεις." In *Μινωικός και Ελληνικός Πολιτισμός. Από την Συλλογή Μητσοτάκη. Μουσείο Κυκλαδικής Τέχνης.* Exh. cat. Athens, 1992, pp. 262–68, nos. 325–38.

Davaras n.d.
Davaras, C. *Μουσείο Αγίου Νικολάου.* Athens, n.d.

Davaras–Betancourt 2004
Davaras, C., and P. P. Betancourt. *The Haghia Photia Cemetery I. The Tomb Groups and Architecture.* Prehistory Monographs 14. Philadelphia, 2004.

Davaras–Soles 1992
Davaras, C., and J. S. Soles. "Ανασκαφές στο Μόχλο Σητείας. Περίοδος 1989." Αμάλθεια 23 (1992): 37–43.

Davaras–Soles 1995
Davaras, C., and J. S. Soles. "A New Oriental Cylinder Seal from Mochlos. Appendix: Catalogue of the Cylinder Seals Found in the Aegean." AE (1995): 29–66.

Day–Wilson–Kiriatzi 1997
Day, P. M., D. E. Wilson, and E. Kiriatzi. "Reassessing Specialization in Prepalatial Cretan Ceramic Production." In Laffineur and Betancourt, eds. Τέχνη (1997), pp. 275–88.

Day–Wilson–Kiriatzi 1998
Day, P. M., D. E. Wilson, and E. Kiriatzi. "Pots, Labels and People: Burying Ethnicity in the Cemetery of Aghia Photia, Siteias." In K. Branigan, ed. Cemetery and Society in the Aegean Bronze Age. Sheffield, 1998, pp. 133–49.

Demakopoulou 1988
Demakopoulou, K., ed. The Mycenaean World: Five Centuries of Early Greek Culture, 1600–1110 B.C. Exh. cat. Athens, 1988.

Dimopoulou-Rethemiotaki 1997
Dimopoulou-Rethemiotaki, N. "Workshops and Craftsmen in the Harbour-Town of Knossos at Poros Katsambas." In Laffineur and Betancourt, eds. Τέχνη (1997), pp. 433–38, pls. clxvii–clxxiv.

Dimopoulou-Rethemiotaki 1999a
Dimopoulou-Rethemiotaki, N. "The Marine Style Ewer from Poros." In Betancourt et al., eds. Meletemata (1999), pp. 217–26, pl. XLIV.

Dimopoulou-Rethemiotaki 1999b
Dimopoulou-Rethemiotaki, N. "The Neopalatial Cemetery of the Knossian Harbour-Town at Poros: Mortuary Behaviour and Social Ranking." In I. Killian, ed. Eliten in der Bronzezeit. Ergebnisse zweier Kolloquien in Mainz und Athen. Verlag des Romisch-Germanischen Zentralmuseums Monographien 43, 1. Mainz, 1999, pp. 27–36.

Dimopoulou-Rethemiotaki 2005
Dimopoulou-Rethemiotaki, N. Το Αρχαιολογικό Μουσείο Ηρακλείου. Athens, 2005.

Dimopoulou-Rethemiotaki–Rethemiotakis 1978
Dimopoulou-Rethemiotaki, N., and G. Rethemiotakis. "Υστερομινωικό νεκροταφείο στο Μετόχι Καλού Ηρακλείου." ΑΔ 33 Α'(1978): 40–109.

Dimopoulou-Rethemiotaki–Rethemiotakis 2000
Dimopoulou-Rethemiotaki, N., and G. Rethemiotakis. "The 'Sacred Conversation Ring' from Poros." In Müller, ed. Minoisch-Mykenische Glyptik (2000), pp. 39–56.

Deshayes 1960
Deshayes, J. Les outiles de bronze de l'Indus au Danube (IVe ou IIe millénaire). 2 vols. Bibliotheque archaeologique et historique LXXI. Paris, 1960.

Dietrich 1998
Dietrich, B. C. "A Minoan Symbol of Renewal." JPR 2 (1998): 13–20.

Doumas 1977
Doumas, Chr. Early Bronze Age Burial Habits in the Cyclades. SIMA 48. Gothenburg, 1977.

Doumas 1992
Doumas, Chr. Οι τοιχογραφίες της Θήρας. Athens, 1992.

Doumas 2000
Doumas, Chr. Early Cycladic Culture. The N. P. Goulandris Collection. Athens, 2000.

Dragona-Latsoudi 1977
Dragona-Latsoudi, A. "Μυκηναϊκός κιθαρωδός από τη Ναυπλία." AE (1977): 86–98.

Driessen–Farnoux 1994
Driessen, J., and A. Farnoux. "Malia. Quartier Nu." BCH 118 (1994): 471–77.

Driessen–Farnoux 1997
Driessen, J., and A. Farnoux, eds. La Crète Mycénienne: Actes de la Table Ronde Internationale organisée par l'École française d'Athènes, 26–28 Mars 1991. BCH Suppl. 30. Athens and Paris, 1997.

Driessen–Macdonald 1984
Driessen, J., and C. Macdonald. "Some Military Aspects of the Aegaean." BSA 79 (1984): 49–74.

Driessen–Schoep–Laffineur 2002
Driessen, J., I. Schoep, and R. Laffineur, eds. Monuments of Minos. Rethinking the Minoan Palaces. Proceedings of the International Workshop "Crete of the Hundred Palaces? held at the Université Catholique de Louvain (Louvain-la-Neuve, 14–15 Dec. 2001). Aegaeum 23. Liège and Austin, 2002.

Effenterre 1980
Effenterre, van. H. Le Palais de Mallia et la cité minoenne. Vols. 1, 2. Incunabula Graeca 76. Rome, 1980.

Effinger 1996
Effinger M. Minoischer Schmuck. BAR–IS 646. Oxford, 1996.

Evans 1899–1900
Evans, Sir A. J. "Knossos I. The Palace." BSA 6 (1899–1900): 3–70.

Evans 1906
Evans, Sir A. J. The Prehistoric Tombs of Knossos. Archaeologia 49. London, 1906.

Evans 1909
Evans, Sir A. J. Scripta Minoa. Vol. 1. Oxford, 1909.

Evans 1914
Evans, Sir A. J. "The 'Tomb of the Double Axes' and Associated Group, and the Pillar Rooms and Ritual Vessels of the 'Little Palace' at Knossos." Archaeologia 65 (1914): 1–94.

Evans 1994
Evans, J. D. "The Early Millennia: Continuity and Change in a Farming Settlement." In. D. Evely, H. Hughes-Brock, and N. Momigliano, eds. Knossos: A Labyrinth of History. Papers presented in Honour of Sinclair Hood. Oxford, 1994, pp. 1–20.

Evely 1993–2000
Evely, R. D. G. Minoan Crafts: Tools and Techniques. An Introduction. SIMA 92. Vol. 1, Gothenburg, 1993; vol. 2, Jonsered, 2000.

Evely 1999
Evely, D. Fresco: A Passport into the Past. Minoan Crete through the Eyes of Mark Cameron. Athens, 1999.

Ferrence (in press)
Ferrence, S. C. "Variety is the Spice of Life: Figurines from the Cave of Hagios Charalambos." In Πεπραγμένα του Ι' Διεθνούς Κρητολογικού Συνεδρίου, Khania, 1–8 October 2006 (in press).

Forsdyke 1926–27
Forsdyke, E. J. "The Mavro Spelio Cemetery at Knossos." BSA 28 (1926–27): 243–96.

Fotou 1993
Fotou, V. New Light on Gournia. Unknown Documents of the Excavations at Gournia and Other Sites on the Isthmus of Ierapetra. Aegaeum 9. Liège, 1993.

French–Wardle 1988
French, E., and K. Wardle, eds. Problems in Greek Prehistory. Papers Presented at the Centenary Conference of the British School of Archaeology at Athens, Manchester, April 1986. Bristol, 1988.

Galanaki 2006
Galanaki, K. "Πρωτομινωικό ταφικό σύνολο στην πρώην Αμερικανική Βάση Γουρνών Πεδιάδος." In Πεπραγμένα του Θ' Διεθνούς Κρητολογικού Συνεδρίου (Ελούντα 1–7 Οκτ. 2001). Α2. Herakleion, 2006.

Georgiou 1983
Georgiou, H. "Coarse Wares and Technology." In O. Krzyszkowska and L. Nixon, eds. Minoan Society. Proceedings of the Cambridge Colloquium 1981. Bristol, 1983, pp. 75–92.

Gerontakou 2003
Gerontakou, E. "Δύο μεσομινωικοί αποθέτες στο νεκροταφείο του Πλατάνου." In Vlachopoulos and Birtacha, eds. Αργοναύτης (2003), pp. 303–30.

Gesell 1985
Gesell, G. C. Town, Palace and House Cult in Minoan Crete. SIMA 67. Gothenburg, 1985.

Gill 1966
Gill, M. "Seals and Sealings: Some Comments. The Knossos Sealings with Linear B Inscriptions." Kadmos 5 (1966): 1–16.

Godart–Kanta–Tzigounaki 1996
Godart, L., A. Kanta, and A. Tzigounaki. "La bureaucratie palatiale: naissance et évolution d'un système de pouvoir en Egée." In E. De Miro, L. Godart, and A. Sacconi, eds. Atti e Memorie del Secondo Congresso Internazionale di Micenologia, Roma–Napoli, 14–20 Ottobre 1991. Rome, 1996, pp. 581–98.

Guarducci 1939–40
Guarducci, M. "Missione archeologica italiana in Creta: lavori dell' anno 1939." ASAtene 1–2 (1939–40): 231–39.

Hägg 1989
Hägg, R. "Sacred Horns and Naiskoi. Remarks on Aegean Religious Symbolism in Cyprus." In Karageorghis, ed. Civilizations of the Aegean (1989), pp. 79–83.

Hägg 1990
Hägg, R. "The Cretan Hut-Models." Op. Ath. 18 (1990): 95–107.

Hakulin 2004
Hakulin, L. Bronzeworking on Late Minoan Crete. A Diachronic Study. BAR–IS 1245. Oxford, 2004.

Halbherr–Stefani–Banti 1977
Halbherr, F., E. Stefani, and L. Banti. "Haghia Triada nel periodo tardo palaziale." ASAtene 55 (1977): 13–296.

Hallager 1996
Hallager, E., ed. The Minoan Roundel and Other Sealed Documents in the Neopalatial Linear A Administration. 2 vols. Aegaeum 14. Liège and Austin, 1996.

Hallager–Andreadaki-Vlazaki 1984
Hallager, E., and M. Andreadaki-Vlazaki. "Two New Roundels with Linear A from Khania." Kadmos 23 (1984): 1–10.

Hallager–Hallager 1995
Hallager, B., and E. Hallager. "The Knossian Bull—Political Propaganda in Neo-Palatial Crete?" In R. Laffineur and W.-D. Niemeier, eds. Politeia (1995), vol. 2, pp. 547–59.

Hallager–Hallager 1997–2000
Hallager, E., and B. P. Hallager, eds. The Greek Swedish Excavations at the Agia Aikaterini Square Kastelli, Khania, 1970–1987: The LM IIIC Settlement. Vol. 2 (text and plates). Stockholm, 1997–2000.

Hallager–Hallager 2003
Hallager, E., and B. P. Hallager, eds. The Greek-Swedish Excavation at the Agia Aikaterini Square Kastelli, Khania 1970–1987 and 2001. The Late Minoan III B:2 Settlement. Vol. 3. Stockholm, 2003.

Hallager–McGeorge 1992
Hallager, B. P., and P. J. P. McGeorge. Late Minoan III Burials at Khania: The Tombs, Finds, and Deceased in Odos Palama. SIMA 93. Gothenburg, 1992.

Hallager–Tzedakis 1984
Hallager, E., and Y. Tzedakis. "The Greek-Swedish Excavations at Kastelli, Khania 1982–83." AAA 18 (1984): 1–20.

Hatzaki 2005
Hatzaki, E. M. Knossos: The Little Palace. BSA Suppl. Vol. 38. London, 2005.

Hawes et al. 1908
Hawes, H. B., B. E. Williams, R. B. Seager, and E. H. Dohan. Gournia, Vasiliki and Other Prehistoric Sites on the Isthmus of Hierapetra, Crete: Excavations of the Wells-Houston-Cramp Expeditions, 1901, 1903, 1904. Philadelphia, 1908.

Hayden 2003
Hayden, B. J. "Final Neolithic-Early Minoan I/IIA Settlement in the Vrokastro Area, Eastern Crete." AJA 107.3 (2003): 363–412.

Hazzidakis 1912–13
Hazzidakis, J. "An Early Minoan Sacred Cave at Arkalochori in Crete." BSA 19 (1912–1913): 35–47.

Hazzidakis 1934
Hazzidakis, J. Les Villas minoennes de Tylissos. Études Crétoises 3. Paris, 1934.

Hencken 1971
Hencken, H. The Earliest European Helmets. Cambridge, Mass., 1971.

Higgins 1961
Higgins, R. A. Greek and Roman Jewellery. London, 1961.

Hogarth 1899–1900
Hogarth, D. G. "Knossos II. Early Town and Cemeteries." BSA 6 (1899–1900): 70–85.

Hogarth 1900–1901
Hogarth, D. G. "Excavations at Zakro, Crete." *BSA* 7 (1900–1901): 121–49.

Hogarth 1902
Hogarth, D. G. "Bronze-Age Vases from Zakro." *JHS* 22 (1902): 333–38.

Hood 1956
Hood, M. S. F. "Another Warrior-Grave at Ayios Ioannis near Knossos." *BSA* 51 (1956): 81–102.

Hood 1961–62
Hood, M.S.F., "Archaeology in Greece, 1961–2." *AR* 8 (1961–62): 3–31.

Hood 2005
Hood, S. "Dating the Knossos Frescoes." In L. Morgan, ed. *Aegean Wall Painting, A Tribute to Mark Cameron. BSA* Studies 13. London, 2005, pp. 45–81.

Hood–de Jong 1952
Hood, M. S. F., and P. de Jong. "Late Minoan Warrior-Graves from Ayios Ioannis and the New Hospital Site at Knossos." *BSA* 47 (1952): 243–77.

Huot–Yot–Calvet 1985
Huot J. L., M. Yot, and Y. Calvet, eds. *De l'Indus aux Balkans: Recueil à la memoire de Jean Deshayes.* Paris, 1985.

Immerwahr 1990
Immerwahr, S. A. *Aegean Painting in the Bronze Age.* University Park and London, 1990.

Jantzen 1951
Jantzen, U. "Die spätminoische Nekropole von Kydonia." In F. Matz, ed. *Forschungen auf Kreta 1942.* Berlin, 1951, pp. 72–81.

Kaiser 1976
Kaiser, B. *Untersuchungen zum minoischen Relief.* Bonn, 1976.

Kanta 1980
Kanta, A. *The Late Minoan III Period in Crete: A Survey of Sites, Pottery and Their Distribution. SIMA* 58. Gothenburg, 1980.

Kanta 2006
Kanta, A. "Monastiraki, a Minoan Palatial Center in the Valley of Amari, Crete." In A. Kanta, and M. Marazzi, eds. *Monastiraki I.* Rome, 2006, pp. 13–34.

Karageorghis 1989
Karageorghis, V., ed. *The Civilizations of the Aegean and Their Diffusion in Cyprus and the Eastern Mediterranean, 2000–600 B.C. Proceedings of an International Symposium, 18–24 September 1989.* Larnaca, 1989.

Karantzali 1996
Karantzali, E. *Le Bronze Ancien dans les Cyclades et en Crète. Les relations entre les deux regions. Influence de la Grèce continentale. BAR–IS* 631. Oxford, 1996.

Karayianni 1984
Karayianni, E. *Μινωικά σύνθετα σκεύη.* Athens, 1984.

Karetsou 2000
Karetsou, A., ed. *Κρήτη-Αίγυπτος, Πολιτισμικοί δεσμοί τριών χιλιετιών. Μελέτες.* Herakleion, 2000.

Karetsou–Andreadaki-Vlazaki–Papadakis 2000
Karetsou, A., M. Andreadaki-Vlazaki, and N. Papadakis, eds. *Crete–Egypt. Three Thousand Years of Cultural Links.* Exh. cat. Herakleion, 2000.

Kilian-Dirlmeier 1993
Kilian-Dirlmeier, I. *Die Schwerter in Griechenland (ausserhalb der Peloponnes), Bulgarien und Albanien.* Prähistorische Bronzefunde IV, 12. Stuttgart, 1993.

Koehl 1986
Koehl, R. B. "The Chieftain Cup and a Minoan Rite of Passage." *JHS* 106 (1986): 99–110.

Koehl 2000
Koehl, R. B. "Minoan Rhyta in Egypt." In Karetsou, ed. *Κρήτη-Αίγυπτος* (2000), pp. 94–100.

Koehl 2006
Koehl, R. B. *Aegean Bronze Age Rhyta.* Prehistory Monographs 19. Philadelphia, 2006.

Kopaka–Platon 1993
Kopaka, K., and L. Platon. "Ληνοί μινωικοί: Installations minoennes de traitement des produits liquides." *BCH* 117 (1993): 35–101.

Kraiker–Kübler 1939
Kraiker, W., and K. Kübler. *Die Nekropolen des 12. bis 10. Jahrhunderts.* Kerameikos. Ergebnisse der Ausgrabungen I. Berlin, 1939.

Krzyszkowska 1990
Krzyszkowska, O. *Ivory and Related Materials: An Illustrated Guide. BICS* Suppl. 5. London, 1990.

Krzyszkowska 2005a
Krzyszkowska, O. *Aegean Seals: An Introduction. BICS* Suppl. 85. London, 2005.

Krzyszkowska 2005b
Krzyszkowska, O. "Amethyst in the Aegean Bonze Age. An Achaeological Enigma?" In Bradfer-Burdet, Detournay, and Laffineur, eds. *Κρης Τεχνίτης* (2005), pp. 119–30.

Laffineur 1990
Laffineur, R. "The Iconography of Mycenaen Seals and the Status of Their Owners." In *Aegaeum 6. Annales d'Archéologie Egéenne de l'Université de Liège.* Liège, 1990, pp. 117–60.

Laffineur 1999
Laffineur, R., ed. *Polemos. Le contexte guerrier en Égée à l'âge du Bronze. Actes de la Rencontre égéenne international Université de Liège, 14–17 avril 1998.* Aegaeum 19. Liège, 1999.

Laffineur–Betancourt 1997
Laffineur, R., and P. P. Betancourt, eds. *Τέχνη: Craftsmen, Craftswomen and Craftsmanship in the Aegean Bronze Age. Proceedings of the 6th International Aegean Conference, Philadelphia, Temple University, 18–21 April 1996.* Aegaeum 16. Liège, 1997.

Laffineur–Niemeier 1995
Laffineur, R., and W.-D. Niemeier, eds. *Politeia. Society and State in the Aegean Bronze Age. Proceedings of the 5th International Aegean Conference.* Aegaeum 12. Liège and Austin, 1995.

Lebessi 1967
Lebessi, A. "Ανασκαφή σπηλαιώδους τάφου εις Πόρον Ηρακλείου." *ΠΑΕ* (1967): 195–209.

Lebessi–Muhly–Papasavvas 2004
Lebessi, A., P. Muhly, and G. Papasavvas. "The Runner's Ring. A Minoan Athlete's Dedication at the Syme Sanctuary, Crete." *AM* 119 (2004): 1–31, pls. 1–8.

Levi 1952
Levi, D. "Attività della Scuola Archeologica Italiana di Atene nell'anno 1951." *Bolletino d'arte* (1952): 4–30

Levi 1956
Levi, D. "Attività della Scuola Archeologica Italiana di Atene nell'anno 1955." *Bolletino d'arte* (1956): 238–74.

Levi 1976
Levi, D. *Festòs e la civiltà minoica. Testo I. Incunabula Graeca* 60. Rome, 1976.

Long 1974
Long, C. *The Ayia Triadha Sarcophagus. A Study of Late Minoan and Mycenaean Funerary Practices and Beliefs. SIMA* 41. Gothenburg, 1974.

Löwe 1996
Löwe, W. *Spätbronzezeitliche Bestattungen auf Kreta. BAR–IS* 642. Oxford, 1996.

Macdonald–Knappet 2007
Macdonald, C., and C. Knappet. *Knossos. Protopalatial Deposits in Early Magazine A and the South-West Houses. BSA* Suppl. Vol. 41. London, 2007.

MacGillivray 2004
MacGillivray, J. A. "The Astral Labyrinth at Knossos." In Cadogan, Hatzaki, and Vasilakis, eds. *Knossos: Palace, City, State* (2004), pp. 329–38.

MacGillivray et al. 1991
MacGillivray, J. A., L. H. Sackett, J. M. Driessen, A. Farnoux, and D. Smyth. "Excavations at Palaikastro, 1990." *BSA* 86 (1991): 121–47.

Mackeprang 1938
Mackeprang, M. B. "Late Mycenaean Vases." *AJA* 42 (1938): 537–59.

Magrill 1987
Magrill, P. "A Minoan Alabastron in Dublin." *BSA* 82 (1987): 155–64.

Mantelli 1992
Mantelli, K. "The Neolithic Well at Kastelli Phournis in Eastern Crete." *BSA* 87 (1992): 103–20, pls.1–2.

Manti-Platonos 1981
Manti-Platonos, M. "Τελετουργικές σφύρες και ρόπαλα στο μινωικό κόσμο." *AE* (1981): 74–83.

Marangou 1990
Marangou, L., ed. *Cycladic Culture: Naxos in the 3rd Millennium B.C.* Athens, 1990.

Marinatos 1931
Marinatos, S. "Η ορεία κρύσταλλος εν Κρήτηι." *AE* (1931): 158–60.

Marinatos 1933
Marinatos, S. "Funde und Forschungen auf Kreta." In *AA* (1933): 298–304.

Marinatos 1935a
Marinatos, S. "Ανασκαφαί εν Κρήτηι, Αρκαλοχώρι." *ΠΑΕ* (1935): 212–20.

Marinatos 1935b
Marinatos, S. "Ausgrabungen und Funde auf Kreta 1934–35." *AA* (1935): 244–559.

Marinatos 1937
Marinatos, S. "Αι μινωικαί θεαί του Γάζι." *AE* (1937): 278–91.

Marinatos 1939–41
Marinatos, S. "Το μινωικόν μέγαρον Σκλαβοκάμπου." *AE* (1939–41): 69–96.

Marinatos 1962
Marinatos, S. "Zur Frage der Grotte von Arkalokhori." *Kadmos* 1 (1962): 87–94.

Marinatos 1971
Marinatos, S. *Excavations at Thera IV (1970 Season)*. Βιβλιοθήκη της εν Αθήναις Αρχαιολογικής Εταιρείας 64. Athens, 1971 (2nd ed.: Athens, 1999).

Marinatos 1977
Marinatos, S. *Excavations at Thera VI (1972 Season)*. Βιβλιοθήκη της εν Αθήναις Αρχαιολογικής Εταιρείας 64. Athens, 1977 (2nd ed.: Athens, 1999).

Marinatos 1986
Marinatos, N. *Minoan Sacrificial Ritual. Cult Practice and Symbolism*. Acta Instituti Atheniensis Regni Sueciae 8, IX. Stockholm, 1986.

Marinatos 1993
Marinatos, N. *Minoan Religion. Ritual, Image and Symbol*. Columbia, S.C., 1993.

Marinatos–Hirmer 1959
Marinatos, S., and M. Hirmer. *Kreta und das Mykenische Hellas*. Munich, 1959.

Marinatos–Hirmer 1960
Marinatos, S., and M. Hirmer. *Crete and Mycenae*. London, 1960.

Melas 1999
Melas, M. "The Ethnography of Minoan and Mycenaean Beekeeping." In Betancourt et al., eds. *Meletemata* (1999), pp. 485–91.

Mikrakis 2000
Mikrakis, M. "Μουσική στην Κρήτη και την Αίγυπτο. Ένα ιδιαίτερο πεδίο ανάπτυξης πολιτισμικών δεσμών." In Karetsou, ed. *Κρήτη-Αίγυπτος* (2000), pp. 162–69.

Momigliano 1991
Momigliano, N. "MM IA Pottery from Evans' Excavations at Knossos." *BSA* 86 (1991): 149–271.

Montelius 1924
Montelius, O. *La Grèce préclassique*, Part 1. Stockholm, 1924.

Moss 2005
Moss, M. *The Minoan Pantheon. Towards an Understanding of Its Nature and Extent. BAR–IS* 1343. Oxford, 2005.

Mosso 1910
Mosso, A. *Le origini della civiltà Mediterranea*. Milan, 1910.

Mountjoy 1974
Mountjoy, P. A. "A Note on the LM IB Marine Style at Knossos." *BSA* 69 (1974): 173–75.

Mountjoy 1976
Mountjoy, P. A. "A Late Minoan IB Marine Style Rhyton from Pseira." *AAA* 9 (1976): 83–86.

Mountjoy 1984
Mountjoy, P. A. "The Marine Style Pottery of LM IB / LH IIA: Towards a Corpus." *BSA* 79 (1984): 161–219, pls. 14–28.

Mountjoy 1985
Mountjoy, P. A. "Ritual Associations for LM IB Marine Style Vases." In P. Darcque and J. C. Poursat, eds. *L'Iconographie Minoenne. Actes de la Table Ronde d'Athènes (21–22 avril 1983)*. *BCH*, Suppl. 11. Athens, 1985, pp. 231–42.

Muhly 1992
Muhly, P. *Μινωικός λαξευτός τάφος στον Πόρο Ηρακλείου*. Βιβλιοθήκη της εν Αθήναις Αρχαιολογικής Εταιρείας 129. Athens, 1992.

Müller 1997
Müller, W. *Kretische Tongefässe mit Meeresdekor. Entwicklung und Stellung Innerhalb der Feinen Keramik von Spatminoisch IB auf Kreta*. Archäologische Forschungen 19. Berlin, 1997.

Müller 2000
Müller, W., ed. *Minoisch-Mykenische Glyptik. Stil, Ikonographie, Funktion: V. Internationales Siegel-Symposium, Marburg, 23.–25. September 1999*. CMS Beiheft 6. Berlin, 2000.

Müller-Celka 2003
Müller-Celka, S. "The Mycenaean Moulded Glass Seals: Some Thoughts about Their Distribution, Use and Manufacture." In N. Kyparissi-Apostolika, and M. Papakonstantinou, eds. *The Periphery of the Mycenaean World. 2nd International Interdisciplinary Colloquium, 26–30 September, Lamia 1999. ΥΠΠΟ ΙΔ΄ ΕΠΚΑ*. Athens, 2003, pp. 87–98.

Myres 1902–3
Myres, J. L. "Excavations at Palaikastro II. The Sanctuary Site of Petsofa." *BSA* 9 (1902–3): 356–87.

Nakou 1995
Nakou, G. "The Cutting Edge: A New Look at Early Aegean Metallurgy." *JMA* 8.2 (Dec 1995): 1–32.

Niemeier 1981
Niemeier, W.-D., ed. *Studien zur minoischen und helladischen Glyptik. Beiträge zum 2. Marburger Siegel-Symposium 26.–30. September 1978*. CMS 1. Berlin, 1981.

Niemeier 1985
Niemeier, W.-D. *Die Palaststilkeramik von Knossos*. Archäologische Forschungen 13. Berlin, 1985.

Niemeier 1990
Niemeier W.-D., "Mycenaean Elements in the Miniature Fresco from Thera?" In D. A. Hardy et al., eds. *Thera and the Aegean World III. Proceedings of the Third International Congress, Santorini, Greece, 3–9 September 1989*. London, 1990, pp. 267–79.

Niemeier 1997
Niemeier, W.-D. "Cretan Glyptic Arts in LM I–III: Continuity and Changes." In J. Driessen and A. Farnoux, eds. *La Crète Mycénienne* (1997), pp. 297–311.

Nillson 1950
Nilsson, M. P. *The Minoan-Mycenaean Religion and Its Survival in Greek Religion*. Skrifter Utgivna av Kungl. Humanistiska vetenskapssamfundet i Lund 9. Lund, 1950 (2nd rev. ed., 1968).

Olivier 1995
Olivier, J. P. "Les sceaux avec des signes hiéroglyphiques. Que Lire? Une question de bon sens." In I. Pini and J. C. Poursat, eds. *Scéaux Minoens et Mycéniens*. CMS Beiheft 5. Berlin, 1995, pp. 169–81.

Olivier–Godart–Poursat 1996
Olivier, J. P., L. Godart, and J. C. Poursat, eds. *Corpus Hieroglyphicarum Inscriptionum Cretae*. Études Crétoises 31. Paris, 1996.

Orlandos 1958
Orlandos, A. K. *Τα υλικά δομής των αρχαίων Ελλήνων, Τεύχος 2: Τα μέταλλα, το ελεφαντοστούν, τα κονιάματα και οι λίθοι*. Athens, 1958.

Pållson-Hallager 1986
Pålsson-Hallager, B. "Mycenaean Pottery in LM IIIA1 Deposits at Khania, Western Crete." In French and Wardle, eds. *Problems in Greek Prehistory* (1988), pp. 173–91.

Palmer 1962
Palmer, L. R. "An Unknown Vessel from Knossos." *Antiquity* 36 (1962): 48–49.

Palmer 1963
Palmer, L. R. *The Interpretation of Mycenaean Greek Texts*. Oxford, 1963.

Palmer 1969
Palmer, L. R. *A New Guide to the Palace of Knossos*. London, 1969.

Panagiotaki 1999a
Panagiotaki, M. "Minoan Faience- and Glass-Making: Techniques and Origins." In Betancourt et al., eds. *Meletemata* (1999), pp. 617–23.

Panagiotaki 1999b
Panagiotaki, M. *The Central Palace Sanctuary at Knossos*. *BSA* Suppl. Vol. 31. London, 1999.

Panagiotaki et al. 2004
Panagiotaki, M., Y. Maniatis, D. Kavoussanaki, G. Hatton, and M. Tite. "The Production Technology of Aegean Bronze Age Vitreous Materials." In J. Bourriau, and J. Phillips, eds. *Invention and Innovation: The Social Context of Technological Change. II, Egypt, the Aegean and the Near East, 1650–1150 B.C. Proceedings of a Conference held at the McDonald Institute for Archaeological Research, Cambridge, 4–6 September 2002*. Oxford, 2004, pp. 149–75.

Papadakis 1984
Papadakis, N. "Παραδόσεις αρχαίων αντικειμένων από ιδιώτες στη Σητεία." *Αμάλθεια* 15 (1984): 133–42.

Papadatos 2003
Papadatos, Y. "Ένα παλίμψηστο λοιπόν..." In Vlachopoulos and Birtacha, eds. *Αργοναύτης* (2003), pp. 277–91.

Papadatos 2005
Papadatos, Y. *Tholos Tomb Gamma. A Prepalatial Tholos Tomb at Phourni, Archanes*. Prehistory Monographs 17. Philadelphia, 2005.

Papadopoulos 2002
Papadopoulos, Th. "Η χρήση του γυαλιού στην κρητομυκηναϊκή εποχή." In Πρακτικά Β΄ Συνεδρίου Μαργαριτών Μυλοποτάμου Ρεθύμνης Κρήτης, Μαργαρίτες Μυλοποτάμου, 26–28 Σεπτεμβρίου 1997. Athens, 2002, pp. 29–38.

Papadopoulou 1997
Papadopoulou, E. "Une tombe à tholos "intra-muros." Le cas du cimétiere MR d'Arménoi." In Driessen and Farnoux, eds. La Crète Mycénienne (1997), pp. 319–40.

Papadopoulou (in press)
Papadopoulou, E. "Νέα δεδομένα από το υστερομινωικό νεκροταφείο στο Μαρουλά Ρεθύμνου." In Πεπραγμένα του Ι΄ Διεθνούς Κρητολογικού Συνεδρίου, Khania, 1–8 October 2006 (in press).

Papadopoulou–Tzachili (in press)
Papadopoulou, E., and I. Tzachili. "Συστηματική ανασκαφή στο μινωικό ιερό κορυφής στο Βρύσινα Ρεθύμνου (Poster presentation)." In Πεπραγμένα του Ι΄ Διεθνούς Κρητολογικού Συνεδρίου, Khania, 1–8 October 2006 (in press).

Papaefthymiou-Papanthimou 1979
Papaefthymiou-Papanthimou, Aik. Σκεύη και σύνεργα του καλλωπισμού στον κρητομυκηναϊκό χώρο. Αριστοτέλειο Πανεπιστήμιο Θεσσαλονίκης, Επιστημονική Επετηρίδα της Φιλοσοφικής Σχολής, Παράρτημα αρ. 23. Thessaloniki, 1979.

Papapostolou 1977
Papapostolou, I. A. "Τα σφραγίσματα των Χανίων: συμβολή στη μελέτη της μινωικής σφραγιδογλυφίας." Ph.D. diss. Aristotle University of Thessaloniki, Thessaloniki, 1977.

Papapostolou–Godart–Olivier 1976
Papapostolou, I. A, L. Godart, and J. P. Olivier. Η Γραμμική Α στο μινωικό αρχείο των Χανίων. Rome, 1976.

Papatsarouha 1998
Papatsarouha, El. "La conception minoenne du monde végétal à travers l'iconographie des sceaux." Ph.D. diss. Université de Paris I, Panthéon Sorbonne, Paris, 1998.

Paribeni 1903
Paribeni, R. "Lavori eseguiti della Missione archeologica Italiana nel palazzo e nella necropoli di H. Triada." Rendiconti dei Lincei. Vol. 12. 1903.

Paribeni 1904
Paribeni, R. "Ricerche nel sepolcreto di Haghia Triada presso Phaestos." MonAnt 14 (1904): 677–756.

Peatfield 1990
Peatfield, A. A. D. "Minoan Peak Sanctuaries: History and Society." Op. Ath. 18 (1990): 117–31.

Peatfield 1999
Pietfield, A. "The Paradox of Violence: Weaponry and Martial Art in Minoan Crete." In Laffineur, ed. Polemos (1999), vol. 1, pp. 67–74.

Pernier 1935
Pernier, L. Palazzo minoico di Festòs: Scavi e studi della Missione Archeologica Italiana a Creta dal 1900 al 1934. Vol. 1. Rome, 1935.

Pernier–Banti 1951
Pernier, L., and L. Banti. Il palazzo minoico di Festòs. Vols. 1, 2. Rome, 1951.

Phillips 1991
Phillips, J. S. "The Impact and Implications of the Egyptian and 'Egyptianizing' Material found in Bronze Age Crete ca. 3000–ca. 1100 B.C., I–III." Ph.D. diss. University of Toronto, Toronto, 1991.

Pilali-Papasteriou 1992
Pilali-Papasteriou, A. Μινωικά πήλινα ανθρωπόμορφα ειδώλια της συλλογή ς Μεταξά. Συμβολή στη μελέτη της μεσομινωική ς πλαστικής. Thessaloniki, 1992.

Pini 1999
Pini, I. "Further Research on Late Bronze Age Aegean Glass Seals." In Η Περιφέρεια του Μυκηναϊκού Κόσμου, Α΄ Διεθνές Διεπιστημονικό Συμπόσιο. Λαμία 26–29 Σεπτ. 1994. ΥΠΠΟ, ΙΔ΄ ΕΠΚΑ. Lamia, 1999, pp. 331–38.

Platon 1951a
Platon, N. "Η αρχαιολογική κίνησις εν Κρήτηι κατά το έτος 1951." Κρητ. Χρονικά Ε΄ (1951): 444–45.

Platon 1951b
Platon, N. "Το ιερόν Μαζά (Καλού Χωριού Πεδιάδος) και τα μινωικά ιερά κορυφής." Κρητ. Χρονικά Ε΄ (1951): 96–160.

Platon 1952
Platon, N. "Η αρχαιολογική κίνησις εν Κρήτηι κατά το έτος 1952." Κρητ. Χρονικά ΣΤ΄ (1952): 471–81.

Platon 1959
Platon, N. "Συμβολή εις την σπουδήν της μινωικής τοιχογραφίας. Β΄. Η τοιχογραφία της προσφοράς σπονδών." Κρητ. Χρονικά ΙΓ΄ (1959): 319–45.

Platon 1960a
Platon, N. "Ανασκαφαί περιοχής Πραισού." ΠΑΕ (1960): 294–307.

Platon 1960b
Platon, N. "Μινωική αγροικία Προφήτη Ηλία Τουρτούλων." ΠΑΕ (1960): 294–300.

Platon 1961
Platon, N. "Ανασκαφή Κάτω Ζάκρου." ΠΑΕ (1961): 216–24.

Platon 1962
Platon, N. "Ανασκαφή Ζάκρου." ΠΑΕ (1962): 142–68.

Platon 1963
Platon, N. "Ανασκαφαί Ζάκρου." ΠΑΕ (1963): 160–88.

Platon 1965
Platon, N. "Ανασκαφαί Ζάκρου." ΠΑΕ (1965): 187–224.

Platon 1966
Platon, N. "Ανασκαφαί Ζάκρου." ΠΑΕ (1966): 139–73.

Platon 1969
Platon, N. "Ανασκαφή Ζάκρου." ΠΑΕ (1969): 197–237.

Platon 1971
Platon, N. "Ανασκαφή Ζάκρου." ΠΑΕ (1971): 231–75, pls. 328–50.

Platon 1974
Platon, N. Ζάκρος. Το νέον μινωικόν ανάκτορον. Athens, 1974.

Platon 1977
Platon, N. "Ανασκαφή Ζάκρου." ΠΑΕ (1977): 421–46.

Platon 1988
Platon, N. "Ανασκαφή Ζάκρου." ΠΑΕ 143 (1988): 219–43, pls. 156–66.

Platon 1990
Platon, L. "Ιδιότυπο τελετουργικό σκεύος από τη Ζάκρο." In Πρακτικά του ΣΤ΄ Διεθνούς Κρητολογικού Συνεδρίου (Χανιά 24–30 Αυγ. 1986). Α2. Khania, 1990, pp. 129–39.

Platon 2002a
Platon, L. "Τα μινωικά αγγεία και το κρασί." In Mylopotamitaki, Aik, ed. Οίνος παλαιός ηδύποτος. Πρακτικά του Διεθνούς Επιστημονικού Συμποσιού. Κουνάβοι 24–26 Απρ. 1998. Herakleion, 2002, pp. 5–24.

Platon 2002b
Platon, L. "The Political and Cultural Influence of the Zakros Palace on Nearby Sites and in a Wider Context." In Driessen, Schoep and Laffineur, eds. Monuments of Minos (2002), pp. 145–56.

Platon–Brice 1975
Platon, N., and W. C. Brice. Ενεπίγραφοι πινακίδες και πίθοι Γραμμικού Συστήματος Α εκ Ζάκρου. Βιβλιοθήκη της εν Αθήναις Αρχαιολογικής Εταιρείας 85. Athens, 1975.

Platon–Davaras 1960
Platon, N., and C. Davaras. "Η αρχαιολογική κίνησις εν Κρήτηι κατά το έτος 1960." Κρητ. Χρονικά ΙΔ΄ (1960): 504–27.

Platonos 1981
Platonos, M. "Τελετουργικές σφύρες και ρόπαλα στο μινωικό κόσμο." ΑΕ (1981): 74–83.

Platonos 1987
Platonos, M. "Γλάστρες και ανθοδοχεία στο μινωικό κόσμο." In Ειλαπίνη: τόμος τιμητικός για τον καθηγητή Νικόλαο Πλάτωνα. Herakleion, 1987, pp. 227–34.

Platonos-Yiota 1995
Platonos-Yiota, M. "Σπονδική τελετουργική πρόχους." In Πεπραγμένα του Ζ΄ Διεθνούς Κρητολογικού Συνεδρίου (Ρέθυμνο, 25–31 Αυγ. 1991). Α2. 1995, pp. 777–88.

Platon–Platon 1991
Platon, N., and L. Platon. "Εργασίες μελέτης και συντήρησης ευρημάτων ανασκαφών Ζάκρου." ΠΑΕ 146 (1991): 392–96.

Podzuweit 1979
Podzuweit, C. Trojanische Gefassformen der Frühbronzezeit in Anatolien, der Ägais und angrenzenden Gebieten. Ein Beitrag zur vergleichenden Stratigraphie. Heidelberger Akademie der Wissenschaften, Monographien 1. Mainz am Rhein, 1979.

Popham 1964
Popham, M. R. The Last Days of the Palace at Knossos. Complete Vases of the Late Minoan IIIB Period. SIMA 5. Lund, 1964.

Popham 1966
Popham, M. R. "The Palace of Knossos: Its Destruction and Reoccupation Reconsidered." Kadmos 5 (1966): 17–24.

Popham 1967
Popham M. R. "Late Minoan Pottery, a Summary." BSA 62 (1967): 337–51.

Popham 1970
Popham M. R. The Destruction of the Palace at Knossos. Pottery of the Late Minoan IIIA Period. SIMA 12. Gothenburg, 1970.

Popham 1972–73
Popham, M. R. "The Unexplored Mansion at Knossos: a Preliminary Report on the Excavations from 1967 to 1972. Part I. The Minoan Building and Its Occupation." AR 19 (1972–73): 50–61.

Popham 1978
Popham M. R. "Notes from Knossos, Part II." BSA 73 (1978): 179–87, pls. 22–27.

Popham 1980
Popham, M. R. "Cretan Sites Occupied between c. 1450 and 1400 B.C." BSA 75 (1980): 163–67.

Popham 1984
Popham, M. R., ed. The Minoan Unexplored Mansion at Knossos. BSA Suppl. Vol. 17. Athens and London, 1984.

Popham–Catling–Catling 1974
Popham, M. R., E. A. Catling, and H. W. Catling. "Sellopoulo Tombs 3 and 4, Two Late Minoan Graves near Knossos." BSA 69 (1974): 195–257.

Poursat 1977a
Poursat, J. C. Catalogue des ivoires mycéniens du Musée National d'Athènes. Athens, 1977.

Poursat 1977b
Poursat, J. C. Les ivoires mycéniens: Essai sur la formation d'un art mycénien. Bibliothèques des Ecoles Françaises d'Athènes et de Rome 230. Athens, 1977.

Poursat 1996a
Poursat J. C. Οδηγός των Μαλίων. Τα παλαιοανακτορικά χρόνια, η συνοικία Μ. Athens, 1996.

Poursat 1996b
Poursat J. C. Fouilles exécutées à Malia, Le Quartier Mu. Vol. III: Artisans minoens: Les maisons-ateliers du Quartier Mu. Études Crétoises 32. Athens and Paris, 1996.

Poursat 1999
Poursat, J. C. "Ivoires chypro-égéens: De Chypre à Minet-el-Beida et Mycènes." In Betancourt et al., eds. Meletemata (1999), pp. 683–87.

Poursat–Papatsarouha 2000
Poursat, J. C., and E. Papatsarouha. "Les sceaux de l'Atelier de Malia: questions de style." In Müller, ed. Minoisch-Mykenische Glyptik (2000), pp. 257–68.

Psilakis–Psilaki 2000
Psilakis, N., and M. Psilaki. Τα βότανα στην κουζίνα. Herakleion, 2000.

Pulak 1988
Pulak, C. "The Bronze Age Shipwreck at Ulu Burun, Turkey: 1985 Campaign." AJA 92 (1988): 1–37.

Pulak 2000
Pulak C. "The Cargo of Copper and Tin Ingots from the Late Bronze Age Shipwreck at Uluburun." In Ü. Yalçin, ed. Anatolian Metal I. Der Anschnitt. Beiheft 13. Bochum, 2000, pp. 137–57.

Rehak 1995
Rehak, P. "The Use and Destruction of Minoan Bull's Head Rhyta." In Laffineur and W.-D. Niemeier, eds. *Politeia* (1995), pp. 435–60.

Renfrew 1969
Renfrew, C. "The Development and Chronology of the Early Cycladic Figurines." *AJA* 73 (1969): 1–32.

Rethemiotakis 1998
Rethemiotakis, G. *Ανθρωπόμορφη πηλοπλαστική στην Κρήτη από τη νεοανακτορική έως την υπομινωική περίοδο.* Βιβλιοθήκη της εν Αθήναις Αρχαιολογικής Εταιρείας 174. Athens, 1998.

Rethemiotakis 2002
Rethemiotakis, G. "Evidence on Social and Economic Changes at Galatas and Pediada in the New-Palace Period." In Driessen, Schoep, and Laffineur, eds. *Monuments of Minos* (2002), pp. 55–69.

Rutkowski 1972
Rutkowski, B. *Cult Places in the Aegean World.* Bibliotheca Antiqua 10. Wroclaw, 1972.

Rutkowski 1986
Rutkowski, B. *The Cult Places of the Aegean.* New Haven and London, 1986.

Rutkowski 1988
Rutkowski, B. "Minoan Peak Sanctuaries: The Topography and Architecture." In *Aegaeum* 2. Annales d'Archéologie Egéenne de l'Université de Liège. Liège, 1988, pp. 71–100.

Rutkowski 1991
Rutkowski, B. *Petsophas: A Cretan Peak Sanctuary.* Studies and Monographs in Mediterranean Archaeology and Civilization, ser. 1, vol. 1. Warsaw, 1991.

Rutkowski–Nowicki 1996
Rutkowski, B., and K. Nowicki. *The Psychro Cave and Other Grottoes in Crete.* Studies and Monographs in Mediterranean Archaeology and Civilization ser. 2, vol. 1. Warsaw, 1996.

Sakellarakis 1968
Sakellarakis, Y. "Ελεφαντοστά εκ των Αρχανών." In *Atti e Memorie del 10 Congresso Internazionale di Micenologia: Roma, 27 Settembre–3 Ottobre 1967.* Rome, 1968, pp. 245–61.

Sakellarakis 1977
Sakellarakis, I.A., "The Cyclades and Crete." In J. Thimme, ed. *Art and Culture of the Cyclades: Handbook of an Ancient Civilisation.* Karlsruhe, 1977, pp. 145–54.

Sakellarakis 1979
Sakellarakis, Y. *Το ελεφαντόδοντο και η κατεργασία του στα μυκηναϊκά χρόνια.* Athens, 1979.

Sakellarakis–Sakellarakis 1973–74
Sakellarakis, J.A., and E. Sakellarakis. "The Adorant of Myrsini." In *Antichità Cretesi. Studi in onore di Doro Levi, I.* Cronache di Archeologia 12. Catania, 1973–74, pp. 122–26.

Sakellarakis–Sapouna-Sakellaraki 1997
Sakellarakis, Y., and E. Sapouna-Sakellaraki. *Archanes. Minoan Crete in a New Light*, I–II. Athens, 1997.

Sampson 1987
Sampson, A. *Η νεολιθική περίοδος στα Δωδεκάνησα.* Athens, 1987.

Sandars 1963
Sandars, N. K. "Late Aegean Bronze Swords." *AJA* 67 (1963): 117–53.

Sapouna-Sakellaraki 1969
Sapouna-Sakellaraki, E. "Συμβολή εις την μελέτην του μινωικού αναγλύφου." *AAA* 2 (1969): 399–406.

Sapouna-Sakellaraki 1971
Sapouna-Sakellaraki, E. *Μινωικόν ζώμα.* Βιβλιοθήκη της εν Αθήναις Αρχαιολογικής Εταιρείας 71. Athens, 1971.

Sapouna-Sakellaraki 1995
Sapouna-Sakellaraki, E. *Die bronzenen Menschenfiguren auf Kreta und in der Ägäis.* Prähistorische Bronzefunde I, 5. Stuttgart, 1995.

Sarpaki 2000
Sarpaki, A. "The Study of Palaeodiet in the Aegean: Food for Thought" and "Palaeoethnobotany and Palaeodiet in the Aegean Region: Notes on Legume Toxicity and Related Pathologies." In S. Vaugham and W. Coulson, eds. *Palaeodiet in the Aegean.* Wiener Laboratory Monograph 1. Oxford, 2000, pp. 115–21.

Savignoni 1904
Savignoni, L. "Scavi e scoperte nella necropoli di Phaestos." *MonAnt* 14 (1904): 501–666.

Sbonias 1995
Sbonias, K. *Frühkretische Siegel, Ansätze für eine Interpretation der sozial-politischen Entwicklung auf Kreta während der Frühbronzezeit.* BAR–IS 620. Oxford, 1995.

Schachermeyer 1979
Schachermeyer, F. *Kreta zur Zeit der Wanderungen.* Vienna, 1979.

Schiering 1960
Schiering, W. "Steine und Malerei in der minoische Kunst." *JdI* 75 (1960): 17–36.

Schiering 1972
Schiering, W. "Ein minoisches Tonrhyton in Hammerform." *Κρητ. Χρονικά ΚΔ΄* (1972): 477–88.

Schliemann 1880
Schliemann, H. *Ilios, the City and the Country of the Trojans.* London, 1880.

Seager 1909
Seager, R. B. "Excavations on the Island of Mochlos, Crete in 1909." *AJA* 13 (1909): 272–303, pl. VI.

Seager 1910
Seager, R. B. *Excavations on the Island of Pseira, Crete.* University of Pennsylvania. The Museum Anthropological Publications III, 1. Philadelphia ,1910.

Seager 1912
Seager, R. B. *Explorations in the Island of Mochlos.* Boston and New York, 1912.

Seiradaki 1960
Seiradaki M. "Pottery from Karphi." *BSA* 55 (1960): 1–37.

Shaw 1971
Shaw, J. W. "Minoan Architecture: Materials and Techniques." *ASAtene* 49 (1971): 5–256.

Shaw 2003
Shaw, M. "Grids and Other Drafting Devices in Minoan and Other Aegean Wall Painting. A Comparative Analysis including Egypt." In K. P. Foster and R. Laffineur, eds. *Metron: Measuring the Aegean Bronze Age. Proceedings of the 9th International Aegean Conference, New Haven, Yale University, 18–21 April 2002.* Aegaeum 24. Liège, 2003, pp. 179–89.

Shaw 2005
Shaw, M. "The Painted Pavilion of the 'Caravanserai' at Knossos." In L. Morgan, ed. *Aegean Wall Paintings. A Tribute to Mark Cameron.* BSA Studies 13. London, 2005, pp. 91–111.

Soles 1992
Soles, J. S. *The Prepalatial Cemeteries at Mochlos and Gournia and the House Tombs of Bronze Age Crete.* Hesperia Suppl. 24. Princeton, New Jersey, 1992.

Soles 2003
Soles, J. S. *Mochlos IA. Period III, Neopalatial Settlement on the Coast: The Artisans' Quarter and the Farmhouse at Chalinomouri. The Sites.* Prehistory Monographs 7. Philadelphia, 2003.

Soles 2005
Soles, J. S. "From Ugarit to Mochlos—Remnants of an Ancient Voyage." In R. Laffineur and E. Greco, eds. *Emporia. Aegeans in the Central and Eastern Mediterranean. Proceedings of the 10th International Aegean Conference.* Aegaeum 25. Liège and Austin, 2005, pp. 429–42.

Soles 2007
Soles, J. S. "Saevus Tridens." In P. P. Betancourt, M. C. Nelson, and E. H. Williams, eds. *Krinoi kai Limenes: Studies in Honor of Joseph and Maria Shaw.* Prehistory Monographs 22. Philadelphia, 2007, pp. 251–55

Soles (in press)
Soles, J. S. "Metal Hoards from LM IB Mochlos." In I. Tzachili and Y. Bassiakos, eds. *Aegean Metallurgy in the Bronze Age. Proceedings of an International Symposium, Rethymno, Crete, 19–21 November 2004* (in press).

Soles–Davaras 1996
Soles, J. S., and C. Davaras. "Excavations at Mochlos, 1992–1993." *Hesperia* 65 (1996): 175–230.

Soles–Stos-Gale 2004
Soles, J. S., and Z. A. Stos-Gale. *Mochlos IC. Period III. Neopalatial Settlement on the Coast: The Artisans' Quarter and the Farmhouse at Chalinomouri. The Small Finds.* Prehistory Monographs 9. Philadelphia, 2004.

Stampolidis 2003
Stampolidis, N., ed. *Sea Routes. From Sidon to Huelva. Interconnections in the Mediterranean, 16th–6th c. B.C.* Athens, 2003.

Stampolidis–Karetsou 1998
Stampolidis, N., and A. Karetsou, eds. *Ανατολική Μεσόγειος. Κύπρος-Δωδεκάνησα-Κρήτη: 16ος–6ος αι. π.Χ.* Exh. cat. Herakleion, 1998.

Stampolidis–Karetsou–Kanta 1998
Stampolidis, N., A. Karetsou, and A. Kanta, eds. *Eastern Mediterranean. Cyprus-Dodecanese-Crete, 16th–6th cent. B.C.* Exh. cat. Herakleion, 1998.

Stos-Gale–Macdonald 1991
Stos-Gale, Z. A., and C. F. Macdonald. "Sources of Metal and Trade in the *Bronze Age Aegean.*" In N. H. Gale, ed. *Bronze Age Trade in the Mediterranean: Papers presented at the Conference held at Rewley House, Oxford, in December 1989. SIMA 90.* Jonsered, 1991, pp. 249–88.

Televantou 1984
Televantou, Ch. "Κοσμήματα από την προϊστορική Θήρα." *AE* (1984): 14–54.

Televantou 1994
Televantou, Ch. *Ακρωτήρι Θήρας. Οι τοιχογραφίες της Δυτικής Οικίας.* Βιβλιοθήκη της εν Αθήναις Αρχαιολογικής Εταιρείας 143. Athens, 1994.

Tilmann–Pöhling 1990
Tilmann, B., and W. Pöhling, eds. *Kreta: Das Erwachen Europas, Begleitband zur Ausstellung im Niederrheinischen Museum der Stadt Duisburg, 22. April bis 29. Juli 1990.* Duisburg, 1990.

Treuil 1983
Treuil, R. *Le Néolithique et le Bronze Ancien Egéens. Les problèmes stratigraphiques et chronologiques, les techniques, les hommes.* Bibliothèque des Écoles françaises d'Athènes et de Rome 248. Paris, 1983.

Tsipopoulou–Little 2001
Tsipopoulou, M., and L. Little. "Καύσεις του τέλους της εποχής του Χαλκού στην Κριτσά Μιραμπέλλου, Ανατολική Κρήτη." In N. Stampolidis, ed. *Καύσεις στην εποχή του Χαλκού και την πρώιμη εποχή του Σιδήρου. Πρακτικά του Συμποσίου. Ρόδος, 29 Απρ.–2 Μαϊου 1999.* Athens, 2001, pp. 83–98.

Tylecote 1976
Tylecote, R. F. *A History of Metallurgy.* London, 1976.

Tsipopoulou–Vagnetti 2006
Tsipopoulou, M., and L. Vagnetti. "Late Minoan III Evidence from Kritsa, Mirabello." In *Πεπραγμένα του Θ´ Διεθνούς Κρητολογικό Συνέδρειο (Ελούντα 1–7 Οκτ. 2001).* A1. Herakleion, 2006, pp. 201–10.

Tyree 1975
Tyree E. L. "Cretan Sacred Caves: Archaeological Evidence." Ph.D. diss. University of Missouri, Columbia, 1975.

Tyree 2001
Tyree E. L. "Diachronic Changes in Minoan Cave Cult." In R. Laffineur and R. Hägg, eds. *Potnia. Deities and Religion in the Aegean Bronze Age. Proceedings of the 8th International Aegean Conference. Göteborg University, 12–15 April 2000.* Aegaeum 22. Liège and Austin, 2001, pp. 39–50.

Tzedakis 1969a
Tzedakis, Y. "L' atelier de céramique postpalatiale à Kydonia". *BCH* 93.I (1969): 346–418.

Tzedakis 1969b
Tzedakis, Y. "Ανασκαφαί ΥΜ ΙΙΙΑ-Β νεκροταφείου εις περιοχήν Καλαμίου Χανίων." *AAA* 2 (1969): 365–68.

Tzedakis 1970
Tzedakis, Y. "Μινωικός κιθαρωδός." *AAA* 3 (1970): 111–12.

Tzedakis 1972
Tzedakis, Y. "Ανασκαφή Καστελλίου Χανίων." *AAA* 5 (1972): 387–91.

Tzedakis–Martlew 1999
Tzedakis, Y., and H. Martlew, eds. *Minoans and Mycenaeans. Flavours of Their Time*. Exh. cat. Athens, 1999.

Tzigounaki 2006
Tzigounaki, A. "Στοιχεία και επισημάνσεις για την οργάνωση του διοικητικού συστήματος κατά την παλαιοανακτορική περίοδο." In *Πεπραγμένα του Θ΄ Διεθνούς Κρητολογικό Συνέδρειο (Ελούντα 1–7 Οκτ. 2001)*. Α3. Herakleion, 2006, pp. 201–18.

Varvaregos 1981
Varvaregos, A. "Το οδοντόφρακτον μυκηναϊκόν κράνος (ως προς την τεχνικήν της κατασκευής του)." Ph.D. diss. University of Athens, 1980. Athens, 1981.

Verlinden 1984
Verlinden, C. *Les statuettes anthropomorphes crétoises en bronze et en plomb de IIIe millénaire au VIIe siècle av. J.-C.* Archaeologica Transatlantica 4. Providence and Louvain-La-Neuve, 1984.

Vlachopoulos–Birtacha 2003
Vlachopoulos, A., and K. Birtacha, eds. *Αργοναύτης. Τιμητικός Τόμος για τον Καθηγητή Χρίστο Γ. Ντούμα από τους μαθητές του στο Πανεπιστή μιο Αθηνών (1980–2000)*. Athens, 2003.

Von Arbin 1984
Von Arbin, H. "The Alabastron-shaped Vases found in the 'Throne Room' at Knossos." *Op. Ath.* 15 (1984): 7–16.

Wachsmann 1987
Wachsmann, S. *Aegeans in the Theban Tombs*. Orientalia Lovaniensia Analecta 20. Leuven, 1987.

Walberg 1976
Walberg, G. *Kamares: A Study of the Character of Palatial Middle Minoan Pottery*. Uppsala, 1976.

Walberg 1986
Walberg, G. *Tradition and Innovation. Essays in Minoan Art*. Mainz am Rhein, 1986.

Walberg 1992
Walberg, G. "Minoan Floral Iconography." In R. Laffineur and J. L. Crowley, eds. *Εικών. Aegean Bronze Age Iconography: Shaping a Methodology. Proceedings of the 4th International Aegean Conference, University of Tasmania, Hobart, Australia, 6–9 April 1992*. Aegaeum 8. Liège, 1992, pp. 241–46.

Warren 1969a
Warren, P. M. "An Early Bronze Age Potter's Workshop in Crete." *Antiquity* 43 (1969): 224–27.

Warren 1969b
Warren, P. M. *Minoan Stone Vases*. Cambridge, 1969.

Warren 1972
Warren, P. M. *Myrtos, an Early Bronze Age Settlement in Crete*. London, 1972.

Warren 1976
Warren P. M. "Did Papyrus Grow in the Aegean?" *AAA* 9 (1976): 89–95.

Warren 1989
Warren, P. M. "The Destruction of the Palace of Knossos." In Karageorghis, ed. *Civilizations of the Aegean* (1989), pp. 32–37.

Warren 1990
Warren, P. M. "Of Baetyls." In *Πεπραγμένα του ΣΤ΄ Διεθνούς Κρητολογικό Συνέδριο (Χανιά 24–30 Αυγ. 1986)*. Α2. Khania, 1990, pp. 353–63.

Warren 1992
Warren, P. M. "Λίθινα αγγεία και σκεύη της μινωικής Κρήτης." In *Μινωικός και Ελληνικός Πολιτισμός. Από τη συλλογή Μητσοτάκη. Μουσείο Κυκλαδικής Τέχνης.* Exh. cat. Athens (1992), pp. 151–55.

Warren 2005
Warren, P. M. "A Model of Iconographical Transfer. The Case of Crete and Egypt." In Bradfer-Burdet, Detournay, and Laffineur, eds. *Κρης Τεχνίτης* (2005), pp. 222–27.

Waterhouse 1988
Waterhouse, H. "The Flat Alabastron and the Last Ritual in the Knossos Throne Room." *OJA* 7 (1988): 361–67.

Whitelaw et al. 1997
Whitelaw, T. M., P. M. Day, E. Kiriatzi, V. Kilikoglou, and D. E. Wilson. "Ceramic Traditions at EM IIB Myrtos, Fournou Korifi." In Laffineur and Betancourt, eds. *Τέχνη* (1997), pp. 265–74.

Wilson–Day 1994
Wilson, D. E., and P. M. Day. "Ceramic Regionalism in Prepalatial Central Crete: The Mesara Imports of EMI to EMIIA Knossos." *BSA* 89 (1994): 1–87.

Wright 2004
Wright, J. C. "A Survey of Evidence for Feasting in Mycenaean Society." In J. C. Wright, ed. *The Mycenaean Feast*. Princeton, 2004, pp. 13–58.

Xanthoudides 1905–6
Xanthoudides, S. "Cretan Kernoi." *BSA* 12 (1905–6): 9–23.

Xanthoudides 1909
Xanthoudides, S. "Μινωικόν σκεύος ενεπίγραφον." *AE* (1909): 179–96.

Xanthoudides 1918a
Xanthoudides, S. "Μέγας πρωτομινωικός τάφος Πύργου." *ΑΔ* 4 (1918): 136–70.

Xanthoudides 1918b
Xanthoudides, S. "Πρωτομινωικοί τάφοι Μεσαράς." *ΑΔ* 4 Παράρτημα (1918): 15–23.

Xanthoudides 1922
Xanthoudides, S. "Μινωικόν μέγαρον Νίρου." *AE* (1922): 1–25.

Xanthoudides 1924
Xanthoudides, S. *The Vaulted Tombs of Mesara. An Account of Some Early Cemeteries of Southern Crete*. London, 1924.

Xenaki-Sakellariou 1985
Xenaki-Sakellariou, A. *Οι θαλαμωτοί τάφοι των Μυκηνών, ανασκαφής Χρήστου Τσούντα (1887–1898)*. Paris, 1985.

Younger 1985
Younger, J. G. "Aegean Seals of the Late Bronze Age: Stylistic Groups. IV. Almond- and Dot-eye Groups of the Fifteenth Century B.C." *Kadmos* 24 (1985): 34–73.

Younger 1986
Younger, J. G. "Aegean Seals of the Late Bronze Age: Stylistic Groups. V. Minoan Groups Contemporary with LMIII A1." *Kadmos* 25 (1986): 119–40.

Younger 1993
Younger, J. G. *Bronze Age Seals in Their Middle Phase (ca. 1700–1550). SIMA* 102. Jonsered, 1993.

Younger 1995
Younger, J. G. "Bronze Age Representations of Aegean Bull-Games, III." In Laffineur and Niemeier, eds. *Politeia* (1995), pp. 507–46.

Younger 1999
Younger, J. G. "Glass Seals and "Look-Alike" Seals." In Betancourt et al., eds. *Meletemata* (1999), pp. 953–57.

Yule 1981
Yule, P. *Early Cretan Seals: A Study of Chronology.* Marburger Studien zur Vor- und Fruhgeschichte 4. Mainz am Rhein, 1981.

Zapheiropoulou 1984
Zapheiropoulou, Ph. "The Chronology of the Kampos Group." In J. A. MacGillivray, and R. L. N. Barber, eds. *The Prehistoric Cyclades: Contributions to a Workshop on Cycladic Chronology.* Edinburgh, 1984, pp. 31–40.

Zeimbeki 2004
Zeimbeki, M. "The Organisation of Votive Production and Distribution." In Cadogan, Hatzaki, and Vasilakis, eds. *Knossos: Palace, City, State* (2004), pp. 351–61.

Zois 1973
Zois, A. Κρήτη. Η εποχή του Λίθου. Athens, 1973.

ABBREVIATIONS

AA	*Archäologischer Anzeiger*
AAA	*Αρχαιολογικά Ανάλεκτα εξ Αθηνών*
ΑΔ	*Αρχαιολογικόν Δελτίον*
AE	*Αρχαιολογική Εφημερίς*
AJA	*American Journal of Archaeology*
AM	*Mitteilungen des Deutschen Archäologischen Instituts: Athenische Abteilung*
AR	*Archaeological Reports*
ASAtene	*Annuario della Scuola archeologica di Atene e delle Missioni italiane in Oriente*
BAR–IS	*British Archaeological Reports–International Series*
BCH	*Bulletin de correspondance hellénique*
BSA	*Annual of the British School at Athens*
CMS	*Corpus der Minoischen und Mykenischen Siegel*
Έργον	*Το έργον της εν Αθήναις Αρχαιολογικής Εταιρείας*
GORILA	*Godart, L., and J. P. Olivier. Recueil des inscriptions en Linéaire A. Études Crétoises 21, Vols. 1–5. Paris, 1976–1985.*
Im Labyrinth des Minos	*Im Labyrinth des Minos: Kreta, die erste europäische Hochkultur. Ausstellung des Badischen Landesmuseums, 27.1 bis 29.4.2001, Karlsruhe, Schloss. Exh. cat. Munich, 20*
JdI	*Jahrbuch des Deutschen Archäologischen Instituts*
JHS	*Journal of Hellenic Studies*
JMA	*Journal of Mediterranean Archaeology*
JPR	*Journal of Prehistoric Religion*
Κρητ. Χρονικά	*Κρητικά Χρονικά*
MonAnt	*Monumenti Antichi pubblicati per cura della Accademia Nazionale dei Lincei*
OJA	*Oxford Journal of Archaeology*
Op. Ath.	*Opuscula Atheniensia*
ΠΑΕ	*Πρακτικά της εν Αθήναις Αρχαιολογικής Εταιρείας*
PM	Evans, Sir A. J. *The Palace of Minos: A Comparative Account of the Successive Stages of the Early Cretan Civilization as illustrated by the Discoveries at Knossos.* Vol. 1–4. London, 1921–36 (2nd ed.: New York, 1964).
SIMA	*Studies in Mediterranean Archaeology*
TUAS	*Temple University Aegean Symposium*